The Telegraph
Book of the
Olympics

The Telegraph
Book of the
Olympics

edited by **MARTIN SMITH**

In memory of David Welch, Fleet Street's finest Sports Editor and the man who provided the catalyst for London's successful bid to host the Games of the XXX Olympiad. The tragedy is that he will not be there to see his dream fulfilled.

First published in Great Britain
2012 by Aurum Press Ltd
7 Greenland Street
London NW1 0ND
www.aurumpress.co.uk

A catalogue record for this book is available from the British Library.

ISBN 978 1 84513 707 6

1 3 5 7 9 10 8 6 4 2
2012 2014 2016 2015 2013

Typeset in Spectrum by Saxon Graphics Ltd, Derby
Printed by MPG Books, Bodmin, Cornwall

CONTENTS

FOREWORD

'The most important thing in the Olympic Games is not the winning but the taking part.' Although this is Baron Pierre de Coubertin's most familiar motto, when the athletes appear for the first time at the Olympics in London it will be something else he said that will be ringing in their ears. 'Citius, fortius, altius' means 'Faster, stronger, higher' – but in its least competitive interpretation it can be taken as meaning: never mind going for gold – just aim to beat your personal best.

This may have been the case with some events at the first modern Olympic Games in 1896, but it has not always been so. Think of Hitler's Games of 1936, or the drug-fuelled Eastern bloc regimes of the 1970s and 1980s, or the unashamed ambition of China to sit atop the medal table at the Beijing Games in 2008. However, the one consistent theme in every Olympics has been, and always will be, the absolute necessity to produce your best on the only day that truly matters during the four-year cycle of an Olympiad. It's the one day when there can be no excuses, no 'if onlys': when there's nowhere to hide. Every athlete aims to peak on this day, and it is the knowledge that your competitors are in the shape of their lives, expecting to deliver their ultimate performance when it's required, that makes the drama of Olympic competition so captivating and winning so special.

And it's not just the athletes who enjoy the countdown to the Games. Journalists know that what they write will be read for years to come by people who might not even have been born when the Games took place. In the instantaneous and disposable world we inhabit today it's vital that special skill and ambition be preserved, rewarded and celebrated. The best writers can place us at events long since past, allowing us to relive the tension, the atmosphere, the action and reaction, and those who were not present to feel the excitement as close to first hand as possible.

My contribution to this book was written in Athens as I reflected on winning my second Olympic gold medal. Retirement followed, and my Olympic role at Beijing 2008 changed from competitor to *Telegraph* reporter. Others in the book who have been both the observed and the observer include Lord Sebastian Coe and my former crewmate and now *Telegraph* colleague Sir Steve Redgrave, true Olympic royalty who won five gold medals at five Olympics. In his piece, Sir Steve describes how he met the legendary American 400-metres hurdler Edwin Moses and was so awestruck he could hardly speak. That may appear illogical, but it somehow sums up the aura of the Olympic Games, where the spirit of 'Citius, fortius, altius' turns men into gods and will be called upon once again in London this summer.

JAMES CRACKNELL
February 2012

INTRODUCTION

The third coming of the Olympic Games to London provides an opportune moment to reflect upon 116 years of endeavour, struggle and glory on sport's greatest stage. As this book illustrates, *The Daily Telegraph* has been there reporting and analysing since Baron Pierre de Coubertin rose to his feet in the Sorbonne in the last decade of the nineteenth century A.D., and made an impassioned plea for a modern version of the Games originally performed by the Ancient Greeks. And the *Telegraph* will still be there when the Flame is extinguished to mark the end of the Games of the XXXth Olympiad in the summer of 2012.

It was the London Games of 1908 that really enthused the *Telegraph*, and every Olympics since have been reported by staff writers. In fact, so enthralled were the *Telegraph* by the Games centred on The Great Stadium at Shepherd's Bush in west London, that they devoted page after broadsheet page of non-illustrated, small-print coverage, day after day. It has not been possible to reproduce here everything that was published during the course of those Games, but it would be considered well nigh exhaustive even by twenty-first century standards. At times it was almost as if the newspaper was the official mouthpiece of the organisers; their every communication was relayed with almost meticulous obsequiousness. You could barely move for information about the Marathon, which was being billed from the start as the centrepiece of the whole shebang. In the days before the race, there were thorough details about the 26-mile 385-yard route from Windsor to the Stadium, where to watch, road closures, instructions to the competitors' attendants about where they could follow on bicycles, what would happen if runners had to drop out, and suggestions of who might win. The reports of the race and its aftermath went on for pages; there really were few angles overlooked. The story of

Dorando Pietri — erroneously called by his forename Dorando initially, but corrected later — was manna from heaven. His stumbling, shambling display on the track, getting up, falling over, helped back up again, and his subsequent disqualification for illegal assistance, was described, picked over and commented upon as the biggest news story of the day. There was reaction from Italy, Pietri's home, reaction from America, home of Johnny Hayes, the eventual winner, and reaction from Buckingham Palace, where Queen Mary was so caught up in it that she announced she was going to present a cup to the little Italian who had touched her heart. There was even a notice to contradict rumours that Pietri had passed away, like Pheidippides, the original Marathon runner, terminally exhausted by his exertions. When a fully recovered Pietri appeared at the following day's prize-giving ceremony, he was accorded a welcome unprecedented in those days but which we would recognise as a forerunner to modern-day celebrity: it was as if David Beckham had entered the arena. The *Telegraph*'s man sought out the hero of the hour for an interview, conducted through enthusiastic interpreters, and was able to pass on to readers details of Pietri's background, as well as news of a plethora of marriage proposals sent by smitten female admirers.

The success of London, and the interest generated for the Olympics themselves, encouraged the *Telegraph* to dispatch an unnamed Special Correspondent to the Games in Stockholm four years later. In today's world of soundbites and mixed zones, reporters are forever bobbing up and down and out of their seats in the stands to chase their stories; for much of the first half of the twentieth century, the journalists would remain in their allotted place and report chronologically what was passing before their eyes. So their report for the following day's paper might start with the Marathon runners leaving the stadium, continue with heats of the 1,500 metres, some Greco-Roman wrestling, news from the halfway mark in the Marathon, the high jump and high-hurdle preliminaries, and conclude with the arrival of the runners some two and a half hours later from their circuit of the world outside. The prose was often purple, the competitors almost swamped by the colour. In 1924 B. Bennison, the first Olympics reporter to be by-lined, only gets to the description of Harold Abrahams's 'Chariots of Fire' 100-metres gold medal after he has noted a world record in the 400 metres hurdles by an American.

Bennison covered the Games single-handedly through Antwerp, Paris and Amsterdam. Then it was back to a 'Special Correspondent' for the long trip to Los Angeles in 1932, and the odd comment on the athletics from Bevil Rudd, of whom more in a sentence or two. However, in the lead-up to the 1936 Games the *Telegraph* promised their coverage from Berlin would 'appeal both to the sports enthusiast and to the general reader'. The two-man team was packed with the type of experience that would form the template for latter-day coverage. Bevil Rudd, 'winner of the 400 metres at Antwerp in 1920 and a leading commentator on athletics', was joined by Howard Marshall, 'the well-known writer and broadcaster on various forms of sport'. Rudd, South African-born, had quite a background: he won the Military Cross in the First World War during which he was one of the original small group of tank officers. At the onset of war, he had put aside his postgraduate studies at Oxford where he was a Rhodes Scholar. He would attempt to join up again at the start of the Second World War, but was deemed unfit for active service, and probably too old, but was appointed editor of the Army fortnightly publication *War.* In the 1920 Games he not only won gold at 400 metres, but silver in the longer relay and bronze in the 800 metres, the only time a British Empire athlete returned with medals of each variety until Mary Rand collected all three in 1964. (Bradley Wiggins, incidentally, would do the same in 2004.) In amongst his journalism, Rudd also found time to be private secretary to the first Lord Birkenhead and a master at Harrow School. Sadly he died in 1948, just months before the second London Games. However, his insight into what was happening on the track a dozen years earlier dovetailed with Marshall, who had been an Oxford Blue at rugby, captain of Harlequins and a decent club cricketer. He was the BBC's cricket commentator in the pre-*Test Match Special* days and reported cricket and rugby for *The Daily Telegraph*. He was the English narrator for Leni Riefenstahl's controversial film of the 1936 Games and moved on to higher things at the BBC after serving as war correspondent and reporting the D-Day landings from the Normandy beaches. He was in his mid-thirties at the time of Berlin and his idiosyncratic reports from the Games painted an intimate portrait of Hitler's Germany.

Similarly, Michael Melford, who covered the 1956 and 1960 Games, was an athletics Blue for Oxford in the late 1930s. He was a half-miler and had been a member of the joint Oxford and Cambridge team who went unbeaten during their tour of the United States and Canada in 1937. He was athletics correspondent of the *Observer* before moving to *The Daily Telegraph* where he would become best known as cricket correspondent in succession to E.W. Swanton. On the Olympic front, Melford had succeeded Lainson Wood, who flew solo during the second London Games in 1948.

Compared to the Games' first visit, forty years before, Wood's reports were considerably shorter, largely due to the post-War shortage of newsprint. Wood, a larger than life character, was also boxing correspondent and assistant sports editor and chipped in on athletics and at Wimbledon.

In Rome, in 1960, Melford was joined by his own successor on the Olympic beat in Donald Saunders, the paper's latest football and boxing correspondent. By the time he covered his seventh and last summer Games, nearly a quarter of a century later, Saunders was supervising a nine-strong team in Los Angeles.

Before then, though, Saunders would find his regular travelling companions during the 1960s and 1970s were athletics correspondent James Coote and swimming correspondent Pat Besford. Coote was the son of Sir Colin Coote, editor of *The Daily Telegraph* between 1950 and 1964. Coote junior was a popular figure among the athletics fraternity and there was shock when he was killed in 1979 while piloting his light aircraft over the mountains on the Swiss-Italian border en route to the Europa Cup meeting in Turin. He had offered Sebastian Coe and a fellow journalist a lift. The writer cried off and Coe was told by the British management that he should travel as part of the team. He is forever grateful he followed their instruction. (So, indeed, should be anyone watching the 2012 Games.) Besford's husband John was a British swimming champion and Olympic competitor, and she attended every Games from 1936 until her last for the *Telegraph* in 1984.

Meanwhile, for more than thirty years, from its launch in 1961, Peter Hildreth oversaw the *Sunday Telegraph*'s athletics coverage. He competed over the high hurdles for Britain at three Olympic Games – 1952, 1956 and 1960 – though he never progressed further than the semi-finals. His father Will, too, had represented Britain in the second Paris Games at 200 metres. As an unusual claim to fame, the son won the 220 yards hurdles at Iffley Road in May 1954 immediately before Roger Bannister ran his sub-four-minute mile. A tribute to his tenacity came in 1980 when he was laid low by illness in a Moscow hospital on the day Coe and Steve Ovett were due to meet in the 1,500 metres final. To the office's solicitous inquiry about his health he retorted, 'I haven't come all this way to let a stupid bug stop me reporting another ding-dong between Coe and Ovett' – and it didn't. He died in February 2011, aged eighty-two, but not before he had been reprimanded for revisiting an old training regime and ascending the down escalator at a store in Surrey on his eightieth birthday.

The comparative proximity of Munich encouraged the *Telegraph*, in 1972, to despatch their largest team to date. In addition to regulars Saunders, Coote and Besford, others accredited included all-rounder David Miller, equestrian correspondent Alan Smith and yachting correspondent Tony Fairchild. It was just as well, too, because it would be all hands to the pump when eleven members of the Israeli team were taken hostage, and later murdered by their Arab captors. The sports team on site were able to provide copy and colour to lead the paper's front page for several days running.

There were relatively few tweaks to the *Telegraph* team for Montreal and Moscow, the death of Coote notwithstanding, but in Los Angeles, Saunders, Besford, Smith and Fairchild were joined by Ken Mays on athletics, Chris Moore on hockey and cycling expert Phil Liggett. In addition, Saunders had sports correspondent Colin Gibson available to mop up any big stories, and the paper's West Coast correspondent Ian Brodie to provide local knowledge. The team had grown to fourteen four years later with Gibson, now chief sports writer, taking over Saunders's lead role and Michael Calvin writing the colour feature articles. Gibson would go on to edit the *Sunday Telegraph*'s sports pages and was head-hunted to mastermind *The Australian*'s coverage of the Sydney Games. He has subsequently held top-level communications posts with the Football Association, the England and Wales Cricket Board and the International Cricket Council.

By Seoul, Anita Lonsbrough had replaced Besford as swimming correspondent. The gold medal she won in the 200 metres breaststroke in 1960 was the last by a British female swimmer until Rebecca Adlington's double forty-eight years later; propitiously Lonsbrough was there in Beijing to record for the newspaper her joy at Adlington's success. In 1964, already an M.B.E. for services to swimming, she became the first woman to carry her nation's flag in the opening ceremony. There was a joke among rival journalists, certainly in Sydney, that the ever-expanding *Telegraph* team should march behind its own flag at the start of the Games; by size, it was considerably larger than a fair number of the two hundred or so nations now participating.

By this time, there was a growing recognition of the part sport could play in the success of the newspaper, with the gradual introduction of stand-alone sports supplements, first at either side of the weekend, later on a daily basis. The increased pagination gave sports editors like the innovative David Welch the opportunity to move coverage outside the routine, though still valuable, round of event reporting and enlist big names from the world of sport and beyond. In 1992, for instance, the Princess Royal led the front page of the sports supplement with an impassioned message ahead of the Barcelona Games; in 2000, Steve Redgrave had taken her place in previewing his attempt to win a record fifth rowing gold. Four years later, Welch had former Olympic champions Michael Johnson and Sebastian Coe providing analysis and comment, as well as James Cracknell reliving his second gold in the coxless four boat before swapping his athlete's pass for a press pass.

The foot soldiers were far from ordinary, either. Welch had put together a writing stable of thoroughbreds that included Paul Hayward, Sue Mott, Martin Johnson, Andrew Baker and, later, Jim White, as well as informed specialists like athletics correspondent Tom Knight. Now there was no need for one 'Special Correspondent' to sit glued to his or her seat all day and watch the Olympic Games process past like items on the *Generation Game* conveyor-belt; writers could be assigned to specific events in the hope of British success or interesting colour stories, involving, say, Ian Thorpe or Usain Bolt. This necessitated the introduction of an on-site organiser, or *chef de mission*, to liaise with the writers as well as the sports desk back in London, plan the journalists' movements on a minute-by-minute basis, ensuring they had access to ticketed events, as well as informing them where that night's ad hoc social gathering would be held. In 1996 sports news editor Brian Oliver, later sports editor of the *Observer*, took on the role. In 2000 and 2004 the privilege fell to the compiler of this book.

Sydney and Athens were three-week tours of exhausting, yet thrilling, duty, where 20-hour days were survived largely on adrenaline. Personal memories: sports minister Kate Hoey, bedecked in a Union Flag, administering a bollocking on a visit to the press centre for not having someone present when Richard Faulds won gold in one of her pet sports, shooting – in a gamble the last available body had been sent to the canoeing where Paul Ratcliffe 'only' managed silver; an angry telephone exchange with the B.O.A.'s press officer when Kelly Holmes was pulled out of an exclusive interview with James Cracknell the day before her 1,500 metres final in Athens – the press officer moved to Australia soon after, though following his heart rather than escaping the wrath of the *Telegraph*; David Welch diving into the back seat of the car taking a distraught Paula Radcliffe away from the Panathinaiko Stadium after she collapsed during the Marathon, with the express purpose of protecting his columnist from rival newspapers; getting up at the crack of dawn to travel to the Schinias rowing course to watch Cracknell win his second gold medal, followed in the afternoon by Bradley Wiggins winning gold in the velodrome, and concluding with an evening's athletics in the Olympic Stadium – it should be mentioned that it was a Saturday and what passed for a day off; the closing ceremony in Sydney in close proximity in the press box to the respected journalist Patrick Collins who was bellowing at the top of his voice: 'Kylie, I love you!' as Ms Minogue paraded past; the general excitement that held both cities in thrall for the duration of the Games, and the cleanliness and efficiency of the streets and public transport. London has some major acts to follow.

All the articles selected are contemporaneous and appear as they were published, original headlines on top, though some reports have been trimmed to help the reader get to the point more quickly; others have been left intact for their quirkiness and to remind us of more leisurely times. The events are reported as the writer saw them at the time, without the aid of hindsight, and in most cases the assistance of repeated television replays. They were often written against deadline and delivered by the most modern means of communication, whether that was carrier pigeon, hansom cab, telegraphic wire, telephone to copytaker or via laptops.

Anyway, you've seen the newspaper, now read the book.

———

Some may decry team sport in the Olympic Games, and they may well be right, but without the support of the following 'team' the Olympian task of producing this book would have become Sisyphean. Consequently, thanks must go to Keith Perry, one of my former sports editors at the *Telegraph*, for coming up with the idea in the first place and pushing it through; to Caroline Buckland, Head of Books and Entertainment, for commissioning it; to Graham Coster at Aurum Books for publishing it; to the unfailingly helpful and cheerful Gavin Fuller, Lorraine Goodspeed and the rest of the staff in the *Telegraph* library for facilitating the research; to Robin Harvie, my editor at Aurum; to my trusted former colleagues Andrew Baker and Sue Mott for their excellent advice and encouragement at crucial moments; to the writers, the men and women who performed every bit as well as the athletes and deserve gold medals of their own; to the production staff who undertook the original editing, and wrote the headlines that appeared in the newspaper; and to David Welch for showing great faith by inviting me to accompany the *Telegraph* team to Sydney and

Athens (as well as the Manchester Commonwealth Games in between) and letting me get on with the job once there. *Citius. Altius. Fortius.*

MARTIN SMITH

February 2012

PROLOGUE

Baron Pierre de Coubertin, widely regarded as the founding father of the modern Olympic Games, and justifiably so, was a French aristocrat. He was also a bit of a romantic and an Anglophile when it came to philosophy and sport. The English public school system, which he studied at Rugby, was his role model, and in particular its approach to physical education. It was also in England that he became inspired with the 'Olympic Games' being held annually at Much Wenlock in Shropshire. The catalyst for the inauguration of his own international games came when he saw a model of ancient Olympia on display at the Paris Exposition of 1889. Three years later, at a meeting of the Union des Sociétés Françaises de Sports Athlétiques, the national sports association for France he had set up in the late 1880s, he put forward the idea of reviving the Olympic Games. He was rebuffed. Undeterred, in 1894 he tried again, this time at a sports conference in Paris he organised himself, and to which the world was invited.

It was at this point that *The Daily Telegraph* picked up on the story through its eagle-eyed, nose-to-the-ground special correspondent who supplied the regular diary column Paris Day By Day. There was little in the way of gossip, intrigue or scandal which did not attract his attention or comment. So the anonymous half-brother to London Day By Day, and uncle to Peterborough, Spy and Mandrake of later years, could not help but notice the gathering of sporting worthies from thirteen nations who were meeting at the Sorbonne, and no doubt retiring to dine in the swankiest restaurants in the capital which were forever on his radar. And there, buried several hundred words into his epistle of 18 June, 1894, was the following:

Votaries of international sport and games conducted something after the Olympic model met in congress yesterday in the large Hall of the

Sorbonne. Delegates from several foreign countries were present on the occasion, and many ladies also attended in order to hear the laudations of physical force and muscularity. The chair was taken by Baron de Courcel, formerly French Ambassador in Berlin. The Baron made an interesting opening speech, which fully explained the object of the Congress. He pointed out that in these days of intellectual overwork and competition it was necessary to encourage everything tending to the development of muscle as well as of mind. The more young men were trained physically the better they would be able to cope with their fellows in the struggle for life. The speaker highly praised cycling as a means not only of cultivating health and strength, but of bringing people together and of leading up to true fraternity. He also expressed satisfaction at the increased number of wheelwomen, as well as of wheelmen. M. Jean Aicard, the poet, next appeared on the platform, and spoke enthusiastically about gymnastic exercise. After him came M. Theodore de Reinach, who narrated the history of the Greek ode which the members were to hear. This composition was first heard at Delphi 50 years before the Christian Era. It was given in Paris a few months since, after having been touched up by a modern musician. Madame Reinach, who sang the Ode, was warmly acclaimed – especially by the students – who crowded the upper tiers of the hall, and who were rather noisy during some of the speeches. The Congress will continue for a week, and a varied programme of amusement, as well as of work, has been drawn up for the French and foreign delegates, who will combine the useful with the pleasant during their stay. This Congrès International des Sports marks another important stage in the progress of young Frenchmen of the present generation towards the cultivation of manly games.

His column the next day managed to squeeze in another mention of the meeting that would have a more far-reaching significance than he or they could have imagined.

At the first business meeting of the International Athletic Congress, held in the Sorbonne this morning, it was unanimously adopted that the reconstituted Olympic Games should be carried on without money prizes. This decision was arrived at after a general discussion on amateur athletics, in which the foreign delegates took part. In the afternoon the members of the Congress were received at the Hotel de Ville by the president of the Municipal Council.

That, however, was as far as Our Correspondent's interest went, as the swirl of Parisian society swept him up again. Sadly he did not report the final outcome of the meeting that 'sports competitions should be held every fourth year on the lines of the Greek Olympic Games and every nation should be invited to participate'.

Baron de Coubertin had initially suggested that his home city of Paris should host the inaugural Games in 1900. But the Greeks were so enamoured with the idea of resurrecting the Games that the date was brought forward four years and the venue changed to Athens (once it was agreed that Olympia was both too remote and full of ruins). However, of the thirteen countries who attended the Sorbonne summit, and another twenty-one who had sent written support, only a round dozen were represented in Athens in April 1896. The *Telegraph*, without a man on site, relied on Reuter's Agency to supply coverage of those first Games, but carried their updates daily under the headline 'The Olympic Games'. As with the reporting of many sporting occasions at the time, the actual sport was subservient to details of which members of Europe's still numerous royal families were present as witnesses, to wit this brief report datelined Athens, Monday, in the edition of 7 April, 1896:

> The opening of the Olympic Games today is observed as a national festival. The city is decorated with flags, and an enthusiastic interest is taken in the sports.
>
> The day was opened with a 'Te Deum' in the cathedral, at which the members of the Royal family and the Russian Grand Duke George were present. The Russian Prince and his fiancée, the Princess Marie of Greece, were heartily cheered by the people. The weather is cloudy.

The following day's competition 'comprised a number of interesting events', and among the results listed was what must rank as Great Britain's first gold medal. In those days newspaper reports only gave surnames, so it is plain Elliott who is credited with winning the 'Lifting the Weight with one hand' competition with sixty-one kilogrammes. However, he was beaten in the two-handed event by Jensen, of Denmark, who reversed the one-handed placings by lifting 111 kilogrammes. 'The Acropolis,' the poetic Reuter's man noted, 'was illuminated in the evening. The city presents a most animated appearance.'

The Games continued with much royal coming and going, escorted invariably by guards of cavalry, and various banquets were enjoyed.

However, it was the Marathon, along the route taken by Pheidippides in 490 B.C, that caught the imagination of royalty, public and scribe. The *Telegraph* of 11 April reported:

> The great event of today was the foot race from Marathon to Athens, the distance according to the official programme being forty-two kilometres (twenty-six and a quarter miles). The start was made from the famous Tumulus at Marathon and the goal was the Stadion in Athens. The prize is a handsome cup presented by Michel Bréal, member of the Institute of France. There were twenty competitors.
>
> The three placed men were all Greeks, the result being: 1, Louis; 2, Vasilakos; 3, Belokas. The winner's time was two hours fifty-eight minutes. Vasilakos came in eight minutes later, with Belokas twenty-eight seconds behind. The fourth place was taken by a Hungarian. Louis is a peasant of the village of Amarousion, and Vasilakos a Laconian, now resident at the Piraeus. The result occasioned the wildest enthusiasm among the multitudes thronging the Kephissia road and the Stadion.

The report went into greater detail further down:

> At the Stadion more than sixty thousand persons were assembled. The Archduchess Charles of Austria was present at all the events. King Alexander of Servia was also among the spectators, and was loudly cheered on his arrival. Among the native population the greatest interest was taken in the race from Marathon. Traffic was stopped along the whole course. When the winner (Louis) entered the Stadion, and it was seen that the great race had been won by a Greek, tremendous cheers arose on all sides, the spectators rising to their feet and waving their hats and handkerchiefs. The enthusiasm reached its height when the Crown Prince, stepping forward, took the winner by the hand. As Vasilakos and Belokas, two more Greeks, arrived second and third respectively, the cheering broke out anew. The result of the race was quickly telegraphed to all the chief towns of Greece, and demonstrations in honour of the victor are reported from many parts of the country. In Athens itself the result has, of course, evoked great enthusiasm. Louis has been presented with a magnificent antique vase.

Spiridon Louis became the first 'star' of the Olympics, and his place in its history was endorsed when the German organisers employed him during the Berlin Games in 1936. Now 63, and dressed in Greek national costume, Louis presented to Herr Hitler an olive branch grown in Olympia as a symbol of peace. 'With this simple but significant gesture the opening ceremony ended,' reported the *Telegraph*.

Back in 1896, on 13 April, the *Telegraph* noted:

> A luncheon was given at the Palace today in honour of the victors in the Olympic Games. Among those present were the members of the various committees, the correspondents of foreign newspapers, and the representatives of the local press.
>
> During the lunch the King proposed the health of M. Georges Averoff, through whose munificence the Pan-Athenian Stadion has been restored, and of other donors, and also of the Crown Prince and his brothers, Prince George and Prince Nicholas, all of whom, said his Majesty, had worked so largely at the preparations for the Olympic Games. The King hoped that the foreign athletes would proclaim abroad the success of the Games and the progress made by Greece.
>
> The chief event today was a bicycle race from Athens to Marathon and back to the Velodrome at Phalerum, a distance of ninety kilometres (about fifty-six miles). The winner was Constantinides, a Greek, whose time was three hours twenty-two minutes thirty-one seconds. Battel, an Englishman, came in second. There were six competitors.
>
> The Greeks are much gratified that their compatriots have won both Marathon races, namely the one on foot and that on wheels.

On 16 April, the *Telegraph* was reporting that the Games of the first Olympiad were over:

> The Olympic Games were formally brought to a close this morning, when the King and members of the Royal family proceeded to the Stadion and presented the awards to the victors. The weather was brilliant, and the Stadion was densely crowded with people.
>
> On the arrival of the Royal party Mr Robertson, of the United States, read a Pindaric ode on the Olympic Games. A herald-at-arms then proclaimed the names of the victors, who received from the hands of the King a wreath of wild olive brought from Olympia, a medal, a certificate, and a prize. The name of the winner of the Marathon race was hailed with the greatest enthusiasm. Those who secured second place received laurel wreaths. A number of diplomas and medals were

also conferred. The victors then marched round the Stadion in separate parties according to nationality, the band playing the anthem of the respective countries as the representatives passed.

The King brought the ceremony to a close by announcing the termination of the Games. The greatest enthusiasm prevailed throughout.

It has been decided that the Olympic Games shall be repeated every four years at Athens. The foreign athletes have promised their active support.

In fact, despite many suggestions that Athens should become the permanent home of the Games, Baron de Coubertin insisted that the 1900 edition would be held in Paris, and form part of the World Fair being staged in the city. However, the organisers of the Exposition Universelle Internationale wrested away control of the Games and sidelined the poor Baron. Events were spread across five months and diminished to such an extent that the term 'Olympic Games' was barely used. Indeed, they almost passed the gaze of Our Correspondent in France, and his infrequent mentions in the Paris Day By Day column seemed to ignore the fact that they were the same entity which had been discussed at the Sorbonne six years previously. On 17 July, 1900, at the end of his column, he wrote:

American athletes who have come over here to join in the international championships now being contested on the Racing Club grounds in the Bois de Boulogne have practically carried all before them in the various events which have taken place up to date. Out of eight contests so far held, for example, the United States' undergraduates have secured the finals in no less than six, namely the 110 metres hurdles, the 100 metres flat, throwing the weight, the sixty metres flat, the 400 metres flat, the high jump. The English competitor Bennett carried off the 1,500 metres flat, and a Hungarian the disk-throwing contest, so that the home champions were nowhere in the field.

A week later, however, he found something into which he could sink his journalistic teeth.

The series of international athletic contests in connection with the Exhibition, which have been held here on the grounds of the Racing Club in the Bois de Boulogne, and in which the United States champions have proved victorious nearly all along the line, have now been completed. The last important event, however, fell not to the American, but to the British team. This was the so-called race of nations, over 5,000 metres, or some 5,400 yards. The places were to be competed for not by individual champions, but by countries, and to be allotted according to the points made by each respective international team. Only two countries turned up at the start – France and England, the United States competitors standing little or no chance on the distance. Bennett, the winner of the 1,500 metres flat race previously, led from the start, then leaving first place to Rimmer. The two Englishmen kept the running to the finish, the French team only securing third place. Counting the positions of the five competitors on both sides, England won by twenty-six points to twenty-nine, although owing to the refusal of the judge to allow Orton – a Canadian born, but an undergraduate of Pennsylvania College – to compete in the British team, Cowley had been compelled to join the latter, and being a sprinter had perforce to be content to walk most of the distance.

Something rather like a scandal has arisen in connection with the awards for the above international contests. The sports as such have been unimpeachable, being both irreproachably conducted and full of interest. But the prizes given were hardly worthy of the occasion of an international athletic championship meeting got up in connection with the Exhibition. The 'cups' presented consisted mainly of cheap bronzes, and, worse still, of porcelain plates of no artistic value whatever. It has been an open secret that the poverty of the prizes has been a standing joke among the English and American competitors who came over here for the contest, but, of course, no complaints were made. Now, however, the French organisers of the meeting, not best-pleased at the prospect of gaining a reputation for meanness, have taken the matter in hand, and an inquiry has, it appears, elucidated the fact that an unscrupulous tradesman made a good thing out of the contract to supply the prizes by furnishing, instead of goods of the value specified, the worthless so-called objects of art which the English and American competitors have carried away, and which they will certainly not display on their mantelpieces when they get home.

The lessons of the disaster that was Paris were not learnt. Initially the International Olympic Committee awarded the 1904 Games to Chicago, but when St Louis threatened to organise a rival competition as part of the

World Fair being held in their city, the intervention of President Theodore Roosevelt forced the I.O.C. to vote again. This time the Games were held over four-and-a-half months, but again they became subsidiary to the exhibition. In fact, they became little more than all-American championships. Only four European and four other nations took part, and the United States swept up; indeed they won every single track and field event. Not surprisingly, the *Telegraph* ignored the event completely. It did find room for the results from the Great Eastern Railway Sports, held at the Essex County Cricket Ground at Leyton, within sight of today's Olympic Park (five thousand people turned up for the annual event in 'delightful weather'). The only event reported from St Louis while the athletics were being staged was a fatal accident between a train and a tram on a crossing. It might have been a metaphor.

Two years later, in 1906, the Greeks held an intercalated (intermediary) Games. At first, Baron de Coubertin was against the idea, but was eventually convinced by the enthusiasm of the organisers and included them under the umbrella of the Olympic Movement. However, more than forty years later, and a dozen years after the Baron's death, Avery Brundage, then president of the I.O.C., chaired a commission that decided the Athens meeting was not an official Olympic Games. No one argued. They were, though, the first Games to restrict the number of entries sent by each country and the first to stage a parade of the teams.

The *Telegraph* had Our Special Correspondent on hand to report on the Opening Ceremony in its 23 April, 1906, issue:

> Brilliant weather, in spite of menacing rain, greeted the opening of the Olympic Games this afternoon. At the British Legation King Edward and the Prince of Wales lunched with Sir Francis and Lady Elliot, the only lady present, the party also including Sir Charles Hardinge, the Mayor of the Piraeus, Lord Desborough and Mr Bosanquet, the two British representatives, Commander the Honourable Seymour Fortescue, R.N., Major Ponsonby, and Earl Howe. The King has shown great interest in the chances of the English athletes.

The Games being duly opened, the Royal visitors sat back and watched, as the *Telegraph*'s man noted:

> A few gymnastic exhibitions followed, the most pleasing of which was the Danish girls, short-skirted and neat-legged, led by a teacher in grave

flowing robes and abundant light golden hair. Their combined curtsy to the Royal personages produced instant cheers, and they went through many graceful evolutions. Colonel Balck's Swedish team also did very well, and for several hours the brilliant spectacle went on until I was obliged to leave to send this message, while their Majesties remained.

Just as it had ten years before, the Marathon proved to be of the greatest interest to the local population. Before it started, however, there was a success for Great Britain at the Stadium, as the *Telegraph* reported on 2 May:

> Glorious weather prevailed today, and the whole of Hellas seemed concentrated at Athens to see the result of the great Marathon race in the Stadium. The day began well with Leahy winning the high jump for England, but our flag did not rise again in the final of the half-mile. The Americans made the pace, as usual, for both the Englishmen, Lieutenant Halswell and Crabbe, had drawn outside places at the start. Before halfway had been reached, Halswell went up, and then Crabbe led, but at the last corner both the Americans spurted, shutting out the Englishmen, and won with Pilgrim, Lightbody, Halswell, Crabbe, in that order. The time was very fast indeed, being two minutes one second for the 800 metres.
>
> The final for the hurdles was rather a surprise, as the Englishman made a bold showing. After one false start all got away level. Healey drew slowly out, and actually led at the last hurdle, but was beaten on the run-in by inches by the American, Leavitt, in sixteen and one-fifth seconds, on a slow track.
>
> Expectancy rose high as the time approached for the finish of the Marathon race, and the enormous amphitheatre of marble seats was fairly humming with voices in every language. The Englishmen remembered that Cormack, a light-built runner, had done a fine long-distance race in the Transvaal over twenty-five miles, and Daly was our other champion, a man of very different style, tall, heavy, hot-tempered, and very plucky. The general opinion was that the better runners, with their greater experience, would beat last year's time, and would be well under three hours for the forty-two kilometres. All the competitors were medically examined before going to Marathon yesterday, and Mr Bosanquet, director of the British School, sent his

own cook with food and wine for the Englishmen. There were also great rumours about the Americans and Greeks practising for weeks on the course, so that the long interval of waiting by the sixty thousand spectators was easily filled up, and every inch of the hill above the marble arena was packed with Greeks from every district south of Turkey, and there was a solid line of soldiers right round the top against the blue sky.

At length news reached the committee within the ring that the Irishman, Daly, was leading within ten kilometres of Athens. At ten minutes to six a sudden roar began gathering in the distance, where a cavalry officer was seen riding ahead of a solitary runner. This was Sherring, of Canada, a small, light man, running happily with a smile on his face. The Crown Prince ran alongside him beside the track, and he finished his long and dusty journey in front of the King and Queen of Greece, who handed him a bouquet of flowers. He then walked steadily to the dressing-room, evidently none the worse. Some time after a Swedish runner came in second, and I myself went out down the long road lined with soldiers and spectators, heading from the suburbs to the Stadium. A barbarian victory was evidently unexpected, and unwelcome to the Athenian crowd. I hurried down the line, and met an American third, and a Dane fourth. I was then obliged to go to send this message, as the city, the telegraph office, and roads are all packed to suffocation. The winner's time for the race was two hours fifty-one minutes twenty-three seconds. This gives the British Empire the greatest race of all, and raises our score to four firsts against the Americans' eleven, the Greeks' three, and Sweden's two firsts.

Nothing remains now but the prize-giving tomorrow, and the memory of the entire Greek nation, which is wildly enthusiastic over the greatest athletic meeting ever seen here.

I

LONDON 1908

13 JULY 1908

LEADING ARTICLE

Today King Edward, accompanied by the Queen, the Sovereigns of Greece and Norway and a brilliant retinue, will open the Fourth Olympiad of the modern series in the greatest athletic arena ever erected, whether in the classic or the later world. Upon the shining success with which all the preliminaries have been accomplished Lord Desborough and his friends are to be congratulated. Between two and three thousand of the finest amateurs in contemporary sport are assembled in London from all quarters of the earth. Twenty-two different nations are represented in an amicable contest, which reminds us once more that by slow but sure degrees civilisation is moving towards the friendly federation of mankind. As 'our aspirations are the index to our capabilities', so the greatest dreams of one age are but the foreshadowing of the ideals which some ultimate generation will practically realise. Our London, as the greatest city in the world, has, as it were, opened her hospitable gates this year to the representatives of all peoples, and we may well believe that the international pleasures of which the metropolis has been the scene in this memorable season have contributed some little towards the cause of human progress.

The great Games which begin in the vast Stadium today will be the most important festival of their kind yet held in modern times. Never has so wide a theatre been prepared. Never have interesting events been arranged in such number and variety. Never has so large an attendance of spectators been secured. Never has there been a more complete certainty that the proceedings will be carried out from first to last in the noblest spirit of sport. London opinion may be trusted to keep the ring fairly, and to greet all our foreign guests with the utmost generosity. If they carry off the greater number of the prizes, we shall not grudge them their victory. The unwritten motto of the London Olympiad is, Let the best men win. If we have, like others, our national preferences, we do not indulge them on this occasion. We are, as Greece, France and the United States have been in their turn, the temporary trustees of the world for all athletic purposes. The origin of the movement for the revival in our own time of the most famous festival of classic civilisations is well known. In 1894 the idea was first advocated by that well-known French publicist, Baron Pierre de Coubertin. The thought fired many imaginations, and was hailed with immense enthusiasm in Greece. There were, as a matter of course, some objections from pedants, and some gloomy anticipations of inevitable failure from the pessimists. In the end, however, all difficulties were overcome, and the Games were revived at Athens in 1896. The occasion was fitly honoured by the splendid patriotism of a wealthy Greek merchant, Mr Averoff, of Alexandria. By his munificence the ancient Stadium of Athens was entirely reseated with marble. The first modern Olympiad, revived under the skies of Hellas, proved a magnificent success, and ensured the continuance of the Games as a recurrent part of international life in the twentieth century. The next assembly of the world's athletes took place in Paris in 1900, the third at St Louis in 1904. It had originally been intended to hold the present festival in Rome. The Italian committee transferred their privilege to this country.

The opportunity happily coincided with the approach of the Franco-British Exhibition and of other events sufficient of themselves to make the present season the most characteristic social episode of King Edward's reign. The conditions were in every respect propitious, and nothing has been left undone which could help to ensure not only that the London Olympiad shall be worthy of its immediate predecessors, but that it shall set a standard which may be again equalled elsewhere, but will not soon be surpassed. In one sense, modern athletics, based as they are upon an intensely scientific method, seem utilitarian in their aspect and in many of their general associations, no matter how enthusiastic they may be in spirit, or how full of the finest temper of amateur sport. Yet, over the scene of modern London which will be opened by The King today, in the presence of his brother Sovereigns, there will brood the august memories of the ages. For nearly twelve hundred years, from the fresh and roseate dawn of Hellenic culture to that critical moment of Christian civilisation when the fall of the Western Empire of Rome was at hand, the athletic contests upon the sacred plain in Elis were a rallying point for the whole Greek race. Greece was fated to political destruction because it could not establish a fighting federation. But there was a racial unity of culture, if not of government, and Hellenic life gained in eager vitality and infinite richness by the very divisions which helped a more compacted race to win the dominion of the whole Mediterranean. Ere that moment came the annals of the Olympiads were already a splendid record. The Games were held every four years, in Midsummer, as the moon drew Hellenic blood. What we call Greece today was as different from the wider Hellas of antiquity as is this island from Greater Britain. The competitors came from every city and valley of those miniature, yet immortal, States of the Peninsula, whose whole life was typified by the 'Bards who died content, leaving great verse unto a little clan'. But the men of Hellas were the men of the shores of the sea. Greek lands bordered more than one side of the Mediterranean. So the proud Ionian cities sent their runners, throwers, and boxers. Hardy colonists coasted down from the ultima thule of classic colonisation, the Black Sea. From Sicily and the south of Italy came champions who never dreamed that their birthplaces would be severed one day from the mother race, and that the very tongue of Hellas would cease to be remembered where it had once reigned. And from still further settlements in the Middle Sea came competitors chosen to appear for the Greek communities at Marseilles and elsewhere. From Alexandria and other cities on the African coast were drawn the Greek athletes of a third continent. Surrounded by solemn ceremony as they were, and full of the sense of sanctity in the living race-tie, no less than in the thought of a common ancestry, which was always dwelt upon with religious feeling by the ancients, the old Olympiads at their height were occasions of an incomparable charm. More than a thousand years, as we have said, they endured, as part of that afterglow of Greek culture, slow in fading, which remained when the sun of Hellenic power and liberty had set.

The feature which will strike foreign visitors to the present festival is the magnificence of the Stadium at the Franco-British Exhibition. This huge structure will seat as many spectators, that is to say about eighty thousand, as found room in the largest of the ancient amphitheatres, the Roman Coliseum itself; and at the same time it affords a much more spacious area for games. If this arena were constructed in a more classic material, it would be easily beyond all compare as an athletic centre. If it does not attempt to imitate the triumphs of antique architecture, it is at least an equally wonderful achievement of modern engineering. M. Paul Bourget, with a flash of insight approaching genius, once said that the American mastery of steel was the modern equivalent of the Greek mastery of marble. A similar thing might be said of the technical ability of the present age upon this side of the Atlantic. As an example of metallic construction the Stadium is no less interesting in its way than the Eiffel Tower or the *Lusitania*. Its lofty tiers, affording room for three or four army corps of onlookers, sweep around an immense ellipse with an exact grace of proportion which rather diminishes than emphasises the effect of mere size. The utilisation of the space within shows that the present world by comparison with the classic is as much more complex in its amusements as in its graver labours. Immediately below the seats runs the cemented cycle-track, which gives over a third of a mile to the lap. Next, in a narrowing series of concentric circles, is a broad ribbon of turf. Within this is the cinder-path, of which three laps make a mile. Then in the centre of all comes what may be called 'the field' – a wide, grassy lawn, where every kind of short distance event may take place in full view. Nor is this all. Upon an edge of the green expanse is erected for the swimming contests a tank of water more than three hundred feet long and about fifty wide, with a staging over the deep water, where a thirty-foot dive may be taken in safety. Among events more various than we have space to catalogue, one of the most popular features will be the revival of the classic exercises of throwing the discus and flinging the javelin. But the crowning day of the great Games will be reached only next week, when the 'Marathon Race' will be run over a distance of twenty-six miles, starting from the walls of Windsor and finishing in the exhibition grounds. The name of the contest, as every schoolboy knows, commemorates the feat of the herald who ran the same distance with the news of the Persian King's defeat and fell dead in the Acropolis. In a more general sense, the chief interest of the sports, from first to last, will attach to the performances of the American delegation. Upon their own soil in St Louis they won, out of seventeen international events, no less than fifteen. Their achievement in any case is almost certain to be magnificent, and London, while hoping that British competitors may hold their own in some trials against all comers, can only congratulate itself on becoming the scene of the greatest display of its kind witnessed in any arena since athletics began.

---

13 JULY 1908
KING EDWARD AND THE OLYMPIC GAMES
TODAY'S CEREMONY
RIVAL NATIONS
MEETING OF THE WORLD'S ATHLETES
Our Special Correspondent

Opened by His Majesty The King today, the great Olympic Games bid fair to be the most remarkable athletic meeting which has taken place in historic annals. The variety and number of the events have rendered necessary a most complicated programme. The King arrives at half-past three, and all spectators wishing to see the opening ceremony must be in their seats by three o'clock exactly.

Only those with special tickets will be able to drive up to the Royal box, and ticket holders for reserved seats in other parts of the Stadium will do well to arrive by one or other of the Wood-lane entrances by half-past two at latest. Ten thousand tickets for standing-room in the north blocks have been reduced from two shillings to one shilling for today. The Stadium and its approaches have been supervised for the occasion by a special committee, so there is no likelihood of the mistakes of last May, and all that is needed to ensure success is the strict observation by the public of that punctuality which is so distinguished a characteristic of our gracious Sovereign.

The Significance of Today

Like all vast and complicated things, this meeting will, to a large extent, progress by its own momentum, and go on from one sensation to another. But in the midst of the cutting of the records, and the shouting of the thousand-headed crowd of spectators, let us try to remember that something more important than a victory in the hurdles, or a close fight for the half-mile, is in reality at stake.

We are on our trial, not only before the eighteen hundred athletes who have trusted us sufficiently to come over here, but before the trained observers who represent the twenty different nations competing, and that trial is not merely concerned with athletic matters: it will be affected by a hundred different details of character, of conduct, of organisation; and it will have a widespread and enduring influence upon the political and social future of the world. We are judged by the older of our visitors; but the most vivid impression we shall make will be upon our younger guests, who are the coming generation in politics, in commerce, in international problems of all kinds. These latter will be at once more ruthless in their verdict, and more direct in their response. It lies with us, during the next fortnight, to say what that response will be.

---

14 JULY 1908

LEADING ARTICLE

Though the immediate spectacle in the Great Stadium was marred by one of the untoward intervals of a glorious summer, we cannot doubt that yesterday's inaugural ceremony by The King was the stately prelude to a magnificent success. The great Games will fill almost another fortnight in July, and we may well hope that the favour of the elements will crown with brilliant weather the conditions that in every other respect have left nothing lacking. The opening scene was direct and brief. Lord Desborough presented the foreign delegates to His Majesty. King Edward fulfilled the purpose of the occasion in one ringing sentence: 'I declare the Olympic Games of London open.' Then followed a scene which lowering skies could not rob of its spirit and impressiveness. The two thousand picked athletes of the world had walked in, nation by nation, and were marshalled in solid array in front of the Royal box. The King's words were no sooner said than the trumpeters blew a fanfare, the National Anthem followed, and after three cheers for His Majesty, as fine a phlanx of young manhood as sport has ever brought together in any age trooped past the Sovereign. Each nation marched, as it were, in character, and the scene as they circled the path was as memorable and stirring a spectacle of its kind as has been witnessed or could be imagined in connection with modern athletics. The pride of place was conceded by all English-speaking delegates to the foreign representatives. These latter ranked according to their nations, taken in alphabetical order. At the head of all, keeping time to the drums, came the Austrians. Each country had its distinctive costume, but there is nothing invidious in saying that, by common consent of all their colleagues in the march and of every spectator in the Stadium, the finest display was made by the Scandinavian nations. Upon this occasion no hint of the political divisions of these splendid sea-races of the North could be detected, and as they went by they seemed in physique and in every aspect of racial type to be practically one people. They moved with military precision, in white costumes which were the scrupulous perfection of neatness. They deserved the volleys of cheering with which they were received. The English-speaking nations were led by the strong column of redoubtable athletes sent over by the United States, to be acclaimed with generous warmth by the whole gathering around them, as well as by the applause and flag-waving from their fellow citizens of both sections. Next came the sons of the Empire, owning their allegiance to a common flag by rendering to their Sovereign as they passed the military salute due from his subjects throughout the world to The King of All the Britains.

In spite of the ill-humour of the elements there was an evident significance and effectiveness in this inaugural procession which will not easily be forgotten by those who beheld it. But almost in a matter of moments these stately preliminaries were over, and the athletes of the London Olympiad came to business. While most of them vanished into the dressing-rooms, alert cyclists appeared upon the cement track, and the Scandinavians put up their gymnastic apparatus. These, however, were harmless exercises. The Great Games were seriously opened by the heats for the race of 1,500 metres, corresponding pretty nearly to an English mile. It looked first as though our American friends were about to repeat their marvellous performance at St Louis. There, as we have already said, they carried off fifteen events out of seventeen. In feats of the most varied kind, in running, jumping, throwing the hammer, putting the shot, and in many other tests of strength or skill, they easily vanquished the delegates of all the rest of the world put together. There is no doubt that the climate of the North American Continent and the traditional temperament of its people tend to create a race of born athletes. They are lean rather than fleshy. There is more abstention from alcohol among very many millions of the American and Canadian peoples than among any similar number of the populations of Europe. Then they are helped by the tremendous power of concentration, in which the average citizen of the New World far excels the ordinary inhabitant of the Old. Every fibre of physique, every faculty of intelligence is exerted together to the utmost and made to bear upon one end. Hence, even if the records at St Louis should not be altogether maintained in London, we may accept it as a fact that the American people have reached and will keep an astonishing level of athletic excellence. At the outset yesterday's running heats threatened to go all one way. Two runners from the United States won the first two places in the opening trial, and a Canadian came third. The next test showed two representatives of the United States again in the front. After that, however, several heats were carried off for Great Britain, and one for Canada, so that at the close of the preliminaries for the 1,500 metres race the Mother Country won five heats out of eight. The final should be a grand struggle, and even if our men do not win through they will have shown that there is still considerable vitality in this island. In the swimming contest we have at present an easy lead, and have held our own in the great bicycle race.

The fascinating thing about the Olympiads of the present and the future ought to be the very fact that they sift out of the general gathering the special aptitudes of each nation. No man, as Macaulay says somewhere, ever made a bad figure in the world if he knew just what he could do, nor a good figure if he failed to recognise his own true bent. The same thing applies to nations. Each of them, by its separate characteristics of physique and temperament, is especially fitted to surpass all competitors in some one form of sport. This is what distinguished the unparalleled festival opened yesterday from the quadrennial games in Greece. There the spirit of the contests was that of race-enthusiasm rising to the fervour of a religion. The barbarians who represented the vast majority of mankind were rigidly excluded. But, in spite of all the terrible fluctuations of human fortune in the recurrent cycles of war, the world progresses, and its peoples are drawn together. 'The mountains look on Marathon and Marathon looks on the sea.' The herald raced the twenty-six miles to Athens, and cried with his last breath that the hosts of Darius were shattered and that Greece was free. The figure of that runner with immortal news is well commemorated by the trophy to be presented to the victor of next week's great race from Windsor to the Stadium, for the herald of Hellas had proclaimed as he died the epoch-making triumph over barbarism of that young Civilisation whose intensely Western spirit still vitalises the international life of today.

———

15 JULY 1908

BANQUET TO COMPETITORS

Covers were laid for over six hundred and fifty at the banquet at the Holborn Restaurant, at which Lord Desborough and the council entertained the competitors and officials of the Olympic Games last night, but many seats were vacant, possibly owing to the fact that athletes were bearing in mind that dinners and success in athletics on the following days hardly go hand in hand. In conformity with the spirit of the great meeting, the decorations of the hall, as well as the music during dinner, were impartially international; the flags of all nations gently waved over the guests, and a fantasia of the national anthems of the principal peoples of the earth was enthusiastically greeted, the whole company rising and joining heartily in the refrain, not only of 'Rule, Britannia', but also of the 'Marseillaise' and the 'Watch on the Rhine'.

The toast list was commendably short, the healths drunk being only two, that of King Edward VII, and that of the Olympic Games. In giving the former, which was received with round after round of applause, the chairman was asked that The King's health should be drunk with special reference to him as the great monarch who opened these athletic games, and the one to whom was due so much of the success that had been achieved.

In proposing the toast of 'The Olympic Games', Lord Desborough promised that he would use but few words. They were all athletes, and knew the value of going to bed early. (Laughter.) Whatever might happen in the future, he was sure that in the past there had never gathered together such wonderful exponents of sport in all its manifold branches, and he, in the name of the British committee, thanked them for attending. One side of the movement was athletic, but there was another, which was to get together men from all nations who might, while contesting with each other, make friends with each other. (Loud cheers.) He himself had been a bit of an athlete, and he knew that whilst one might feel nettled at the time at being beaten, the vanquished felt in his heart a warm regard for the victor. For each, the aim was not only to do the best for himself, but to remember he was fighting for his flag and his country – (cheers) – and that in the sport of sportsmen there was give as well as take. It was the aim of those who organised the games to carry them through without fear or favour to man or country. (Cheers.) He wished also to thank those who had contributed so liberally to the entertainment of the country's guests. (Cheers.) He hoped that the visitors would be able to see something both of the capital and of the country to which they had come, and it was proposed to take some four hundred athletes each day to see something of the sights, not only of London, but of the surrounding places of interest.

———

17 JULY 1908
NEW 100 KILOMETRES RECORD
A TIME-LIMIT FIASCO

Apart from the drenching of rain, the most vivid incidents to be remembered in connection with yesterday's continuation of the Games at the Stadium occurred in the cycling races. They proved singularly unfortunate to the two crack Continental riders. Coeckelberg, the Belgian long-distance celebrity, was thrown from his machine when well leading the field in the 100-kilometres race. The cause was a collision with an official of the Amateur Athletic Association, who had strayed upon the track. Schilles, the magnificently-proportioned young Frenchman, who is *facile princeps* on the Continent, if not in this country also, at shorter distances, was robbed of the honours attaching to a win in the final of the 1,000-metres race. It cannot be said that the sweets of victory were denied to him, however, as he and his countrymen have the satisfaction of knowing that he defeated three of our best cyclists in the first test. These happenings, it must be stated, gave great dissatisfaction to the French and Belgian visitors, particularly in the case of Coeckelberg's regrettable fall.

If one fact was made more evident than another it revealed Coeckelberg as the only man likely to beat our champion, Meredith. Riding easily out of himself, the Belgian took the eye of the critics as the probable winner of the race. The sickening thud with which his head came into contact with the track would have deterred most men from continuing. But he duly delayed doing so long enough to recover from the shock, and very palpably express his feelings to the creator of the trouble. Taking a towel to staunch the blood that was flowing from several injuries, he gave an exhibition of pluck and will-power that can seldom have been surpassed in the annals of cycling.

There were still some twenty miles to be traversed, and Coeckelberg set himself to try and recover the two-thirds of a lap that separated him from the leading file of riders as he resumed the saddle. To his infinite credit, and thereby adding to his great reputation, he struggled on and on. Only in the last two laps did he get within hail of his field. He finished seventh, within one hundred yards of the winner, Meredith. But to the general satisfaction he qualified for the final, although out of the first half-dozen leaders, by reason of having gained the second highest number of points for lap-leading. Meredith, with his most dangerous rival so sorely handicapped, won the race in a time that lowered the previous best on record for the one hundred kilometres by nearly six minutes. A fast pace was maintained throughout, and all the riders who went the full distance were inside the record. Other mishaps occurred, two men actually falling in the last lap. Early on one of the French representatives, J. Madèlaine, was so badly hurt that he had to be carried from the track on a stretcher. Puncturing of tyres played a prominent part, and, as usual, Meredith was one of the sufferers in this direction. Over-inflation or very thin tyres are probably the cause of his frequent breakdowns in this way.

There is a time-limit fixed to every cycle race, with the sole exception of the pursuit race. The limit set for the 1,000 metres – one minute forty-five seconds – cannot be said to have erred on the side of excess. Had it been extended to two minutes the unpleasantness which followed the victory of Schilles, well and honestly won, in the final test from three British opponents would not have happened. A rule is a rule, of course, and for many months the foreign Olympic executives have had copies of the terms relating to the conduct of the cycling races in their possession. It is only reasonable, therefore, to infer that these were made known to their representatives taking part in the Games. Yet a distinct feeling arose in impartial minds that, in such exceptional circumstances and on such an occasion, the time-limit might well have been discarded. A race is a race, whatever the length of time it may occupy. And in cycling, especially, the race does not always go to the speediest rider. A good tactician will, as often as not, beat a pedaller of superior ability by his opportunist methods. There are no more brainy riders than the French, whose best riders are past-masters of track craft. Schilles justified this impression to the full by the way he outrode and outmanoeuvred our two cracks, Johnson and Jones, after that, perhaps, more dependable performer on such a heavy track, Kingsbury, had fallen early in the race.

The 400 metres swimming race proved to be the medium by which the Union Jack came to the masthead. It was thought that the Australian, Beaurepaire, was the strongest force competing. But these opinions were not borne out in the race, as the British first string, H. Taylor, practically led from start to finish. But for steering a most erratic course he would have won even more easily than he actually did. It was in the last of the four lengths that his stamina told. Beaurepaire turned almost simultaneously with him, the Australian's smartness in this direction being very much remarked, with the Austrian, Scheff, in close pursuit. From that point Taylor went away fast. In a good fight for second place Beaurepaire finished three yards ahead of Scheff. He has, however, to run the gauntlet of an objection – apparently urged with reason – for impeding the third swimmer.

---

17 JULY 1908
LADY COMPETITORS
IMPRESSIONS OF LONDON

The gentle invasion of the domain of sport by ladies is, of course, no new thing. Apart altogether from the hunt, which ladies have adorned for generations, we have in modern times expert lady tennis players and archers, and more recently still lady golfers and lady rifle shots. Even at the great carnival of sport which is being continued from day to day at the Stadium, the greatest affair of its kind which the world has yet seen, lady competitors are playing a much larger part than is apparent to the eye of the casual visitor to the vast arena in Shepherd's-bush. The fact that a Swedish lady has carried off one of the Olympic medals for covered courts lawn tennis would of itself prove that ladies have not entered the lists in vain; and in the archery events, too, ladies are only maintaining a position which they have honourably won. To that extent, therefore, the Danish ladies whose gymnastic exhibitions have evoked such admiration at the Stadium are not the sole representatives of the foreign lady element at the fourth Olympiad. It is, however, the proud boast of these clear-skinned and bright-eyed Danish damsels that their nation furnished the first team of ladies who ever participated in an Olympiad. This was at Athens in 1906. And it is pleasant to recall that when King Edward and Queen Alexandra visited the Greek capital a couple of years ago, and witnessed the Olympic Games, they evinced the greatest interest in the performances of Denmark's fair daughters, and His Majesty expressed the hope that they would pay the London Olympiad a visit in due course.

His Majesty's hope has been fulfilled, for, as we know, the gymnastic exercises of the Danish ladies' team at the Stadium this week have been the subject of general and favourable comment. But the group of Danish ladies now participating in the gymnastic exercises at the Stadium is not the same group which introduced so charming an innovation into the round of sports at Athens. The band of twenty-four young ladies over whom Mrs Lonborg Nilsen so capably presides as instructress and directress was only chosen little more than a month ago. They were selected to represent their country from amongst the pupils of the Danish Gymnastik Austalt in Copenhagen, and the only special preparation they received for their appearance at the Stadium had to be imparted subsequently. This preparation, however, was more in the nature of rehearsal than tuition. The ladies had all been thoroughly grounded in the gymnastic exercises which are so integral a feature of the Danish system of education, and all that really required to be done was to arrange the precise number and sequence of the exercises that were to be given. How thoroughly the work has been done under Mrs Lonborg Nilsen's care is well known to all who witnessed the performance of the young ladies at the Stadium on Monday and again yesterday.

From a conversation a representative of *The Daily Telegraph* had at the Stadium yesterday afternoon with Mrs Anna Glane, who has had not a little to do with the arrangements for the young ladies travel to and from Denmark, and for their stay in London, it would appear that Mrs Lonborg Nilsen and her fair charges entered the arena on Monday afternoon with a good deal of trepidation. Monday, as it happened, was the first occasion on which the young ladies had ever drilled on grass, and, needless to say, it was the first time they had ever appeared before so large a gathering of spectators. Now, however, they were extremely delighted to be told that their performances had made a favourable impression upon the cosmopolitan multitude at the Stadium. If they have upheld the honour of their country – and of that there can be no shadow of doubt – they feel amply compensated for all the pains that have been taken over their four weeks' preparation.

It is to be hoped that the lessons derivable from the exhibitions given by these young ladies from Copenhagen are not being lost upon those who in this country are directly interested in and responsible for the physical culture of the rising womanhood of the nation. Indulgence in superlatives is always dangerous, but really there is no getting away from the fact that the display which these young ladies give is in some respects unique. 'The point of the Danish system,' said Mrs Glane, yesterday, 'is to develop beauty with strength. Everything in our country is based on scientific principles.' And then, she added, with an arch smile, 'From our butter-making upwards.' The grace which these ladies maintain their exercises, no matter how difficult they may seem, is beyond dispute; and that is one reason why some of our instructors in callisthenics might do well to see them at work.

It would be the greatest mistake to imagine that there is nothing to be learned from this Danish team. We can even, perhaps, learn something from them in the matter of costume. It was impossible to watch their performance on Wednesday afternoon, when two teams of English young ladies were in the arena at the same time, without seeing that the English costume compared unfavourably with the Danish. The conventional English navy blue, with its trimmings of scarlet or white, did not seem nearly so neat, or even so businesslike, as the simple cream serge and light brown hose of the visitors. Not only was the English garb not so presentable to the eye, but it did not display the shapeliness of the limbs from the knee downwards nearly so well as did the attire of the ladies from Denmark. Opinions, of course, may differ on these points; but the fact remains that the neatness and simplicity of the Danish costume was the subject of general remark.

---

17 JULY 1908

LETTERS TO THE EDITOR
EMPTY SEATS AT THE STADIUM

Sir – I think it would be a good idea if one-half of the Stadium was closed entirely, leaving the portion nearest the winning post for its patrons. I was in the two shillings part yesterday, and could not distinguish the numbers on the boards, owing to the fact that the boards were not turned in our direction. If the present show cannot draw – and it will not under the present exorbitant prices – what is to become of it in the future? I tried – two days running – to get a seat on the winning-post side, but was told that they were not selling any for those parts, as it would spoil the sale of the higher-priced seats.

S. Blanchett
Shaftsbury-avenue, W.C.

Sir — Would you kindly allow me to point out that the real reason why the public do not patronise these Games is the prices, which are so high and uneven on all sides? On Monday last, when His Majesty arrived, I saw a large number of persons, English and foreigners, actually turned away from Block B (the 1s section), whilst in the adjoining area, the price being 4s, there were hardly any spectators at all. I would respectfully suggest that a charge of 6d or 1s be made only for fifty thousand out of the eighty thousand seats provided, and that a uniform charge of 6d for all parts be made to those who have paid to enter the Exhibition, and desire also to enter the Stadium. The weather has really nothing whatever to do with the shrinkage in the attendance, for, as an old sport myself — and I believe I speak on behalf of all real Britishers who possess that splendid instinct of sport within their breasts — we do not care a brass-button top whether it rains, thunders, or snows if there is sport to be seen, and the prices are commensurate with the capacity of our pockets. The great British public will not in the main patronise anything where the prices are prohibitive, and I am certain, if my suggestion is adopted, they will flock in their thousands, as they do to a football match. In such a magnificent spectacle of such classic encounters between all the nations as can now be beheld near our very doors, it is a great pity the management cannot drop their mistaken policy, and realise that the prices are dead against the success of their worthy enterprise.

Walter Stephens
London

---

18 JULY 1908

IN THE COMPETITORS' STAND
A STUDY IN CONTRASTS

Visitors to the Stadium during the past few days must often have been puzzled by the positively frantic keenness with which the Olympic Games are followed by the occupants of one of the stands on the side of the arena opposite to that in which the Royal box is situated. It is really the only quarter of the spacious arena in which the spirit of international emulation is maintained from day to day at fever heat. The shilling stands at the extremities of the Stadium obviously contain the sporting crowd. The impartial fashion in which the spectators there located greet every brilliant finish, every plucky, even if unsuccessful, effort, no matter what the nationality of the competitor who may be the hero of the moment, shows that here, at all events, is the democratic multitude which cheers sportsmanship for its own sake.

The huge covered stand between which and the Royal box the full breadth of the arena interposes, wears its enthusiasm with a difference. It makes the welkin ring with its applause in sections, rather than as a separate entity in the meagre but cosmopolitan crowd which follows the sports from day to day. The reason is obvious. You might almost have guessed it from the first. It is the competitors' stand – the clean-cut section of the amphitheatre, in which the athletes of all nations gather together incidentally to witness the sports, but primarily, as it would seem, to cheer their competitors and to acclaim with frenzied applause their national standard when, as the signal for victory, it happens to be run to the masthead.

An interesting quarter of the Stadium is this competitors' stand. It is at once a pandemonium of patriotism and a babel of tongues. As you sit in the midst of its steep sloping benches, you can listen to nearly all the languages of Europe at once. What is more, you have a sort of ethnographic chart of the full-blooded manhood of Europe, and of the English-speaking peoples across the seas, spread in front of you. If you are fond of that sort of thing you can compare the physique of the swarthy Italian or Hungarian with the fair-haired Scandinavian, Dane, or Finn, or with the keen and strenuous Colonial and American. Even the materials for a comparative study of national dress are thrown at you without the asking. The caps, indeed, would make a special study by themselves.

But it is neither the dress nor even the physique of this congress of the youth of all nations that most impresses the spectator. It is the limitless vivacity of these young men, their overflowing patriotism, their faculty for rising from their seats as one man on the slightest provocation, and rendering volley after volley of cheering as a tribute to pluck, endurance, or success. They have crossed the seas to compete at the Stadium, and if the Stadium does not hear of them as the aspiring representatives of their country, it is not their fault. But there are degrees in this effervescent patriotism of the different sections of this cosmopolitan multitude – a multitude that is to be numbered by the hundred, and perhaps by the thousand. The Americans comfortably bear off the palm for cock-a-whoop demonstrativeness. When their nation scores a win, everybody knows of it. If he does not know of it, he must be either blind or deaf, because, as soon as a competitor from the United States overcomes anything or anybody, dozens of Stars and Stripes are whipped out, and the air is rent with wildest shouting. If runners-up to the Americans had to be found they might be looked for among the fair-haired and white-capped representatives of the races of Northern Europe. But the Swedes, the Norwegians, the Danes, the Finns are modesty itself compared with the hustling young men from the other side of the Atlantic. The Swedes shout right lustily – and yesterday, it will be admitted, they had very good grounds for doing so – but theirs is the shout of honest pride and genuine glee, and has nothing of the sting of cocksure exultation in it. But the liberty to shout your loudest is one of the cherished privileges of the competitors' stand, and it is never allowed to lapse for want of exercise. The right to shout is apparently as freely recognised as the right to compete, and consequently everyone is happy, particularly when the star of his own country happens to be in the ascendant.

The competitors' stand is an infallible thermometer by which to judge the temperature of athletic rivalry at the Stadium. Yesterday morning, when the archery contests were in progress, the competitors' stand, in common with the remainder of the Stadium, was practically deserted. In the afternoon, however, when walking, cycling, steeplechasing, swimming, diving, and javelin-throwing events were in process of decision, the ample capacity of the stand was sorely taxed, and its occupants were in their most demonstrative mood. The superb javelin-throwing of Lemming, the Swede, was applauded to the echo, not only by his fellow countrymen, but by the whole population of the stand. G.E. Larner got the warmest of ovations when he completed his magnificent ten-mile walk in record time; the successes of Sweden and Norway were fervently acclaimed by the fair-skinned hardy Norsemen, and the keen finishes in some of the cycling contests produced a perfect furore of excitement.

It was indeed an afternoon of tense athletic endeavour, relieved by but one humorous incident. The first heat of the great tug-of-war contest provoked one of the most amusing episodes of an eventful week. Seven teams were entered for this trial of strength and skill – one from the United States, a second from Greece, a third from Germany, a fourth from Sweden, and three more, representing as many sections of the police force in this country – namely, the City Police of London, the K. (Plaistow) Division of the Metropolitan force, and the police force of Liverpool. The accident of the draw set the American team and the Liverpool team face to face in the very first heat. Nobody seemed to pay very much attention to the Liverpool policemen, big and powerful though they were, when they filed out into the arena. All eyes were riveted upon the team of American giants who were to do battle with them, and who, of course, were going to 'lick creation'. That was why they had gone to the trouble of putting on their athletic costumes. A magnificent team they were truly – men of might and muscle, who from their appearance might well be expected to beat anything that might be set up against them. And so they strode out into the open, a team of champions, amid the cheering of their fellow countrymen in the stand. The preliminaries were all settled with scrupulous care, the signal was given, and positively before you could say 'Knife!' the American Goliaths were sprawling on the sward, their feet to the foe. The men from the Mersey had pulled them over. It was a glorious moment for the shilling gallery, which laughed till it was sore. The Liverpool constables smiled a modest smile. The Stars and Stripes in the stand did not flutter. While ends were being changed one of the Americans darted to the dressing-room for another pair of shoes, but before he had regained the vicinity of the rope, his companions were already marching off the ground, followed by the ironic cheers and laughter of the multitude, leaving the stalwart constables of Liverpool the easiest of victors. And then it transpired that the Americans had lodged a protest against the Liverpool team because they wore their ordinary boots. 'I saw the moment they laid hold of the rope that they were not up to it.' So spoke a burly constable of the K. Division.

Now mark the contrast. Later in the day the Liverpool team were required to pull against the Swedes. With them they did precisely as they had done before with the Americans. They pulled the Swedes over the line almost as soon as the signal was given. At the second essay they repeated their success, and were once more the victors. But the Swedes lodged no protest about boots. They shook hands, man for man, with their opponents, and gave them three rousing cheers – a courtesy which the Liverpool men cordially reciprocated before the teams left the ground. It was truly a study in contrasts.

---

18 JULY 1908

LETTERS TO THE EDITOR
SEATS AT THE STADIUM
SIR A. CONAN DOYLE'S VIEW

Sir – You would confer a favour upon the public if you could convince them of the great loss which they will themselves sustain if they fail to visit the Olympic Games. No such opportunity will ever come in the lifetime of most of us to see the finest sport with the minimum of expense and trouble. After visiting the Stadium on two successive days I can testify that everything is done for the comfort of the spectator. There are two points which are worth emphasising. One that the seats are very cheap — an excellent one can be had for three or four shillings, which covers ten hours' amusement; secondly, that it is the very place for a wet day, as most of the stands are covered, and the performance goes on all the same. The present apathy of the public is very little to our credit as a sporting nation.

Arthur Conan Doyle

---

20 JULY 1908

CITY POLICE WIN THE TUG-OF-WAR

If lacking an international flavour, there was still a decided spice of interest left to the tug-of-war, wherein the two eights representing the City of London Police and the Liverpool Police, Nos. 1 and 2 British teams, were due to meet. Two more powerful sets of men it would be difficult to imagine. In the first pull, after a tough struggle, the Londoners had their rivals over. Then the rain commenced to fall, and the second pull was taken while it pelted down, making a foothold no easy matter. For the second time, despite the uncertain conditions prevailing, the City of London Police asserted their superiority. The pull was again resolutely fought out, but the Liverpool eight was mastered in decisive fashion. Inspector Duke, who has played such a prominent part in police athletics, coached the winning team. None was more pleased than he, that was evident. He shook every man of the eight by the hand, and they, in their turn, walked over to the losers, and a good hearty hand-grip all round was exchanged. Then, in the contentment of his heart, Inspector Duke marched his band of conquerors the better part of a circuit of the cinder-path, or nearly a quarter of a mile, in a heavy rainfall. They met with a most hearty greeting as they steadily swung round in single file.

---

20 JULY 1908

ATTENDANCE AT THE STADIUM
PRICES TO BE REDUCED

Late last night it was announced that the Franco-British Exhibition and the British Olympic Association have jointly decided to make very important changes in the prices of seats in the Stadium for the Olympic Games, commencing from today. Of the side which runs parallel to the swimming-tank – that adjoining the Exhibition – the prices for blocks G to S, inclusive, remain as at present. On the left the prices of blocks F to A are reduced from 2s to 1s. The north stand has been reduced from 1s to 6d. From block ZZ to TT the prices have been reduced from 2s to 1s.

The British Olympic Council held a meeting on Saturday afternoon to consider what steps can be taken to improve the attendance. It has been decided to have the proceedings in the Stadium advertised in the grounds of the Franco-British Exhibition. For this purpose it has been arranged that four trumpeters shall be stationed at the top of the Stadium at each end and overlooking the Exhibition. Half an hour before the sports commence the trumpeters will blow one blast, and a quarter of an hour before the time of starting two blasts from the trumpets will be given. At the actual commencement of the sports the trumpeters will give three blasts, whilst at the beginning of each event there will be a fanfare. The council have also decided to make a large reduction in prices of admission for large parties, schools, colleges, etc., and the larger the block of tickets taken the cheaper will be the price.

———

21 JULY 1908

OLYMPIC GAMES
BRITISH FAIRNESS
FRENCH AND AMERICAN CRITICS
LORD DESBOROUGH'S REPLY
Our Special Correspondent

Among several points of criticism which have been raised, both in the American and in the French press, the main one concerns the tug-of-war. As far as I am aware, not a man in the American teams desired to be associated with the protest made by their manager. The gentleman cannot have been acquainted with the conditions usual in such contests; or he would never have allowed his team to appear in clothing and footgear so unsuited to their work, or to pull without keeping the right distance between man and man. They had not, in fact, studied the necessary details, and, therefore, they were beaten by a team which had specialised in this form of exercise, which wore the same boots (with level heels and soles neither hollowed, spiked, nor grooved) as they wore at Stamford Bridge and in the exercise of their daily avocation as policemen. When the Americans work at the tug-of-war as they have worked at other things they will probably beat us as they have elsewhere, for if a team containing Sheridan, Flanagan and Rose are taught the elements of the game, there will be no holding them.

———

21 JULY 1908

CHEAPER SEATS
POPULAR POLICY VINDICATED

The policy of cheaper seats at the Stadium has triumphed, as anybody with the least knowledge of the public taste – and the public temper – could have foreseen from the very beginning. Business-like methods of running the great athletic carnival at Shepherd's-bush were put into operation yesterday, and the result was immediate, convincing, almost startling. With the single exception of Saturday's gathering – which in the nature of the case was bound to be a large one – the crowd assembled within the Stadium yesterday was by a long way the largest that has yet overlooked the capacious arena. The attendance far exceeded even that of the inaugural day, when The King formally opened the Olympiad, and sat with Her Majesty in the midst of a memorable gathering of well-nigh a score of Royal personages. Tier upon tier of seats that from the beginning have been void of tenants, and have in their gaunt vacancy exercised a most depressing influence upon all concerned with the games, competitors and spectators, were yesterday occupied for the first time – always, of course, with the single exception of Saturday.

There was an atmosphere of animation and bustle about the Stadium yesterday that was wholly absent in the earlier days of last week. Somehow, one felt that the Olympic Games were at last a living reality, not a half-dead semblance of international sports, as they were a week ago. There were not only competitors to be cheered, but spectators by the thousand to cheer them. Just after two o'clock when preparations were being made for the resumption of the sports in the afternoon, the appearance of the Stadium approaches was quite exhilarating. There was probably no more crowded region of the whole exhibition than the broad passage-way from which access is obtained to the various blocks of seats all the way round the Stadium. There must have been thousands of people bustling about looking for their particular entrances, and yet such is the capacity of the arena that within half an hour, or less, the Stadium had swallowed them up, and was still gaping for more patrons.

Though there were certainly many thousands of seats still unoccupied, the Stadium wore an aspect of pulsating animation that was quite comforting to behold. The sixpenny northern stand was crowded right back to the skyline, but it was somewhat significant that in the opening up of so many new blocks of seats to shilling patrons, the old shilling stand at the southern end of the Stadium had distinctly fewer occupants than it showed on certain days last week. The simple reason was that the shilling patrons had just migrated to other quarters of the Stadium from which they could obtain a better view of the proceedings. The two-shilling stands were a complete success, and must have added a considerable sum to the Stadium coffers.

———

23 JULY 1908

A GREAT SPRINT FINAL
THREE RECORDS ECLIPSED

Seven final heats of the games were decided yesterday at the Stadium, in the most brilliant weather imaginable. A vast concourse of people witnessed them, and found satisfaction in a series of interesting contests, chief among which was the deciding race for the 100 metres sprint. There is nothing to compare with a sprint final in point of tension and excitement, when runners of the highest quality are engaged. The fact of its being the decisive test is most strongly felt. It was so in the days of the pedestrian Derbys, the old Sheffield handicaps, when we always had some sprinters of unmatchable quality in this country. The assembled thousands at the final struggles sat down close to the ground, and every head was bared so that all might see. Yesterday's final heat in the 100 metres at the Stadium recalled those bygone days vividly to the mind of the old-timer. But it was not now thousands of pounds depending upon the swiftness of the men engaged, as at Sheffield. A higher motive, in the pure glory of winning and upholding the honour of one's nationality.

Two Americans, in Rector and Cartmell, the one an alert, if comparatively diminutive young man, the other an upstanding heavyweight, met the Canadian crack, Kerr, and the little South African, Walker. Rector was the man on whom the fortunes of the United States rested. His admirers said that he was sure to win and that he would do record time for the 100 metres if called upon.

Within the four lines of strings Kerr, the red maple leaf on his jersey showing up vividly, was on the outside station, the one nearest the western covered stand. The two Americans were placed in the two central lines, Cartmell next to Kerr, and Rector beside Walker, who had inside berth and who was therefore closer to the swimming lake. The South African could be easily picked out by his olive-green costume. Hollowing out holes in the cinder-path to get their push-off from, they were the centre of all eyes. A few leg-stretching short run-outs preceded their taking up positions for the start. Down the four crouched on the ground amidst a silence that could be felt. Then that slight movement in hunching up the back in taut, strained fashion, legs, arms, and body at rigid attention, awaiting the crack of the pistol behind them to set them loose and in motion, could be observed, the firer in his white jacket with his pistol held above his head, completed the view of the starting-point.

Bang! and the four men bounded away, running as though for dear life itself. A view of flying feet and straining forms, of which the green-clad one was already prominent. It was silence still with the great majority until some fifty yards short of the winning-posts. Then there burst forth a tornado of cheering which simply swept the whole enclosure. Little Walker, straining every nerve and muscle within him to cracking point, was in front. Rector was clearly behind him, Kerr might be second, but Cartmell was out of the race. For a moment only was the issue not absolutely certain. But any such thoughts did not deter the frantic shouts for the flying little South African. And as the shouts went up he made his victory assured by finishing stronger than his rivals. He flew through the tape the winner by a full yard and a half, wild excitement reigning everywhere.

With all due respect for the official decision, there is barely a shadow of doubt but that Kerr, the Canadian, was second in this race. Several expert critics in the stand directly in front of the worsted and nicely overlooking the finish at a distance of some twenty yards, which favours a better view than standing close up to the winning-post, were unanimous in this belief. Moreover, we are told on good authority that three of the judges declared Kerr to be second, that the fourth disagreed, and that the referee gave the position to Rector. Thus, the consensus of opinion all round – and more particularly of those best placed to see the line of the posts in the clearest perspective – was all in favour of Kerr. Had the Canadian been placed second, this paper would have successfully consummated the daring prophecy put forward yesterday that Rector, the greatest of all the American certainties in these games, might possibly not be first nor second.

The intensity of feeling was so strong when the race was ended that the winner was carried shoulder-high and amid showers of congratulations and applause across the arena to the dressing-room. He later was invited to the Royal Box, where the Duke of Connaught congratulated him on his splendid win, adding these words: 'Yours was the best race of the afternoon; may your kick ever continue.' It was in a sense a British victory and the people regarded it as such. The time of ten and four-fifths seconds equals the Olympic record.

Short-distance running was to the fore in the semi-final trials of the 200 and 400 metres races. Nothing of an uncommon character was seen in connection with the first mentioned. The four finalists, Cloughen, Kerr, Hawkins, and Cartmell, should supply a close finish, and they may finish in the order named. But it is a very near thing all round on the watch. There are no such doubts hedging the 400 metres race, however. All along this has by general consent been allotted to the British champion, Lieutenant W. Halswelle. Yesterday presented the best opposition the Americans can provide, and suffice it to say that, barring accidents, it is not nearly strong enough to keep Halswelle away from the first prize. If he cannot be first at the bend, and so make the very advantageous inside bend, our hope for the 400 metres must bide his time patiently, until he turns into the straight, and, fit and well, there need be little apprehension about his winning. He cut out such a pace yesterday that he lowered the Olympic record by four-fifths of a second – his time was forty-eight and two-fifths seconds.

———

24 JULY 1908

'NO RACE' FIASCO AT THE OLYMPIC GAMES
AN EXCITED CROWD

A regrettable incident – one of the very few that have occurred – marked the doings at the Stadium yesterday. It was in connection with the final of the 400 metres flat race, in which an Englishman, Halswelle, and three Americans were opposed. It was known, after his wonderful running of the last few days, that Halswelle's chance of winning the 400 metres (or quarter-mile) for England against his three American opponents was at the least a good one. He lay back at the start, as usual, and was beginning to close up with the leaders at the corner, when first one American ran wide and then the other, until finally the Englishman was almost off the cinder-track altogether, and on to the cement by the side. He had, of course, no chance of finishing ahead.

The opinion of the crowd in the North Stand, which was close to the corner, was immediately made manifest. Signs of disapproval were heard even from the sacred precincts close to the Royal box. Every spectator on the finishing straight must have clearly seen what happened. The fatal words, 'No race', were hoisted on the telegraph board as soon as the judges in the corner had had time to communicate with the referee. Any competitor wilfully jostling, or running across, or obstructing another competitor, so as to impede his progress, shall forfeit his right to be in the competition, and shall not be awarded any position or prize that he would otherwise have been entitled to.

Punctual to time the runners filed through a gateway on the eastern side of the ground, bareheaded and with running shoes on, one in his clothing, which he divested himself of, and the others in overcoats or gowns. Halswelle was mightily cheered as he did a leg-stretching burst around the southern bend. The Americans sent up shouts for Taylor as he followed the Englishman's example. There was little delay on the marks, where Carpenter had the inside station next to the turf, with Halswelle, Robbins, and Taylor in their order extending to the outside position. At the crack of the pistol Carpenter jumped away with the lead, and Robbins, quicker into his running than the long-striding Britisher, who is not a good beginner, went up second. They strung out in Indian file, with Halswelle lying third, close on the heels of Robbins, Taylor being several yards behind. So they ran to the first corner of the bend at the northern extremity of the track, which has to be negotiated before the finishing straight is reached. Carpenter was nicely ahead, with anything from a four to five yards' advantage, as he swung round this first corner. Looking back at the others it did not take an experienced judge to see that Halswelle was making efforts to get by Robbins. Eventually he managed to do so, but he seemed to lack his usual dash and straightaway rush for the tape. He looked to have run terribly wide at the corner, and he was within very measurable distance of the cycling track all the way along to the winning-posts, Carpenter keeping him close company.

A hundred yards from home the race, as viewed from almost the end of the press stand, looked a desperately close one. Gallantly Halswelle made effort after effort, and nearly got upon level terms with Carpenter and Robbins, of whom the last-named was running by the inside edge. Suddenly the worsted was broken by one of the judges to a shout of 'No race'. But the struggle continued until the posts were reached, with Halswelle sorely tired and his nearest attendant, Carpenter, some two or three yards ahead of him. Unpleasant sounds were heard which overpowered the yell of triumph that the American contingent, believing that their man had won the race, endeavoured to send into the air. Many of them came rushing across from the farther side of the ground to congratulate Carpenter on his unexpected victory over the great British quarter-miler. As for Halswelle, he looked downcast and regretful, but he said not a word then, whatever he may have done afterwards.

When the notice 'No race' was posted on the telegraph board a great outburst of cheering came from all corners of the arena. There could have been few present who did not feel, even if they hardly knew how it had been done, that Halswelle had not had fair play. Yards out of his true course to the finishing points as he had been forced to run indicated that something was wrong before the drastic action of breaking the tape was performed. A loud hooting from the southern arc of the stands gave a clue that something was happening which did not meet with the approval of that section of the crowd stationed there. Altogether the scene at the close of what should have proved to be a great race was a deplorable one. Heated controversy raged at every other step. There were few, perhaps, who knew the exact cause of the trouble. One thing, however, on which nineteen-twentieths of the assembly remained satisfied was that the fair rules of the road, as concerns cinder-path racing, had been infringed. And they were right.

In the years to come this race is bound to be a subject wherewith to point many an athletic moral and adorn a tale. So it may be as well that an unvarnished version, as seen and as grasped in its inner details by one who has had a long experience of foot-racing, both professional and amateur, can be presented. There is no partisanship in this story, but just a diligent attempt to show the actual happenings and the tactics which brought them about. With three runners the Americans had a strong hand to play. They knew none was nearly the equal of Halswelle. So they were set to help one another on their journey. It is the writer's view that all had a separate mission, although Taylor was not party to the plan laid down. He had no need to have it divulged to him.

The race supplied the evidence that Carpenter, the faster man off the mark, sped down the first straight at top pressure, and not at all as though he were hopeful of getting the tiring four hundred and thirty-seven yards and odd inches which constitute four hundred metres. Behind him came Robbins. The last-named American did all that lay in his power to keep Halswelle back, as the Britisher, seeing the leader so well in front, tried to go after him. Robbins impeded Halswelle, and ran him out at the corner to the outside edge of the path, which is some eight yards wide. But, refusing to be kept behind in this way, Halswelle fairly wrested his way to the front. Then occurred the crowning impediment to the British runner. Instead of having taken a bee-line for home, Carpenter, the leader, got in the way of Halswelle, who was made to travel on the extreme edge of the path and almost out to the adjoining cycle-track. The tracks were subsequently followed round by the representative of *The Daily Telegraph,* and they showed, as nothing else could, how Halswelle had been hampered. He had been made to run anything from ten to fifteen yards out of his reasonably proper course. All the way up to the straight Carpenter was by his side.

Forty-nine seconds and one tenth was the time that Carpenter took to complete the distance, as taken unofficially yet capably. On that showing Halswelle must have been returned the winner, and it is a fair assumption to make that he might have lowered the record. The Americans, and their trainer and manager Kelly with them, hold to the extraordinary idea that none but a runner in the rear of another can foul or infringe the rules of the path. If they do so seriously, then, in a measure, the tactical opposition of keeping Halswelle covered, first by one man and then another, so as to give other members of the same team a clear, straight road for the winning-post, is to be accounted for. But it can never be condoned on the score of good sportsmanship.

The pity of it all is that a suggestion made on Wednesday to have the curve of the cinder-path where the impediments befell Hallswelle set with lines of strings was not adopted. With a pathway for each of the runners around the corners none of these boring actions could have been pursued.

————

25 JULY 1908

MARATHON RACE
PRINCESS OF WALES STARTS THE CONTEST
AMERICAN VICTORY
HAYES THE WINNER
DORANDO, THE ITALIAN, DISQUALIFIED
MAGNIFICENT STRUGGLE
REMARKABLE SCENES
POPULAR ENTHUSIASM
THE QUEEN AT THE STADIUM

Yesterday the Marathon Race, run from Windsor Castle to the Stadium, a distance of some twenty-six miles, produced as dramatic and unexpected a finish as any lover of sensation might desire. The British representatives were strongly in front for half the course; then the running was taken up by Hefferon, the South African. Longboat, the much-fancied Canadian athlete, retired at the twentieth mile, and Appleby, one of the best of the English contingent, gradually disappeared from the contest. Just before the Stadium was reached, Hefferon, who was leading at this point by a few yards, was passed by Dorando. The Italian entered the enclosure amid a scene of wild excitement, followed by Hayes, a representative of the United States, the latter having succeeded in passing the South African, after a gallant struggle. Then ensued the most remarkable, and also the most painful scene of a day which had obviously tried the strength of the competitors to the uttermost. Dorando, in going round the Stadium enclosure, fell through sheer exhaustion, more than once. Helped by the officials, who immediately came to his rescue, he managed to breast the tape somehow. But as it was due to the assistance of others that he finished first, the race was very properly given to the American representative, Hayes, and Dorando was disqualified.

Hundreds of thousands of people witnessed the gallant efforts of the fifty-five runners of sixteen countries who were started by the Princess of Wales on the East-terrace of Windsor Castle. In the Stadium there were between fifty and sixty thousand persons awaiting the arrival of the first man. Her Majesty the Queen, the Duke of Connaught, and other members of the Royal family were in the Royal box when at about twenty minutes past five a rocket denoting that the first runner had passed the 26-mile mark was fired. It was known that the Italian, P. Dorando, was leading.

An opening in the stand running parallel to Wood-lane, through which the runners had to pass, was cleared. No runner was seen in the archway. Presently some ambulance men ran across the cycle track with a stretcher. The multitude was all excitement. Could it be that like the Greek runner, in whose honour the race was initiated, the plucky little Italian had fallen when within an ace of grasping his wreath of olive? There were tense, drawn faces in the stands, and the silence was unnerving. In a moment or two the diminutive figure in a wet, white vest and crimson drawers came into view. A deafening roar greeted him. The noise seemed to make no impression on the champion. He walked slowly, painfully, and was obviously only half-conscious of what was going on around him. He wanted to walk the track the wrong way. A friendly hint in a foreign tongue was unheeded. Some one touched him on the arm and pointed the path along which the gallant fellow was to win honours for his country and himself. He still shook his head. Then he was turned round and, with friends on his right and left, he began to walk so slow and so laboured that one wondered if he would ever get round the track.

Twenty yards and Dorando faltered and fell. This heroic little Southerner whose determination had worn down the opposition of champions for twenty-six miles seemingly could not stride out the last three hundred yards. In half a minute Dorando was on his feet again and a trot, or a roll, carried him to the bend near the competitors' stand. Great cheering, full of whole-hearted sympathy, greeted him, but he was again to falter. A crowd of officials, attendants, and of people with no business in the ring, stood around the pathetic figure of a champion about to be robbed of his own. He could not move. Then, possibly knowing full well that the rules of the game prohibited such assistance, a friendly hand lifted the Italian to his feet. He again went his weary way, and before entering the straight once more fell. Everyone felt the tragic situation. A roar from the crowd outside the Stadium indicated the approach of a second runner. The Italian's time was short. Coaxed, entreated by attendants who had watched him every inch of the way, he was once more lifted to his feet. He was set going. Facing him, a hundred yards away, was the tape. The spectators were sighing for him to break it when a shout from the American stand proclaimed that Hayes, a United States representative, had reached the path.

Hayes was running. It was a short, rickety stride he had. The man's powers were almost spent, but a great heart urged him forward. Dorando led him by two hundred yards. But he only moved by inches, and it was by no means certain that Nature would allow him to finish. Twenty yards from the worsted, at the moment when the sturdy American was in the straight, Dorando fell a fifth time. Two friends lifted him up and almost pushed him on the tape, where was received by friends and placed on a stretcher. His was a moral victory. Nature robbed him of his triumph, and though the Olympic Council very properly under the rules adjudged him disqualified from taking the prize, there were sixty thousand persons ready to proclaim him the Marathon champion.

DORANDO'S HEALTH
UNFOUNDED RUMOUR

Last night it was reported that Dorando, the Italian competitor, was dead. We are happy to state, however, on the authority of the Olympic Games Committee, that the rumour is unfounded. Count Brunetta d'Usseaux, who left Dorando at half-past ten last night, informed our representatives that the Italian runner had quite recovered, and would appear at the prize-giving in the Stadium today. Dorando was deeply disappointed at being disqualified, but expressed great delight at the gracious gift of a cup by the Queen.

---

27 JULY 1908
THE QUEEN AND THE OLYMPIC GAMES
PRIZE-GIVING DAY IN THE STADIUM
HISTORIC SCENES
WORLD'S ATHLETES DISPERSE

Saturday brought to a splendid conclusion the long series of contests in the Olympic Games. The great outstanding feature of the city's ceremony was the distribution of prizes by Her Majesty the Queen, including her special gift of a gold cup to Dorando in memory of the Marathon Race, run under such trying conditions on Friday. The little Italian athlete, as the hero of a remarkable contest, was acclaimed with genuine enthusiasm by a vast body of spectators, who gave to each prize-winner in turn the meed of generous and unstinted applause. Amongst other memorable features of a day which set the final seal on a highly successful athletic carnival was a marvellous performance over ten flights of hurdles by an American, the victory of an Englishman in the swimming race of 1,500 metres, and Lieutenant Halswelle's 'run over' – with no competitors – in the 400 metres race, which he accomplished in fifty seconds. The hearty cheers given for the Queen at the close prove, if proof were necessary, how sincere is the gratitude felt by all those who have borne a part in the proceedings for the unremitting interest and sympathy which Her Majesty has shown towards the Olympic Games of 1908.

In the middle of the prize-giving by Her Majesty the Queen, the magnified voice of the red-coated gentleman with the megaphone was silenced by a mighty shout which went up from the southern arc of the Stadium. All eyes sought to discover the cause. The figure of a man in cycling dress moved over the cycle-track, below the competitors' stand. It reached the cinder-path, and then came one long, deep, welcoming shout of 'Dorando'. The man who in the popular belief is the real winner of the Marathon of 1908 had arrived! The Queen turned to Princess Victoria and clapped her hands. Here was the little man with the big heart, who less than twenty-four hours previously had fought with Nature, which had willed it that he should not, unaided, get round that three hundred yards of cinder-path which stood between him and laurels for his country. 'Nature's soft nurse' had brought back power to his strong limbs, and he paced with soldierly stride around the track full of pride that, though an unkind Fate had denied him the prize he had coveted for his nationality, he was to receive a special trophy from the gracious lady who had witnessed his helplessness on the previous day – the Queen.

Dorando, the hero of the Games, was the unwitting cause of the complete cessation of the prize-distributing proceedings. Tax his voice as he would, the megaphonist, from his exalted platform, could not make himself heard. He called for prize-winners to come up for their medals. His voice was lost in the sea of plaudits which rolled from one end of the Stadium to the other, and then rolled back again. The megaphone gentleman gave it up. The prize-winners were watching Dorando. His appearance had electrified them, as it had done the people and the men who had been giving a gymnastic display in the arena. The latter left their places on the grass and sprinted towards the Italian. They reached him, and would have lifted him in their strong arms to bear him in their delirious excitement before the multitude, but the police were before them, and warned them back. Dorando, instead of completing the half-circuit of the cinder track, cut across the grass and hurried to take up his position at the rear of the column of champions. He had to run the gauntlet of more cheers. He repeatedly raised his cloth cap, and now and again he put his hand on the lapel of his coat and bowed. In his buttonhole he wore a large bunch of the leaves of The King's oak, and to these his fingers continually wandered, apparently anxious that he should not lose a single leaf.

The Italian joined the more fortunate of his friends and fellow Olympic competitors. An enthusiastic fellow countryman had brought with him the Italian national colours on a gilt stand. He was prevailed upon not to display his flag until after the Queen had rewarded the Italian with the signal mark of her approval and her sympathy. Dorando waited in the rear of the gold medallists until the whole of the latter had been handed medals for their efforts. The Italian was all smiles. He was smart, alert, and save for the paleness of his cheeks, for which the noise of the crowd may have been responsible, was without a trace of the exhausting race of the previous day. Presently his name was called through the megaphone, and, doffing his cap, he marched to the platform. On his approach the Queen clapped her hands several times, and from the packed stands the delight of the multitude was expressed in a tremendous volume of cheering. Her Majesty bent over the balustrade to say a word or two in congratulations, and then handed to Dorando, as her personal gift, a gold cup of exquisite design. Accompanying the cup was a card, headed with the Crown and 'Buckingham Palace', and on it were the words, in the Queen's handwriting:

'For P. Dorando,

In remembrance of the Marathon Race,

From Windsor to the Stadium.

From Queen Alexandra'.

Pressing the cup to his left breast, Dorando bowed and retired, and, after receiving his sprig of oak leaves, followed his instructions to complete his circuit of the cinder-path. There could be no doubting the fact that the popular mind will always associate Dorando with the English

Marathon Race. The torrent of cheering which marked the Italian's triumphal procession to the dressing-room of his compatriots was unmistakable evidence of this. The competitors took off their hats to him. Athletes swarmed about the course and repeated their applause of the previous day, when he was too dazed to hear their vociferous congratulations. There was only one little knot of spectators who viewed the demonstration of the people without favour. In the American competitors' stand were heard expressions deprecating an incident which might rob Hayes, the winner, of some applause. But there was not unanimity among Americans on this point, for a member of the United States party observed: 'He's not the real winner. That's right enough. But he's a game little man, and he deserves all his popularity.' As Dorando passed through the competitors' gate he was lifted shoulder high, and he left the arena to the accompaniment of three tremendous cheers.

---

27 JULY 1908
'DORANDO' RECOVERED
HIS VIEWS ON DEFEAT

The first thing to be said about 'Dorando', the Italian runner who, although entering the Stadium first in the Marathon Race on Friday, was subsequently disqualified, is that Dorando is not his surname at all. Dorando is his first name. His surname is Pietri. Full name – Dorando Pietri. It seems rather extraordinary that the Olympian authorities should from the first have set down his name in the official list as 'P. Dorando'. One might as well call John Smith, 'S. John'. The only possible explanation is that the authorities confused 'Pietri' with 'Pietro', the Italian equivalent of Peter. But Dorando the Stadium officials christened him at the outset; the name stuck to him right through; and by 'Dorando' no doubt he will continue to be known in the annals of sport – so far, at least, as Olympic records go.

The next point to be mentioned about Pietri, and for the moment it overshadows the other in importance – is that he is happily quite recovered from his exhausting exertions of Friday. It seemed almost incredible that the wiry little fellow who was the recipient of such a tremendous ovation on Saturday afternoon, as he walked round the arena in order to receive the magnificent cup which Her Majesty so thoughtfully and so generously bestowed on him, was the same man who was in such a distressing plight not twenty-four hours previously. No one in all the vast multitude who witnessed the pitiable scenes of Friday afternoon would have imagined for an instant that a man in such parlous case could possibly have recovered so speedily.

By nine o'clock on Friday night – that is to say, within less than four hours of the close of the race – Pietri was himself again. He went upstairs to his room unaided, and on Saturday morning he was out of doors before seven o'clock, feeling somewhat tired, no doubt, but quite well. The rapidity, no less than the completeness, of his recovery has been quite remarkable. It only shows of what grit these trained long-distance runners really are. He visited the Stadium comparatively early in the day, and lunched at the Garden Club in the Exhibition as the guest of Count Brunetta, one of Italy's representatives on the International Olympic Committee, before playing the conspicuous part he did in the prize-presentation ceremony.

Dorando Pietri speaks no English, but through the medium of a brother, now resident in London, who speaks English more than fairly, and of some admiring compatriots, who, crowding around him, showed considerable command of our tongue, a representative of *The Daily Telegraph* was enabled to carry on a conversation of some length with him as he lay resting on a table in the Italian competitors' dressing-room at the Stadium on Saturday afternoon. Pietri is small, almost diminutive, in stature, and spare of build, but his bright eyes speak of his athletic fitness. He is a modest little man. That is one reason why the public interested in the Olympic Games knew so little about him beforehand. Pietri is undoubtedly sorely disappointed to think that the frantic efforts which he made to reach the goal have merely resulted in his disqualification. What is more, he cherishes something like a grievance against the people, officials and others, who assisted him in his final endeavours to gain the tape. It was his aversion to interference that was mainly responsible for the spurt which he essayed on the cinder-path. He and his friends stoutly maintain that if he had only been left alone, he had so much time in hand that he could quite well have finished the race unaided. 'Why,' he said, 'if I only crawled on my hands and knees, I could have finished.' There were doubtless many spectators of Friday's memorable scene in the Stadium who would hesitate to share Pietri's view as 'to his ability to finish the race without assistance'. But, unfortunately, that can only be a matter of opinion. There is now no means of determining whether, if assistance had been withheld, he could have staggered, half-blind, half-senseless, to the tape; but, in the light of the wonderful recovery he has made, it may well be that he could have finished without help. No one will doubt for a moment that the aid which was proffered to the little Italian was prompted by the very best motives — by no other motives, indeed, than common humanity and sympathy with suffering; but, in view of subsequent events, it is perhaps a pity that, once within the Stadium, Pietri was not given a proper opportunity of proving whether or not he was actually able to finish his arduous task. The kindness shown him was certainly well-intentioned, but Pietri's friends are quite positive that it was mistaken.

Pietri has received shoals of congratulations and the messages of sympathy which have poured in upon him since the final issue of the race became generally known. Among the messages which he prizes most highly is one from Lord Desborough, in these terms: 'Lady Desborough and I are sending you some flowers, with every wish for your speedy and complete recovery, and heartiest congratulations on your splendid achievement yesterday, which has the sincere sympathy of every man and woman in the vast crowd at the Stadium.' Accompanying this sympathetic communication was a lovely bouquet of roses. Pietri's reply, which his friends cast into English for him, was this: 'Please accept my thanks for the beautiful roses and your charming letter of congratulations, which I shall always treasure in remembrance of your great kindness.' Another message which Pietri greatly values was one of congratulation from the boys of Eton College. It is the sportsmanlike instinct of this message which appeals to him so strongly. 'Ah!' he exclaims, 'you English are real sportsmen. It is a pleasure to be associated with them in sport.' Pietri is gratified with the good feeling which the English multitude has displayed towards him in the situation in which he finds himself. 'It was fine,' he says — 'so kind and so encouraging.' As you listen to him, and mark his manner, you see that he means it, and that the demeanour of the crowd along the Marathon course and in the Stadium has deeply touched him.

So much for the gratification that his pluck and prowess have gained him. But his fame has brought certain penalties in its wake. The autograph-hunters have swooped down upon him in swarms. And so many impressionable young ladies have couched their requests for his autograph in such sympathetic terms! They are so sorry he failed where he so richly deserved to succeed. And, accordingly, they enclose a stamped envelope for his reply. And the doughty young Italian complacently complies with their request. His friends, of course, have chaffed him good-naturedly on the sudden and serious inflation of his letter-bag. 'Ha! Ha!' said one of his fellow-countrymen to him on Saturday afternoon, as he opened yet another letter written in a pronounced feminine hand, 'there's a wife for you.' 'All right,' says Pietri, with a merry twinkle in his eye, 'I am free.'

Pietri's explanation of his failure is interesting, and in some respects curious. It is partly psychological, partly physical. The very kindness of the spectators along the line of route seems to have contributed to his undoing. So he suggests. What he says is that so dense were the crowds of spectators about three miles from the goal, and so vociferous their cheering, that somehow he got it into his head that he was but a mile from the Stadium, and so adopted a quicker pace than he otherwise would have done. On the other hand, it may be said that he ought to have known the course better than to have allowed himself to make such a mistake; but, on the other hand, it is just possible that, in the physical condition in which he was, it was not so very difficult to misapprehend the actual distance that lay between him and the winning post.

That is the first reason he gives for this failure in the concluding phase of the great struggle. His second is still more interesting. Freely translated, what he says amounts to this: 'When I was running on the hard road – and it was on hard roads that I did most of my training – I felt all right; but when I came to the softer path through Wormwood Scrubs, and later on to the cinder track at the Stadium, I felt that somehow my legs would not work. The sensation I had was that I was sinking into the ground, that my legs would not carry me on, and that I must fall. I believe that, had the whole track been on the hard road, I should never have fallen as I did. It was a most peculiar sensation. I cannot account for it, but there it was – my legs simply seemed unable to carry me from stride to stride. You know what happened.'

But the third reason he assigns for his failure at the finish is most interesting of all, inasmuch as it seems to have a sort of psychological basis. He remembers perfectly well coming down the hard road in Wood-lane and turning into the Stadium. But once arrived within the arena, and confronted with a multitude of eighty thousand people cheering him frantically, a sudden change came over him. The sheer joy of having entered upon the last scene of all, and a feeling that now at last the prize was within his grasp, coupled with the moral influence of the enthusiastic spectators, upset him completely. His own expression is that, not in any figure of speech, but literally, the breath seemed to go out of him. As we should phrase it, the greeting of the densely packed thousands who lined the terraced Stadium 'took his breath away'. The capacity for movement momentarily left him, and he fell to the ground. But exhausted though he was, the sense of the necessity of his reaching the tape never quite forsook him. What some spectators may have mistaken for paroxysms of exhaustion — if such a phrase be admissible — were simply his frantic endeavours to cast himself free of interference, so that he might be allowed to finish alone, and in his own way. But, as he puts it, the misguided kindness of certain people within the arena denied him the brief respite which he thinks was all that he needed, and that respite being denied him, and the assistance being given which at the moment he was too exhausted to reject, he made the spurt of which all witnesses of the finish have such a painful recollection.

And now it is high time to say something about Pietri and his athletic record. He is a young man of twenty-three years. Born in Reggio, in the department of Emilia, in Northern Italy, his home is now in Carpi, a town no great distance from his birthplace, and situated a few miles due north of Modena. In Carpi he keeps a confectioner's shop. Pietri's is a record of specialisation in long-distance running, and of steady progress from success to success. It is only some four years ago that he took to running as a pastime, but from the beginning it was distance-running in which he indulged. His first race was run at Genoa, and the distance was twelve kilometres — approximately, about seven and a half miles. He came out third. Next he ran from Milan to Monza and back, a distance of twenty-five kilometres, and was placed second. Then it was that he found definitely that distance-running was his forte, and so, some three years ago, he went in for two months' training; and with such success that he was proclaimed champion of Italy. In a race which lasted an hour and a half he out-distanced his nearest rival by some three minutes. But a still greater triumph was his when, at a Marathon race held at Paris, in October, 1905, he ran thirty kilometres (between eighteen and nineteen miles), and came out first in a large field, in one hour fifty-four minutes and fifty-three seconds. The next man was seven seconds behind him. A fortnight later he engaged in a race around the outskirts of Milan, a distance of some twelve kilometres, and in the end was beaten by a yard by his trainer, who happened to be none other than Lunghi, another Italian competitor at the Stadium, whose running was one of the discoveries of the Olympic sports just concluded. It was Lunghi, it may be remembered, who ran second to the American flyer, Sheppard, in the half-mile race.

Since then Pietri has done eighteen months' soldiering, but amidst all the calls of military duty, he always managed to find time to keep up his running. A story is told that one day the captain of another company in his regiment wished to see the young soldier who was said to be such a great runner. His exclamation when he saw Pietri was, 'That a runner?' He refused to believe that a man of such diminutive stature and fragile frame could be a stayer. In November last, at Rome, Pietri won fresh honours on the track, and in one of his races had as his second Pagliani, whose running at the Stadium also attracted some attention during the earlier stages of the recent Olympiad. Pietri's success in his own country has been almost phenomenal.

---

28 JULY 1908
OLYMPIC YACHT RACES
Our Special Correspondent
RYDE, Monday Evening

The first of the three days' racing for the Olympic yachting medals was held from Ryde Pier today over the courses of the Royal Victoria Yacht Club. The weather was delightful, although the wind was light throughout the day. The Solent was shining a sapphire blue in the full heat of the July sun, and, whilst fleecy white clouds promised a breeze, it remained rather light until the finish. The British boats really outsailed the foreign competitors, and by the end of the day they had scored no fewer than thirteen out of fifteen points. The yachts were exclusively steered and handled by amateurs of the nationality to which the craft belonged, but in the eight-metres class, which was the largest provided for (26.2 feet by English measurements), a local pilot was allowed in addition to the amateur crew. Neither of the British competitors availed themselves of this privilege, and their hands were entirely amateurs.

Mr Blair Cochrane steered his own boat *Cobweb* to victory, after an extremely close race with the last season's champion, *Sorais*. The latter was splendidly handled by Captain Philip Hunloke, who, although finding himself placed in a decidedly slower boat, with heavier scantlings and smaller canvas, managed to give his opponent a desperately close race. Captain Hunloke quite outmanoeuvred his adversary at the start, but subsequently was beaten by sheer speed on the part of the newer vessel. Both yachts were designed by Fife, *Cobweb* being specially built for these matches, while *Sorais* was built in 1907 for Mrs Allen. This season the latter vessel was bought by the Duchess of Westminster. In today's race the Duchess sailed on board her own yacht in the race. Just before the start it was said that the Duchess of Westminster's name was not entered as one of the crew in the Olympic competitions, and such being the case, it was thought that she would not be allowed to sail. She was able to do so, however, by the regulation permitting an extra person to be on board as a pilot, and as a fact there were only five on board *Sorais*, all told, during the match.

In the six-metre class the success of the British boats was phenomenal. They finished first and second, after a close struggle, the winner being the pretty little Burnham boat *Dormy*, designed by Mr G. Laws. The performance of all the foreign competitors was disappointing, and the Swedish boats were particularly sluggish. It was altogether the most successful day's racing in the small classes held at Ryde for many years, and, from the crowd of fashionable people and spectators lining the head of Ryde pier, one might almost have supposed that the palmy days of the Solent classes had suddenly returned after a long lapse of years.

---

1 AUGUST 1908

OLYMPIC REGATTA
BRITAIN WINS EVERY RACE
FINE BELGIAN EFFORT
An Old Blue

After all the flag is flying still. A tremendous race between two of the finest crews I ever saw together has finally settled the question of styles that has agitated the English world of rowing for over three years. If the Belgians had won we should have been obliged at least to reconsider, if not to change entirely, all those principles of oarsmanship on which the crews of Eton and Radley, of Oxford and Cambridge, of the great metropolitan clubs, had founded their tuition. For, if Leander had been beaten yesterday afternoon, there would have been no doubt whatever about the real superiority of the Belgian style.

But Leander won in such fast time, and by so large a margin, that every hesitation has been set at rest, and I am personally in the happy position of having nothing to withdraw, nothing to alter. Perhaps there is, however, one thing that must be said. Much as we admired the Belgians in bringing over crew after crew to Henley until they were rewarded by victory twice repeated, we must admire still more the splendid race they rowed against a finer crew than they have ever met before, and the magnificently sportsmanlike way they took their honourable defeat.

The great race of yesterday began in splendid weather and perfect conditions at a quarter-past three. When Mr Pitman gave the word to go, the Belgians started at their full pace and perfectly together, rowing twelve, twenty-three and forty-three in the full minute. Leander, showing beautiful precision and great power, went off at eleven, twenty-two and forty-two. For an instant it looked as if the Belgians were ahead, but in the next the bows of the Leander boat had taken the lead they were never again to lose. Only, however, by about six inches did the English crew keep ahead until they had passed the island, up which both eights went at a tremendous pace and nearly dead level. But Leander were gaining about an inch at every stroke, and though their superiority was so slight and so slowly won as to be almost heartbreaking to watch, it was still a definite superiority, and by the first signal they had half a length in hand, and were going splendidly.

Belgium was not one whit less taking to the eye, and apparently travelled even faster when they spurted suddenly at about half a mile from the start. Leander answered them at once in no uncertain fashion, and Bucknall's timely quicken brought his men three-quarters of a length ahead at halfway, which the leaders passed in three minutes forty-five seconds. Once more the Belgian stroke made a great effort, and his men responded gamely, but it took too much out of them. They had faltered once before, and recovered themselves with the greatest courage. This time they rolled badly, and for a moment seemed to go to pieces. Like a flash the English crew went away from them, and, with a quarter of a length clear water between the boats, at last Leander were able for the first time, to take a much-needed 'breather' at a long and hard thirty-five, which they rowed in very good style all through.

But those indomitable Belgians were never done with. They had had their 'breather', too, and the next minute every Englishman's heart was in his mouth, for they rushed up their stroke to over forty with one of those electric sprints for which they have long been famous, and made a desperate effort to get on terms. And up they came − nearer and nearer, until that glorious effort in its turn died away. At exactly the right instant

Bucknall, who was beautifully backed up by Etherington-Smith, gave his 'ten strong strokes', and at the old mile post Leander were again a length and a quarter ahead, and again rowing their long, steady thirty-five.

Not much time was left now, and the Belgians realised it. They spurted again and again as they neared the grandstand, but human nature could do no more. They were willing to the end, and they never for a moment stopped their legwork, but as a crew they could do no more. Leander, keeping together, though every man was tired, swung past the finish some two lengths ahead, and Mr Fenner's flag fell in seven minutes fifty-two seconds from the start. Both the Belgian coaches, to whom the rowing of their country owes so much, were with us on Mr Pitman's launch *Consuta* for that historic struggle, and in the bows beside him were Baron Pierre de Coubertin, president of the International Olympic Committee, and Mr Herbert Thomas Steward, chairman of the Olympic Regatta Committee. None of them are likely to see so great a race again for many a year to come.

2

THE INTER-LONDON YEARS

STOCKHOLM 1912

9 JULY 1912

CITY POLICE DISQUALIFIED
A PRACTICAL JOKE
Our Special Correspondent
STOCKHOLM, Monday

When you receive the rather astounding intelligence of the City of London Police, the Olympic champions of 1908, and fondly believed by those who know and respect them as well to be invincible as tug-of-war specialists, do not be alarmed at this further indication of the degeneracy of our races. This tug-of-war business was only a little practical joke arranged by the Swedish Olympic officials to gain their country some more winning points. They knew that if the pull had been carried out on turf or solid ground of some sort our policemen would have had their men off their feet and beaten in double-quick time. So, with a touch of Swedish humour, which, by the way, is akin to the pawkiness of the Scot, they had arranged a pulling ground of loose sand or gravel. Naturally, in making a foothold for pulling purposes, the men of both sides could not help ploughing up holes. Then, with the most humorous touch of all, profound in its irony, the armletted officials kept poking at our men when their feet sank at all with little flags, probably carried for this express purpose. But the foot-burrowing of the Swedes, the rear man actually getting his hind knee into the soil to make sure of getting a purchase, was left unnoticed.

One of the most exquisitely conceived jokes, executed with such seriousness of expression as quite to deceive the onlookers, had its climax in the disqualification of the London Police when they refused to enter again into the spirit of it by declining to be pulled over a second time. An eminent magistrate once philosophically observed that what the soldier said to the girl was not evidence, and even if *The Daily Telegraph* would open its columns to my story, I am not going to tell what one of the policemen said to the London reporter.

––––––

10 JULY 1912
THE TUG-OF-WAR
Our Own Correspondent
STOCKHOLM, Tuesday

With reference to yesterday's tug-of-war, in which the City Police lost to Sweden, the vice-chairman of the committee has submitted the matter to every member of the British team, and all admitted that they were beaten by their stronger opponents. I have personally consulted Mr Pelling, the secretary of the London Athletic Club, who supports the judges' decision.

––––––

11 JULY 1912
THE TUG-OF-WAR

We have received several letters from Swedes resident in London with reference to our Special Correspondent's account of the tug-of-war, in which the City Police were defeated by Sweden. Yesterday morning we published a telegram from our Stockholm Correspondent which stated that the British team had frankly admitted the superiority of their opponents, and that the judges' decision was approved by the secretary of the London Athletic Club, so that any misunderstanding which may have arisen is satisfactorily cleared up. The mutual friendship existing between Swedes and British, and the hospitable and sportsmanlike nature of the nation which is the world's host on this occasion are sufficient guarantee that the amicable rivalry of these games will continue unmarred to a successful close.

13 JULY 1912
THE TUG-OF-WAR
STOCKHOLM, Friday

Some of the comments passed in London upon the tug-of-war contest, in which the redoubtable City Police team were unsuccessful, have created a good deal of feeling among Swedish sportsmen, who make the following statement on the subject: 'In the tug-of-war the City Police were at a disadvantage in the loose gravel. They sank very deeply before they were able to obtain a firm foothold, but it is held that they should have been prepared, because the rules stated that the competitions would take place upon sandy ground. The second and third men on the rope were too close together. Consequently, when the third man slipped, he was practically held down by the men in front of him, and was unable to rise. In these circumstances, the judge had no option but to disqualify the British team. The first tug took about three minutes, and was in favour of the Swedish team.' – *Reuter's Special Service.*

15 JULY 1912
SATURDAY'S EVENTS
Our Special Correspondent
STOCKHOLM, Saturday

Again today the games were greatly favoured by the weather. The opening hour found the wrestling stages occupied, and the standing high-jumpers with the competitors for the decathlon ready for action. This last competition is an all-round proficiency test. It is of a more exacting character than the single-handed pentathlon, which was decided in favour of a pronounced type of American Indian. He figures here again. The Americans are enthusiastic about him, as the greatest athlete the world over. High and long jumping, javelin, hammer, and discus throwing, a run of a hundred yards or one mile, all come alike to him. More than this, an Indian only knows victory or disgrace. He will exceed the real limits of his strength, and try as few are able to do. We saw the tenacity of his temperament most practically put in force the other day when he plodded on and on, though in a half-fainting condition long before the end; to take second place to the world-beating Kolehmainen in the 10,000 metres run.

Today, Thorpe, the pentathlon candidate, is very much to the fore. He comes through a winner in the bustling heats of the 100 metres sprint, which open the competition. The times recorded here were generally quite good, and in one instance eleven seconds was all but touched. This may sound too fast, yet those who are here and able to appreciate the ideal conditions surrounding the very lively path can clearly see that the sprinters are getting through the tasks a full quarter of a second quicker than if running in England. Having finished the sprinting tests, the decathlon men started long jumping. In a farther corner of the arena the qualifying stages of the standing high jump were disposed of. Here is seen the most difficult form of jumping. With nothing but their own unaided lifting power to take them over a crossbar, which seems to be suspended midway between two posts, the jumpers still contrive to spring up and over it. You see them stand sideways to the bar, then the arms go aloft, and, with a bend of the knees, their legs leave the ground, and by a mighty compression, over the bar they go, some lightly and gracefully, others clumsily. The percentage of failures is small, and the jumping goes on until the Greek – who won the standing broad jump – qualifies at nearly five feet, in company with five Americans. This is wonderful jumping of its kind.

Shot-putting by the decathlon men sets the afternoon programme in progress. This is not the most heavily fixtured day by any means, yet there is the assurance of another large gathering of spectators. The people on the northern and western, upper and lower, tiers of seats are beating the bear with their national flaglets, their handkerchiefs, and dainty little Japanese fans to create a cooling draught. Parasols are not so lavishly displayed as they would be in more southerly parts, although here and there a miniature splash, a dot of brighter colouring, is perceptible among the seated ranks. The shot men made their casts in quick succession. As usual, the wearers of the white singlets, with their badge of the Stars and Stripes and maroon-edged shirts, keep doing well. But a big Finn and a blue-hosed Swede do even better. Having taken their turns at the shot they go on with the discus.

To the general satisfaction of those who dislike those unpleasant happenings which seem to crop up automatically in speed races around a bend when the Americans furnish the greater portion of the competitors, the course is being stringed out for the 400-metres run. With the German, Braun, having to oppose in this final four of the United States team, one felt that he would otherwise have been most severely handicapped. That the Swedish officials hold a similar view is shown by their departure from the method of giving a free track in the heats. The Americans, especially the athletic section, are not too well pleased with the change. They suggest that the revised conditions reflect upon the wish of their athletes to give Braun a clear run. This running through avenues of strings gives each man a clear path. Allowances are made for the extra distances to be covered in the stations so that the runners in the outside berths will be put on equal terms with the inside man.

Not until the fourth attempt were the 400 metres men sent on their mission. None of them seemed to know quite how to run his race, and they were keeping their distances fairly well as they stretched out into the further straight. Here Braun was seen to be going as well as any of them, and he had the beating of one of his opponents at least, in Meredith, his lucky conqueror in the 800 metres. Swinging round the last bend, Lindberg, Reidpath, and Braun were racing pretty well abreast. It was anybody's race coming up the straight, but the thick-set Reidpath got in front, and kept there, with Braun hunting him right through to the worsted, with Lindberg at their heels. Not more than a yard and a half equally separated the three leaders. Haff was close up, fourth, but Meredith, all out, was some six or seven yards behind. The time of forty-eight and one-fifth seconds will indicate the fine quality of the whole field.

Information comes that on the application of the united British contingents, the Olympic Games Committee has agreed that no refreshments shall be given to the competitors en route for the Marathon race tomorrow except at authorised control stations. These will be under the superintendence of certificated medical men, who are sworn not to dispense any but natural foods or drink, to the utter exclusion of any falsely stimulating drugs.

---

15 JULY 1912

THE MARATHON RACE
SOUTH AFRICANS' VICTORY
Our Special Correspondent
STOCKHOLM, Sunday

It is Sunday, and while the churches are at morning service in dear old England, the people of Stockholm – man, woman and child – are wending their various ways to the Stadium. For today the culmination point of the Games is reached. It brings us at last to the Marathon race, for which the best distance runners of four continents have these many months been physically fitting themselves. As in London four years ago, the heat is nothing short of tropical. The heart of Sweden beats among the densely-packed seats, and the thousands who are outside the building, unable to gain admission, but none the less agitated with the burning hope and cherished ideal that one of the native competitors will carry off the prize.

By all accounts the Marathon course is a teaser. It is twenty-five English miles in length. But if well over a mile less than our accustomed run from Windsor to London, the vastly different nature of the roads here more than counterbalance the deficit. Men who have trained over it say that there are many short, steep hills, and corresponding declivities constantly to be met. Certainly, the course follows the track of the high roads. But the nature of Swedish soil in this dry weather means an overspreading layer of powdery dust. In places they say, too, it is ankle deep. So, what with the tremendous heat, the state of the roads, and this dust annoyance, the Marathon men are going to be tried in a manner for which no previous experience could amply prepare them.

While the people are trooping into their seats, the wrestling bouts, now understood to be near their close, are in progress. The big hammer-throwing men also make their appearance, and whirl Dervish-like in their appearance and their human fly-wheel effects, before launching out on an unsuspecting atmosphere and a more suffering turf a great metal ball suspended to a wire which by sporting courtesy is termed a hammer. The scene is brightening up fast. From all sides, up the subway steps, in from the various gateways, and even down from the stands, the Marathon runners are making for the neighbourhood of the Royal box, beyond which stands a retinue of officials. Very few of the men are so unwise as not to have some head protection throwing a shade on to that vital spot, the nape of the neck. Most are handkerchiefed, although many sport wide-brimmed linen or American disc-like soft hats, and one shows a Swedish cap with peak reversed.

Preparations are made for the start of the race, with the runners marshalled in extended lines beside the broad white mark which has been struck sheer across the cinder-path. They stand seven files deep, and about eight men in each line on the inner half of the path. Bang goes the pistol, and they are off, and well on towards a hundred pair of legs set in motion. They make a compact, moving body until the first turn, then three blue-shirted Swedes, to wild cheering, are out by themselves in the lead. But a white handkerchiefed Russian goes racing past them as light-heartedly as though he were off upon a far less strenuous run. Unless he be superhuman, the Marathon will read him the old lesson that early pace does not mean winning the race. Again the people are impelled to cheer when they see a Swede flatter the national pride by passing ahead again, just before the leaders disappeared from sight. An answering shout comes from the enormous crowd without. Already there is a train, two hundred yards long, of stealthy runners.

Now the gaze, if not the thoughts, of the Stadium people is fixed on the competitions within. Then came the megaphoned intelligence that another member of the Kolehmainen family – a brotherhood of four gifted runners – was leading the Marathon field, with the South African McArthur figuring prominently among a batch of Swedes. Later we hear that there is only a matter of three minutes dividing the first half-dozen Marathon men at the half-distance, and that three of these own allegiance to the British flag. The little South African, Gitsham, who was second in our Olympic trial Marathon, is leading; his fellow countryman, the much-fancied McArthur, is third; and the Englishman, Lord, sixth; while the three intermediate places are occupied by a Finn, a Swede, and an Italian.

One feels the strain of the preparation that goes on in the arena and among the crowd for the reception of the returning runners. A new station for the winning posts, and a whitened line drawn across the track, increase the tension. They must be well on their way back now. The discus-throwing and the hurdling by the decathlon strivers do not veil the greater struggle that is being waged, surely by now within clear sight of the Stadium watch-towers. We try to compute how far the leaders are still off. By common consent it cannot be much more than three miles. The tape is stretched from post to post, and all is in readiness, and waiting for a right royal reception to the first man back. They must be getting very near now, as a batch of officials have come to the entrance. The sun is at burning heat, and one pictures the stress of the advancing runners. The unshadowed parts of the stands hold limp, perspiring occupants, who brace themselves up at the palpable agitation out on the field.

A scout boy runs out with a message, and all ears are set to catch its import. Three little flags, the Union Jack on top, an American second, a Swedish third, another Union Jack fourth, and an Italian fifth, figure on a miniature flagpole erected on the judge's box. They indicate the nationality of the leading men. Suddenly there is a commotion, and a blare of bugles. The leader is in sight! Every sound is hushed except the hum of the cheering outside. Then there bursts in a stalwart figure in the familiar green and gold South African uniform. It is McArthur. May your representative here express his own feelings of delighted satisfaction at the victory of this grand stayer and enthusiastic running champion? The files of *The Daily Telegraph* bear impress of a prophetic sally, made three weeks ago now, which has borne fruit. The big Afrikander strode sturdily round the track. Halfway to the finishing point an admirer wreathed him with a sash of the South African colours, and he went on to the winning mark, tired but happy. There was something on his face, and a glint in his eye, that no artist could portray, as he answered to the freely-given cheering of the people.

An interlude of about a minute before the second man entered. And the spectators rubbed their eyes when, for the second time, the runner was to be seen clad in green and gold. But for all their disappointment, the Swedes, like the best of sportsmen, cheered these two men from the far-off country south of the Line. Later, when the South African team, proud of their comrades' success, chaired them round the eastern bend to their dressing-room, the incident, long to be remembered, drew a torrent of congratulatory shouting, which seemed to overwhelm McArthur and Gitsham by its force and sincerity.

————

16 JULY 1912

OLYMPIC GAMES
CONCLUDING EVENTS
Our Special Correspondent
STOCKHOLM, Monday

Today the story of the fifth Olympic Games revival comes to a full stop. Its opening chapters were enticing enough to compel one to go through the whole. Never, surely, have the Olympiads, ancient or modern, been enacted under more glowing skies. Stockholm has indeed been well favoured. This closing day is as bright as the first. Though the morning programme is but a scant one, with only the decathlon rivals undertaking their pole-jump test, the public attendance is quite good. It is as nothing, however, compared with the mass of humanity which flooded the arena and the amphitheatre last night. After the flush of excitement induced by the Marathon race, with its establishment of a principle that the South Africans possess lasting powers second to none, the evening was devoted to a sort of anti-climax. Notwithstanding the several events still to be decided, a farewell dinner was given in honour of the assembled athletes. To the number of some four thousand strong, they sat at long lines of covered tables. While they dined a very powerful choir sang Swedish folk songs, and a fine military band interspersed the vocal music with instrumental selections. The Stadium was lit up with many lights, a feature of the illumination being the use of red and green Greek fire at the top of the battlemented towers. It threw a radiant glow far beyond its especial requirements.

This morning the sad news is given out that one of the Marathon runners, the Portuguese Lazaro, has died from over-exertion in the big race. He did not complete the journey, but dropped out exhausted some six and a half miles on the return journey. Poor little fellow! It is easy to realise how, coming from a race not too well versed in the virtues of good physical training, he entered upon this very severe trial in an unprepared state, and as a consequence paid life's highest penalty. Much sympathy is expressed on all sides, and it is not a mere figure of speech to state that this tragic incident, brought about by the biggest race of the gathering, has cast a heavy shadow upon this final day's doings.

Quickly the large field engaged in the cross-country race comes forward to line up for the start. Kolehmainen, already the winner of the 10,000 and

5,000 metres, is seen to be there. For a few moments there are doubts as to whether the Frenchman Bouin will also compete. The sun is burning hot, but the cross-countrymen step swiftly towards the outlet from the Stadium when the pistol report releases them. They are not to be envied. Suddenly the well-known figure of Kolehmainen comes into view again. He is running easily, with arms set square by his sides and those supple, lengthy legs of his going stealthily along. He has made two hundred yards before the second man, who is just ahead of four blue-shirted Swedes, appears. The general impression seems to be that the race is over, instead of only one-half of the course having been traversed. So the leader and the long, struggling trail of perspiring athletes, with the Manchester man, Scott, our chief representative, about midway along its length, again leave the Stadium.

A bugle blast commands silence. The cross-country men are returning. To a wild burst of shouting and Finnish adaptation of Hurrah – which sounds very much like 'Harva' – Kolehmainen comes in running easily, and apparently as fresh as when he first went out of the enclosure. For the next few minutes there is a procession of leading Swedes and Finns. They have shown their stamina in this blazing heat. But for the intervention of Richardson, who carried the redoubtable South African colours into sixth place, these two little northerly nations would have filled the ten leading positions. The three English runners who finished were Hibbins, Glover, and Humphreys, respectively fifteenth, sixteenth, and eighteenth.

There was left but the 1,500 metres race among the ardent all-rounders who have been at the decathlon these past two days. Three poor mile heats of the decathlon, each serving to attract the sympathies of the crowd to the two successful Swedish athletes figuring in them, witness the due completion of the games within the Stadium. They leave America head of the poll, with Sweden second and England third. The concluding scenes mark the triumph of the American-Indian Thorpe, who, by winning the decathlon, in addition to the pentathlon, stamps himself as a proficient, all-round athlete. With the presentation of the prizes in front of the Royal box, photograph taking, souvenirs, and cheers for everybody, the latest of the Olympiads, as concerns its most popular contests, is numbered with the past.

ANTWERP 1920

PICTURESQUE SCENE AT THE OPENING CEREMONY
KING ALBERT PRESENT

B. Bennison

ANTWERP, Saturday

King Albert, with his Queen radiant and happy by his side, young Princess Marie José, and her brothers, Prince Leopold and Prince Charles obviously delighted, and the lean, ascetic Cardinal Mercier, an arresting figure, were saluted this afternoon by the world's best athletes, men of countries knit together by the Great War, and who, on the wonderful playground here, have come to engage in sports that, properly understood, go to the very root of life. Belgium has built some three miles from the centre of Antwerp a stadium which has cost two million francs, and in it picked men and women of twenty-seven nations who will compete in Olympic Games. They came into the arena this afternoon in a wonderful sunlight, and the parade was unique. I have never seen anything like it before. It suggested a world untroubled, a world supremely young, buoyant, and laughing, and yet splendidly disciplined.

It was a truly thrilling and dramatic moment when M. Victor Boin, proudly carrying the Belgian flag, mounted a rostrum in front of the Royal box, and with uplifted right hand affirmed that his countrymen were about to enter the games as sportsmen for honour and glory, to help conserve the spirit of sport, and to bring out all the chivalry that was in it. In a fierce, dazzling sunlight trumpeters blew a triumphant blast, guns thundered, overhead was an aeroplane that capered strangely, and in the centre of the enclosure the world's athletes, making a picture rich in colour, stood at attention. Then, King Albert having declared the stadium open, guns crashed, and from out of little wicker baskets pigeons were liberated to fly to all corners of the world to tell that the seventh Olympiad had begun. It was stage management *in excelsis*. There could have been no better prelude to what promises to be an historic carnival.

During the next fourteen days there will be many great battles for supremacy on the track, in the field, on the lawn tennis courts, in the water, and between the fencers of the nations. Runners and athletes generally are saying, with justification, that they have had very little practice, that there has been little scope to loosen their limbs. Very largely they will take their chances without having had preliminary canters. The condition of the track is not conducive to fast times. Indeed, we look for no records, though America will probably excel in short-distance events. For my part, I am counting on a long round of capital sport, and that the purpose of the Olympic Games, which is to keep alive and spread the gospel of physical fitness the world over, will be abundantly realised, for in the words of the venerable Cardinal Mercier, who preached in the cathedral this morning, a world built up of high ideals, such as are begotten by sport, will be a better world.

------

19 AUGUST 1920
HILL'S WONDERFUL RUN
THE 5,000-METRES HERO
B. Bennison
ANTWERP, Tuesday

On this day of blistering sunshine we have witnessed a round of wonders, and we who have come to Antwerp for the Olympic Games have been deeply stirred and thrilled. Englishmen are pardonably proud and happy; France may claim that in Guillemot she has one of the greatest runners of modern times; experts, for the most part, have been confounded. The victory of Albert Hill, the Herne Hill Harrier, in the 800 metres, exploded form and poked fun at the prophets. This fair-haired, well-knit, stout-hearted athlete, when we were almost sure that Rudd, the Rhodes scholar, wearing the bright-green colours of South Africa, would win; when Americans had only eyes for their magnificent runner, Earl Eby, and when there was more than a possibility of his countryman, Campbell, finishing first; when King Albert and every one of the several thousand people in the Stadium were gripped tight by the desperate, punishing battle for victory, flew to the front not more than thirty yards from the tape, and as he did so a mighty shout went up.

We had scarcely thought of the young Londoner; Edgar Mountain certainly – a well-set-up, strong young man. For Hill, until Rudd took the lead just before rounding the bend for the straight, had occupied no sort of place from which it seemed likely that he would eventually beat all opposition. It is possible that when Rudd kind of wobbled and told plainly of distress, and Eby was almost touching the South African's shoulder, Hill was encouraged to make the effort of his life; until that moment he could scarcely have supposed that he would win. The condition of Rudd, I am sure, gave him inspiration; in the last few yards of this truly memorable race Hill was as a man who would do or die. With chin held high, jaws clenched, his eyes half-closed, his face distorted by the greediness with which he had already eaten his strength, he forced himself to the first position. But there were more than ten or a dozen yards to go – awful, soul-breaking yards – and Eby, with characteristic grit, challenged Hill to a fight to the last gasp, and this little American, slipping past Rudd, stuck to Hill like some terrier. But Hill never faltered; on he went to break the tape, with the hot breath of Eby on his shoulders. Rudd, on the heels of Eby, was third, and as he passed the post he fell all of a heap, utterly and completely spent. Campbell, a worthy American, also collapsed, and for quite a long time lay on the turf in a semi-conscious condition. Hill, though he could never have engaged in such a battle before, was, by comparison with the others, tolerably fresh, and the while his countrymen cheered and shouted, and everybody roared their admiration for him, he hurried to lend a helping hand to the prostrate Campbell. Great, chivalrous man is Hill. He will never run such a race as he did this afternoon. It was all very wonderful. No athlete ever fought so nobly for his country.

And now about Guillemot. A pastrycook by trade, he is at present a soldier of France. He is a ruddy-faced, black-haired, 22-year-old man, almost boyish in appearance. See him run, and the stickler for style would say that he was all wrong. He pushes his head well forward; he has not the ideal carriage. And it is said that he is no believer in hard, systematic training; that he is just a natural runner; that he runs because he feels he must run. That he runs according to the ethics of any school other than that of his own creation I can well believe, and he won me to him because of his originality. No such long-distance runner has France had since Jean Bonin, who fell in the War. He is the type of young man who knows no tiredness. Guillemot had set his heart on winning; and the faith of Frenchmen in his chances was spoken openly and without qualification. Italy had Speroni, who proved his worth in his heat; a thick-shouldered, deep-chested, little man is Speroni. He was the first to set the pace, but the race was but in its infancy when Paavo Nurmi, the Finn, declared by many to be a second Kolehmainen, strode out and led the way. This Nurmi is tall, and has an action at once easy and graceful, and his physical strength is obvious.

A little fellow, indeed, did Guillemot appear to be as he ran and seemed to glue his shoulder to that of the Finn. So they ran far ahead of the others, who could not live up to the pace which they set. It was in every way a tussle between these two sharply different men; Englishmen, Swedes, Furmas, the American, and Speroni, were all out of the hunt, tailed off hopelessly; they were of a different class to Guillemot and Nurmi. Indeed, after the first two or three laps, it was all a question as to whether Guillemot or the Finn would crack. Almost imperceptibly, but none the less surely, Nurmi would increase his rate. Guillemot, as if he were of the same machine as personified by the Finn, would do likewise; he would not budge a fraction of an inch from Nurmi's shoulder; he would not get in front, though the temptation to do so must have been terribly hard to resist. No, Guillemot preferred to ape the ways of a limpet and hang on until the time arrived for a supreme effort. Half the distance of the last lap had been completed, and it looked as if Nurmi would beat the Frenchman by sheer strength and staying power. From the press box Guillemot appeared to be tired; he leaned forward in rather ominous fashion, but some little distance before entering the straight he darted forward in a way astonishing, almost after the manner of a sprinter. Nurmi winced and beat himself into a quicker pace, but to catch the Frenchman was impossible; it could not be done, and so Guillemot was the hero of the 5,000 metres. With Nurmi he had outclassed all others. As he went past the post he rushed into the arms of his waiting, overjoyed countrymen, and was kissed and embraced and cheered vociferously.

The London policemen, whose average weight is fifteen stones twelve pounds – huge men every one of them – would appear to have the tug-of-war in their pockets. It was ridiculously easy for them to beat the American team in the first round. They took hold of the rope, and in a twinkling the American giants were pulled into defeat. Surely our policemen are unbeatable in this gloriously old-fashioned game of tug-of-war!

———

20 AUGUST 1920

ENGLISH SUCCESSES
Our Special Correspondent
ANTWERP, Thursday

Albert Hill, the Herne Hill Harrier, won a second great victory for England, finishing first in the 1,500 metres final, after a particularly desperate race. His triumph was almost as thrilling as that won by him on Tuesday in the 800 metres. Phillip Baker (England) was a fine second, and Shields (America) third, the time being four minutes one and one-fifth seconds. Ray (United States), from whom much was expected, cracked under the pace. Hill was carried shoulder-high and warmly cheered. As expected, the London policemen won the tug-of-war, beating Holland.

---

21 AUGUST 1920

WIN FOR RHODES SCHOLAR
Our Special Correspondent
ANTWERP, Friday

Harry Edward, the British runner, has been pursued by bad luck for the second time in these Games. He suffered from an indifferent start in the sprint, and this afternoon, in the semi-final of the 200 metres, he strained a tendon in his left leg. Still, he qualified for the last stage, but he went to the mark obviously unfit and lame. It was, in the circumstances, wonderful that he finished third. Woodring (America) was first, and Paddock, also of America, second. The time was twenty-two seconds. The crack American, Murchison, was fourth.

Rudd, the Rhodes scholar, won a triumph for the British Empire in the final of the 400 metres, Butler (England) being second, and Engdahl (Sweden) third. It was a stirring race. The surprise of the day was the defeat of the Frenchman, Guillemot, in the 10,000 metres, which was won by Nurmi, of Finland. Wilson (England), who ran splendidly, was third. Nurmi beat Guillemot in the last fifty yards. Percy Hodge (England) won the 3,000 metres steeplechase by one hundred yards in front of Flynn (America), Ambrosini (Italy) being third. Foss (America) took the pole jump. He did thirteen feet five and one-eighth inches, which is a world's record.

PARIS 1924

7 JULY 1924
BRITAIN'S PROMISING START
ABRAHAMS EQUALS RECORD

PARIS, Sunday

We have had a crowded and, to many sporting writers who have come to Colombes, a perplexing and severely trying afternoon. There was much wanting in the arrangements and accuracy of the result-board, and to those who had an elementary knowledge of the French language the information offered by means of a loudspeaker conveyed little or nothing. Perhaps, as at Antwerp, details of events that are to follow will be supplied in both French and English; otherwise I am afraid there will be much unnecessary groping after facts. And surely a mistake has been made in holding back the day's sport until three o'clock on each afternoon. The result, as I saw it today, was a tremendous hustle. For instance, heats in the 400 metres hurdle, the qualifying stages of the high jump, and the javelin, were decided simultaneously, and to appraise the worth of each and particular competitors was out of the question.

It was left to H.M. Abrahams to put up the most striking performance. In the second round of the 100 metres his time was ten and three-fifths seconds, which equals the Olympic record set up by the American D.F. Lippincoff at Stockholm twelve years ago. Abrahams, in this particular heat, had the race in his pocket. The moment he jumped out of his hole his long, raking stride kind of annihilated the other five competitors. He can never have moved better. He reduced the sprint to a thing all so simple, and, though one may never know how this race will shape itself tomorrow when the semi-final and final are to be decided, the running of Abrahams was such this afternoon that even with such redoubtable fliers as Murchison, Bowman, and Charles Paddock amongst the survivors, no one who saw the Cambridge Blue today would like to say that the blue riband of the track would go to the United States. My countrymen may be in high feathers today, though I would insist that Charles Paddock appears to be no less speedy than at Antwerp, and unquestionably Murchison is faster than he was four years ago. Most Americans I have met believe that they will fill the first three places in the sprint, with Murchison as the winner. This much is certain: the final may produce a tremendous and thrilling battle. Liddell, as has been announced, did not turn out, but Great Britain have Nichol as a real live second string to Abrahams, who was first in the opening round and was a good second to E.W. Carr, the Australian, in the next stage. France has one survivor in the sprint, Degrelle, a young Paris fireman who was not thought of the same class as André Mourlon, who failed to qualify in the second round.

---

8 JULY 1924

WORLD'S RECORDS AT OLYMPIC GAMES
VICTORY OF H.M. ABRAHAMS

B. Bennison

PARIS, Monday

The semi-final of the 100 metres had no sooner been completed at Colombes this afternoon than a new world's record was established. It was J.C. Taylor, a tall, fair-haired American, who added a fresh page to the history of the Olympic Games in the final of the 400 metres hurdles, covering the distance, after what was an unsatisfactory race, in fifty-two and three-fifths seconds. Taylor, I would hasten to add, was in no way to blame for what happened, and I would have it known that there can be no question that he is one of the finest examples of an athlete sent to Paris by his country. It transpired, however, that Brookins, who made such a marked impression in his heat yesterday, was disqualified, after finishing second, for what, it was announced, was bad jumping, while F.J. Blackett, of Great Britain, was also ruled out for having toppled over three hurdles. The placings for the second, third, and fourth positions were: E. Vilen, of Finland; Ivan Riley, of America; and George André, of France, respectively. The last-named, for his age and remembering his long and strenuous life in the world of sport, put up a really remarkable performance. The American contingent were pardonably elated at the success of their champion, and the ceremony of saluting the American flag was one of the most impressive things of the day. Taylor reduced the previous world's best, done at Antwerp four years ago by F.J. Loomis, also of the United States, by a fraction less than two seconds.

But it was the final of the sprint, which rounded off the afternoon's sport, that we most wanted to see. It was past seven o'clock when the speed team began to prepare. From the inside of the track the positions were Paddock, Scholz, Murchison, Abrahams, Bouman, and Porritt. When the leather-lunged announcer gave it out that all was in readiness for the start the silence was awe-inspiring. Not a whisper could be heard. Holes had been carefully dug, and, to a perfect start, off the men went like a shot. This and that man's name was screamed. On they flew, with Abrahams, in the centre, showing just a suspicion of daylight between himself, Scholz, and Porritt. And then at fifty yards Abrahams, amid yells of joy from the British, made his effort. It was Herculean in its mightiness, and he took a lead of a quarter of a yard from Scholz, with Porritt only inches behind. The flying American, Bouman, was next, and then the awkward Paddock and Murchison.

Would Abrahams live through? He did. He tugged at his big heart, his jaws seemed to snap, his finely-chiselled face was distorted, telling a tale of iron determination. There was no cracking of Abrahams, and on he flashed to break the tape in front of Scholz. It was one of the closest finishes; it was the merest trifle that the Cambridge Blue won by. But it was enough, and there was given off a crack of enthusiasm. No more popular victory could have been. For the first time in the history of the Olympic Games, as they have come to be, an Englishman has won the sprint. Except in 1908, when Reggie Walker, the South African, won at Shepherd's-bush, the 100 metres has been captured by America, and we had only come to regard the winning of the blue riband of the track by the United States as a matter of course.

The placings were: Abrahams (1), Scholz (2), Porritt (3), Bouman (4), Paddock (5), Murchison (6). Abrahams did ten and three-fifths seconds, which was precisely the time in which he won his heat yesterday. That Murchison was last of all came as something like a bombshell in the American camp, but there was no begrudging Abrahams of his triumph. On every hand he was warmly congratulated, and when he stood and saluted the British flag as it was unfurled in token of his victory, there was one long cheer, and then, as the British National Anthem was played, all the thousands of people present stood at attention. It has been a memorable day for England.

———

9 JULY 1924

ANOTHER BRITISH WIN IN THE OLYMPIC GAMES TRIUMPH OF D.G.A. LOWE PRINCE A SPECTATOR

B. Bennison

PARIS, Tuesday

It was good to be again at Colombes this afternoon, for the weather remained gloriously fine, and quite unexpectedly the Prince of Wales, together with Prince Henry, looked into the Stadium. His Royal Highness, accompanied by the Count Clary and other officials at once made his way into the enclosure, greeted the prodigious weight-putters, and then took up a position at the start of the 200 metres race, and, appropriately enough, Abrahams was about to prepare to get to his mark and engage in his second battle with Paddock, the flying American. The Prince chatted with the hero of the sprint and others of the competitors, including the Irishman, S. Lavan, and for some time watched the progress made in the different events. The visit of the Prince of Wales was of a strictly informal character. He came to the Stadium after the manner of several thousands who had found their way there.

We are immensely proud of our D.G.A. Lowe. For Great Britain he won the 800 metres flat in grand style. A punishing race it was. Though it did not produce any record time, it was, from the point of view of the English, the shaping of it that captured the imagination. Almost with the firing of the pistol the long-legged Stallard who had run so impressively in the heat, forced himself into first place, and from this point he acted as pacemaker to Lowe and Houghton. So long as his two compatriots were at his heels, ready if need be to take the lead, Stallard carried himself as if he were supremely happy. It looked as if he would go on and win, so telling, so easy, so gallant, his style. But there was always lying handy, and chockfull of grit, Martin, the Swiss. When round the bend for the last time, and the straight had been reached, Martin made his effort. Immediately Lowe, who had nursed himself ever so judiciously, put on speed ahead, and fifty yards from home he was in front. Then it was that Stallard, with much of his stamina spent, dropped back, and Lowe went on to finish a strong winner. The time was one minute fifty-two and two-fifths seconds. Martin was second; Eric, United States, third; Stallard, fourth; Richardson, United States, fifth; and Dodge, also of America, sixth.

I I JULY 1924

EXCELLENT SPORT AT THE OLYMPIC GAMES
GREAT DAY FOR FINLAND
B. Bennison

When my Finnish confreres sought me out on the eve of the Olympic Games and insisted that to them belonged the greatest long-distance runners in all the world they did not exaggerate. They came to France, and in a way cold-blooded gave it out that this and that event was already in their pocket. They said: 'We have reduced our athletics to a science; we have cut chances out of our reckoning; that which we have created at home we shall recreate at Colombes. You shall see. We have our Nurmi, our Ritola, Katz, and there are others of a younger generation. The capacity of each we know to a nicety.' I have seen, and known, most men since the days of Sid Thomas and Alfred Shrubb who have made distance racing a speciality. I recall, also, Sonny Morton and E.W. Perry, heroes of my days before I trekked south from the big industrial North. These idols of my youth have, this afternoon, been smashed to smithereens, for nothing have I seen that has bordered more closely upon the wonderful than the performance of P. Nurmi in the final of the 1,500 metres.

This tall, broad-shouldered man, with fair hair and stamina unbelievable, won, so it appeared, at his leisure. But although I am ready to accept him as unapproachable, it is possible that, had not Stallard suffered a mishap to his right ankle yesterday, even this phenomenal Finn would not have romped home in the absurdly easy fashion he did. For Stallard, in his heats, had made such a valiant show that we felt that he, together with Lowe, would provide us with at least an outside chance of capturing this particular prize. News of Stallard's doubtful condition I learned when lunching with Earl Cadogan, and it was an agreeable surprise when I found him on the track ready to fight the best of them. The ankle of Stallard was bound up, and he gave off a tell-tale limp. That he completed the distance, and even got into third place, was remarkable. I do believe that Stallard would have turned out had it been necessary for him to be carried to his mark, such was his keenness, enthusiasm, and deep-rooted determination not to let his country down. I expected that he would fall by the wayside early. At least he had no more than one leg and a swinger, but he stuck to Nurmi and Scharer (Switzerland) like a leech. I was prepared to see Lowe give most trouble to these two men, who showed the way from the start, but in a way amazing Stallard, remembering his sorry plight, was more in the thick of the fight than the rest. Only a quarter of a lap had been covered when Nurmi, with but little effort, assumed the leadership, Watson (United States) lying second, and Switzerland's hope third.

At the end of the second round Nurmi flung the watch which he carried away, and got so far ahead that there was never any question that he would win. So he broke the tape without, I thought, having really extended himself. Scharer followed him, and, as I have said, Stallard was next. Stallard reached the post only by reason of instinct, for no sooner had he drawn abreast of the judges than he fell heavily, and for a time he lay stretched out on the enclosure. His great efforts had been unavailing, and the last I saw of the brave Stallard was his being carried on an improvised stretcher to the dressing-room. His failure was, indeed, a gallant one, but, upon reflection, I am sure he was ill-advised to run. Lowe, his countryman, was fourth, R.B. Baker (United States) fifth, and Hahn (also America) sixth. The time was three minutes fifty-three and three-fifths seconds, which set up a new record for the Olympic Games. Had Nurmi been thoroughly extended it is highly probable that he would have beaten the world's record of three minutes fifty-two and three-fifths seconds, of which he is the holder. The race, to him, took the form of a pleasure trip.

Later the final of the 5,000 metres made the day's sport the best we have yet seen at Colombes. It resolved itself into another story of Nurmi and his compatriot Ritola, for Nurmi was the winner and Ritola a splendid second. We had for our representatives F.C. Saunders and C.T. Clibbon, but, from what we had previously seen of them and other finalists, we decided that there was only one man likely to cause any anxiety to Finland. That man was Wide, of Sweden, thought by his fellows to be about the best man his country has yet produced. And we were right in our deductions. Wide set out to make the pace, but Nurmi and Ritola only allowed him to hold it so long as they pleased.

At the half-distance Nurmi, who never turned a hair, having consulted his watch, evidently decided that it was time to quicken his paces. Obviously, it was his business to try and run Wide to a standstill and so make way for Rastas and Seppala, who were the other Finns beside Ritola out for glory. He quickly left Wide very many yards behind, and, making pace for Ritola, the two made a race of it all to themselves. And when the last lap came to be done I really believe that one tried to beat the other. But Nurmi was too much for Ritola. There was no robbing Nurmi of first position, though Ritola tried ever so hard to do so. Wide was third, and he was pretty well all out. J.L. Romig (United States) was fourth, Seppala (Finland) fifth, and our man, Clibbon, sixth. Nurmi did fourteen minutes thirty-one and one-fifth seconds, which was better than Guillemot's figures at Antwerp, and only fell short of a world's record by three seconds.

---

12 JULY 1924
ERIC LIDDELL THE HERO
NEW WORLD'S RECORD
B. Bennison
PARIS, Friday

Eric Liddell is today's Olympic hero for Great Britain. After an electrifying race, he won the 400 metres, in forty-seven and three-fifths seconds, a time which has never been equalled. Enthusiasm was unbounded when this fair Scotsman broke the tape; men and women of all nations cheered him unrestrainedly, and when the British flag was run up the mast in token of his mighty achievement, the thousands of folk who had come to the Stadium at Colombes jumped to attention. The scene, on an afternoon radiant with sunshine, was one of immense splendour; we Britishers had dared but only to whisper hopes that this flying Scotsman, who, as you know, because of his religious scruples, refrained from taking part in the sprint last Sunday, would capture the prize. We knew him to be fit and well; on many occasions he had given ample proof of his fighting qualities. Liddell is of the do or die breed, but that he would put up a world's record-breaking performance scarcely entered into the calculations of even the most optimistic of us.

It was fast approaching seven o'clock when Liddell, Fitch, Butler, Johnston, and Taylor, the finalists, were called to the track. The going was appreciably better and faster than on the preceding day. So much had been demonstrated earlier, and I would here set out the extraordinary fact that in the heats of the 400 metres the record was broken three times. First, Imbach, the Swiss, did forty-eight seconds; then Fitch, United States, followed, with forty-seven and four-fifths seconds; and Liddell, in the last stage of the semi-finals, covered the distance in forty-eight and one-fifth seconds, all of which times were in advance of that previously set up. B.G.D. Rudd, the famous South African and Oxford University athlete, did but forty-nine and six-tenths seconds at Antwerp four years ago, and small wonder was it that we ached for the coming of the last battle.

Happily, the start was as perfect as any start could be. Every man was off his mark simultaneously and as if they had been shot out of their holes by some machine. Liddell set up a terrific pace. He ran as if he were wild with inspiration; like some demon. And as he flew along, to the accompaniment of a roar, we experts fell to wondering whether Liddell would crack, such was the pace he set out to travel. 'Liddell' was screamed; 'Imbach' was thundered by the Swiss; 'Taylor' was shouted by a finely-drilled American claque. 'Butler', 'Fitch', in turn, was yelled. Liddell, yards ahead, came round the bend for the straight, and as he did so he pulled the harder at himself, for Fitch was getting nearer; there was Butler, too, and Imbach had to be reckoned with. It was the last fifty metres that meant the making, or breaking, of Liddell. Just for a second I feared that he would kill himself by the terrific speed he had set up, but to our great joy he remained chockfull of fight. Imbach, perhaps fifty yards from the tape, fell; the little man was out of it. It was then Liddell or Fitch. The Scotsman had so surely got all his teeth into the race that the American could not loosen his hold, and Liddell got home first by what, considering the formidable opposition, was almost a remarkable margin. Butler was third, Johnson next, and then Taylor, who had the bad luck to stumble a yard or so from the finish. Congratulations were simply showered upon Liddell; not in all athletic history has a man done what he accomplished this afternoon.

————

14 JULY 1924

NURMI'S REMARKABLE FEAT
NEW WORLD'S RECORDS

B. Bennison

PARIS, Saturday

On a day of blinding light and terrific heat there was spread before us in the Stadium of Colombes a spectacle which I would never wish to see again – magnificent, amazing, terribly cruel: a fight almost to the point of death. And only for honour and glory. Of thirty-nine lion-hearted men, drawn from all parts of the world, who set out on the 10,000 metres cross-country race, only fifteen reached and passed the finishing post. The other twenty-four had crumpled up and fallen prostrate by the wayside. Wildest rumours reached the Stadium long before Paavo Nurmi, the phenomenal Finn, had won with something like half a mile to spare from his countryman, Ritola. The Spaniard Andia was reported dead; Wide, the Swede, had been found with his feet bleeding, a helpless wreck. Ambulance men rushed hither and thither; men and women stood as if transfixed as they saw this and that man come into view, reeling, rocking, their eyes glazed, their wet, grimy faces distorted as they struggled to complete what had proved to be the most gruelling, heart-breaking race I have ever seen.

The condition of a slip of a Frenchman named Marchal was pitiable in the extreme. When there were, perhaps, only fifty yards to go he fell sprawling on the red-hot track, and then only by instinct, I am sure, he forced himself up, and away he went, swaying this way and that, to the post, which, I am certain, he could not see. Again he collapsed, and he was carried off, his feet cut and stabbed by the hard, rough, jagged roads; a man he was who had eaten every ounce of his stamina. Except for Nurmi and Ritola, every single one who completed the course was *in extremis*. One man, oblivious to all else but a determination to finish or die, jogged round the track minus shoe and stocking, and the bandages, with which he had strapped his ankles, had become so loosened that they gave him a curious appearance. Four Swedes and the Spaniard Andia were taken to hospital. Word came to me that Wide, Bergstrom, and Andia had all died. Happily the news was untrue, but they, and many others as I write, are in a shocking state of prostration, and it is almost certain that more than one of them will never draw on a pump again; they have run their last race.

And now I would tell of the wonder man Nurmi. At once he led the field; whether on grass, or cinders, or whatever conformation the course took, he was just his giant self. He ran as if heat and sun to him, though a Finn reared in a country of hardiness, meant nothing. He bent his elbows so as to give them the appearance of piston rods, and with head held high, and without a cover, he strode along with a smoothness and an indifference to his awful task that left us spellbound. And when he came through the archway leading to the track such was his condition, so strong was he within himself, that he might have only run a few hundred yards instead of having raced more than six miles. He was greeted in a way you would expect — we shouted a welcome to him that took the form of a thunderous roar that grew in volume so as to become deafening when he broke the tape.

Having done so, he trotted a few yards beyond the finishing line, wheeled round on to the grass, took off his pumps, and marched, like a grenadier on parade, to the dressing-room. He never moved a muscle. He was less overwrought than the many thousands of men and women who looked on. As he was about to disappear from view he took one sharp glance at Ritola, who was coming up the straight, and a half-smile played about his thin lips as he saw his fellow Finn finish second. Earl Johnson, an American giant, came third. Harper, the Englishman, came next, and then, as so many others had done, collapsed. Nurmi's time was thirty-two minutes fifty-four and four-fifths seconds, which represents an altogether extraordinary performance. I am sure that no other living man could have done that which Nurmi achieved today. He is the wonder of all athletic ages, and of Ritola I would say that no country, other than his own, has a greater long-distance runner. The 3,000-metres team race, thanks to Nurmi and Ritola, went to Finland in Olympic record time — eight minutes thirty-two seconds. Great Britain was second and the United States third.

———

22 JULY 1924

FINAL SCENES AT OLYMPIC BOXING
UNPARALLELED INCIDENT

B. Bennison

PARIS, Monday

In the early hours of this morning, following many ugly and distressing scenes that can never have a place in sport in this or any other country, the Olympic boxing, which had been spread over the week, ended. The last of many days of storm and stress was begun by the withdrawal of the two Italians, Castellenghi and Sarandi, from the semi-finals, as a protest, so it was given out, against the judging. The withdrawal of these men was done without any great fuss or ceremony, but in a way, such was the atmosphere at the Vélodrome d'Hiver, so as to prepare us for almost anything. I had the feeling that we were always sitting on a volcano; and sure enough, long before the night's work had been completed and we were free to get back to Paris, our little sorely-troubled world was erupted.

One H. Mendez, a swarthy son of Argentine, was declared to have lost to the Belgian middleweight, Delarge. Thereupon men and women of his country broke loose. Up they jumped; screamed and shrieked and yelled; they whistled and catawauled; they fumed and blustered and stamped. It was Argentina's night with a vengeance. There was Mendez, standing with his back to the ropes like one transfixed; 'Mendez!' 'Mendez!' 'Mendez!' a thousand voices roared; elaborately-gowned women mounted chairs that set a-cracking and waved little flags, what time they screeched; a band struck up the Belgian National Anthem; it was drowned in the din. What Lord Cadogan and other distinguished sportsmen who had seats at the foot of the ring thought of it all I may only surmise; to me the shindy can have no parallel in amateur sport. There were moments, especially when a Belgian, all hot and over-wrought, rushed into the centre of a crowd of hot-blooded Argentines and unfurled the flag of his country in their faces, as if to say, 'Tread on the tail of my coat if you dare'. Donnybrook *in excelsis* could never have produced scenes more distasteful. There was nothing else for it but to sit tight and allow the champions of Mendez to let off steam. A man here and there suffered to be ejected; soldiers were requisitioned, and slowly did the fire peter out, and for the rest of the evening we had comparative calm.

There was not the slightest excuse for the pandemonium. Mendez, a good, if a fantastic, boxer, lost for the reason that he did not make his effort until it was too late; he seemed to take it for granted that so soon as he pleased he could knock the Belgian cold. Those of his country apparently regarded him as a certain champion; it was entirely forgotten that in boxing, as in all sport, there can be no foregone conclusions. However, Mendez and his camp followers took the view that his defeat was the last straw. They had seen the verdict go against A.Copello, also one of their boxers, in the preceding bout, and they were in no sort of humour to reconcile themselves to the downfall of yet another. And they signalled the same in a way that shocked every man who would be accepted as a sportsman. Even one of the seconds of Mendez thought it necessary to fling himself on to the neck of an over-wrought compatriot and cry hysterically. However, the ring was not uprooted; the judges were not molested, and no material damage, so far as I could ascertain, was done, but the row was still raging furiously when the two English middleweights, Harry Mallin and J. Elliott, entered upon their final. To concentrate upon their job was impossible; so long as they remained in the ring there was a danger that a considerable section of the crowd would run amok.

Mallin and Elliott, however, stuck to their guns and did their best in abnormal conditions. But Mallin, though he was a clear winner, did not box up to form; it would have been astonishing had he done so. Like Elliott, who has won much praise from the critics, he was inexpressibly glad when he was free to take his departure. Mallin had the immense satisfaction of knowing that for the second time there was not a middleweight his equal among the world's amateurs; and I doubt whether there is one who does his boxing with a closer appreciation for all that is best in it. Great Britain not only captured the middleweight championship, but also the light-heavyweight crown, through the agency of H. Mitchell.

And this by the way of conclusion: I trust that if boxing is again given a place in the Olympic Games, those responsible for it will have put their house in order. If it is not possible to have more competent judging than I have seen in Paris, then boxing must be ruled out of the next Olympiad. Boxing, whenever it is done as part of a tournament, embracing all the countries, must at best be difficult, but when bad decisions are given, when there can be little or no confidence in the judgment of the arbiters, then a repetition of the scenes we have had daily at the Vélodrome d'Hiver is inevitable. Any game so conducted as to make for bad blood can never be worth the while. I would forget that which I have witnessed in Paris.

23 JULY 1924
LEADING ARTICLE
THE OLYMPIC GAMES

Those who hoped most for the establishment of the Olympic Games must have read with the deepest regret the story of the contests in Paris. Some gallant races were run, some brilliant victories were won, before a sportsmanlike crowd. But such events were rare. Day after day we have read of disputes between competitors and judges, or dubious, or less than dubious, tricks, and uninformed, or worse than uninformed, decisions. The spectators again and again showed their partiality to individuals and nations by loud and violent abuse, hysterical disorder and rioting. The amazing turbulence which the boxing competitions produced has been vividly described by Mr Bennison. The incredible decision which declared a man a winner who had not only been thoroughly beaten on points but earned disqualification by biting his opponent led to an ultimatum from the English-speaking nations. That judgment was reversed under a threat from the United States and the Dominions, as well as our own country, to withdraw their men. In spite of this rather emphatic criticism of the organisation of the Olympic boxing, there was so little improvement that its finals were fought out amid a disturbance which required troops to subdue it. We hear without surprise that the British Olympic Committee have now informed the International Committee that in future British boxers will not compete at the Olympic Games. But it is not only in boxing that there have been unpleasant incidents. In fencing the Italian foil team were dissatisfied with the judging and declined to go on. In the sabre contest there was another quarrel. One or more duels are announced to be the inevitable consequence. We say nothing of the booing by the spectators, free fights among them, and their attempts to drown the national anthems of countries so unfortunate as to incur their dislike. British competitors in general seem to have fared better than those from other nations. Compared with the Americans, for example, we are assured that our men received quite a cordial welcome. But could there be a more severe criticism than such comparisons on the organisation and conduct of the Games? It has become plain that if they are to be resumed four years hence there must be a thorough and drastic process of reform. Their present scope is perhaps too large, and by its abundance of events prevents adequate supervision and control by a competent governing body. Some phases of the Games – we may point to the best track events, for example – have been tolerably well conducted. But there can be no denying the conclusion that the total result of the contests just concluded has been an injury to sport and to international amity. Those who believe that the Olympic Games may yet do good service to the world must make very different working plans for the future gatherings.

AMSTERDAM 1928

30 JULY 1928
LEADING ARTICLE
THE OLYMPIC GAMES

The ninth Olympic Games were opened at Amsterdam on Saturday by Prince Henry of the Netherlands, the representatives of forty-four nations taking part in the picturesque ceremony of marching past and saluting, each after its traditional fashion, the Royal box. During the next fortnight all lovers of sport will eagerly follow the fortunes of those picked athletes from Great Britain who will, without any doubt, maintain the very high standards which this country has always set, even if they fail to carry off the supreme trophies. It is now thirty-four years since that splendid Frenchman, Baron Pierre de Coubertin, with the aim of introducing into his country the English public school attitude to games, revived the old Greek idea of Olympic Games. It has taken many years to make all the different nations realise the benefits that accrue from these meetings, but even the most cursory comparison between the general attitude towards sport all over the world in the Nineties and today shows how swift has been the spread of interest in games and athletics. This has been largely due to the Olympic Games Movement, which set out with the ambitious aim of fostering a better understanding and good fellowship between all the peoples of the world by bringing them together on the common ground of sport. No one could pretend that such a task is an easy one. Where many men of widely differing temperaments and standards of what is and what is not honourable are vying with one another to secure success for their country there are bound to be occasional hitches and adjustments. The marvel is that there have been so few misunderstandings. The way to world peace is, however slowly, at least surely being paved by these contests, which are becoming more and more the modern counterpart of the mediaeval tournaments, notable as much for the spirit of chivalry as for skill, courage and fortitude.

Everyone hopes that our representatives will give a good account of themselves at Amsterdam, but there will be no feeling that the country is going to the dogs if they return home without any single garland, nor would there be any feeling of undue superiority if they happened, by a miracle, to sweep the board. The Olympic Games to us are first and last an opportunity for fostering international good-fellowship, and it is a wholly admirable thing that once every four years the sportsmen and sportswomen of all races should meet thus in keen and friendly rivalry.

---

31 JULY 1928

EMPIRE DAY AT OLYMPIC GAMES
NOTABLE TRIUMPHS
LORD BURGHLEY WINS THE HURDLES
AMERICANS SURPRISED

B. Bennison

AMSTERDAM, Monday

This has been Empire Day at the Olympic Games. We have won two of the most coveted prizes offered by the world of sport – the 100 metres and the 400 metres hurdles – the heroes are P. Williams (the Canadian), not yet twenty years of age, whose home is in British Columbia, and Lord Burghley. The triumph of Lord Burghley I will refer to later; that achieved by Williams in the sprint brought to a close a memorable day. It was a thrilling race, as it was bound to be with everybody keyed up to the highest pitch of excitement. The six men went to their marks, with the various claques of Americans rooting for all their worth for McAllister and Wykoff. J.E. London was in the middle position; the two Americans on the outside. There were two false starts, W.B. Legg and then Wykoff beating the pistol. Silence gave way to a mighty shout as the six men jumped out of their holes. There was little or nothing in it at the quarter distance; at halfway there was daylight between Williams and London, the Canadian just in front. It was still Williams and London for it, and Williams just did it; he broke the tape a foot in front of London. Lammers was third a couple of feet behind. The time was ten and four-fifths seconds. Not to have a man in the first three was a staggering blow to the Americans, who, despite previous disappointments, had counted upon the sprint as near to a certainty for them. Like Lord Burghley, earlier in the afternoon, Williams was carried around the arena shoulder high.

Lord Burghley has joined the ranks of world's champions, and was acclaimed as such to the hoisting of the Union Jack, the singing of his country's National Anthem, and the ringing cheers of his fellows. He won the 400 metres final in a manner so gallant as to win the thousands of onlookers over to him entirely. I would tell the glory of his triumph with regard to every detail of a race that burned itself into the imagination. Together with T.C. Livingstone-Learmouth, he occupied an outside lane. Cuhel, the American, had an inside position; Petterson (U.S.A.) came next, then Taylor (U.S.A.), and Facelli (Italy). Cuhel hung somewhat at the firing of the pistol; the others got away beautifully. Lord Burghley cleared the first seven hurdles with a good grace and ease which none of the others possessed. He never touched a single obstacle; over each he went like a deer. Coming into the straight he was abreast of the two Americans. Almost imperceptibly, but none the less definitely, he increased his pace to get, perhaps, half a yard in front of Cuhel and Taylor before clearing the final hurdle. This he jumped without apparent effort, and then, with jaw set tight, his fair head shot back, he went on to win by a couple of feet from Cuhel in fifty-three and two-fifths seconds, which equalled the Olympic record put up by Morgan Taylor yesterday. Taylor, by the way, was third, Petterson was fourth, Livingstone-Learmouth fifth, and Facelli last. Douglas Lowe was the first to congratulate Lord Burghley, who was carried shoulder high.

————

1 AUGUST 1928

OLYMPIC GAMES
D.G.A. LOWE'S GREAT VICTORY
800 METRES RECORD

B. Bennison

AMSTERDAM, Tuesday

Douglas Lowe, the old Cantab, has done that which no man has ever accomplished in the Olympic Games; for the second time he has won the 800 metres race; no competitor has been successful twice in the same event. His victory today gave rise to one long British roar; it was magnificent, tremendous in its intensity, dramatic in its finish. It was all that we had expected – a battle royal between nine mighty runners. And it was one that will never be forgotten by those privileged to see it. Lowe and his rivals came on to the track towards the close of the day, and before they disrobed they drew for positions. Lowe was in no hurry to chance his luck; he was, in fact, the last to put his hand in the hat. And then, with a broad, self-satisfied smile, he discovered that he had drawn the inside position.

When they prepared for the start Edwards was pulled back because his fingers were over the line. But that was the only contretemps. The start was as perfect as anything could be. Lowe at once jumped into his stride, to take the lead with Edwards at his elbow. Round the second bend Hahn, the American, with a fierce spurt went ahead; then Fuller took first position, with Edwards, stride tremendous, close up. Lowe, it was plain, was not in the least perturbed. He was running well within himself, his action and style generally delightful and telling of the poetry of motion. Lying second, he was in a position to take the lead when he decided it would best serve his purpose to do so. Hahn thought to crack the Englishman by putting on speed, and he was aided and abetted by Edwards. But Lowe could neither be cracked nor held. He maintained his raking stride, and when he came to the last bend of all into the straight, he had carved out a comfortable, an unbeatable lead. Bythlen, the Swede, was the only danger, and he was yards behind. How the British shouted their joy as Lowe, with nodding head now all out, went on to win by six yards from Bythlen. Engelhardt was third, Edwards (Canada) fourth, Hahn (U.S.A.) fifth, Martin (France) sixth, Keller (France) seventh, Watson (U.S.A.) eighth, and Fuller (U.S.A.) last. Lowe's time was one minute fifty-one and four-fifths seconds, which set a new Olympic record. On all hands was Lowe congratulated, one of the first to do so being Engelhardt. Judgment and pace reduced to a science was the secret of Douglas Lowe's conquest.

---

4 AUGUST 1928

OLYMPIC GAMES
NURMI DEFEATED IN THE 5,000 METRES
THRILLING STRUGGLE

B. Bennison

AMSTERDAM, Friday

Nurmi, the mighty Finn, has been defeated. He has fallen before Ritola, his countryman. For once in his extraordinary career his pace and stamina failed him today; the nicely adjusted machinery which he suggests rusted and almost stopped; only his heart kept him in motion until he had run the 5,000 metres race. Then, as he finished second, just in front of Wide, the Swede, he turned with unsteady gait on to the turf, his hard, immovable, inscrutable face blanched, his jaws clenched tight, to throw himself on to his back and stretch as if he were wholly spent. With a tug he pulled himself upright and stiffened like a guardsman on parade, he marched with measured step, his fair head held high, to gather his overall before making for the dressing-room. Meantime, Ritola stood with arms limp, the muscles of his thin wiry legs quivering, before the camera; his unusual, drawn face bronzed by the sun, alight with exultation. So soon as he had won he was shaken heartily by the hand by Wide; Nurmi had offered him no congratulations. Maybe it was that the renowned Nurmi was a sick man; at least I would like to think so, though I am assured that on the track the rivalry between the two is such as to make almost for a vendetta.

I will tell the story of the race. Great Britain had for her representatives Oddie and Johnston; the Finns numbered four, the Swedes three, there were two Americans, and Latvia had one runner. Oddie and Johnston showed the way in the early stages, but they were never to be seriously counted. They both fought as Britons will fight, to the last gasp. One could see with half an eye that the race was bound to go to Finland long before halfway had come. If there was a surprise it was that Lermond, of

America, had the capacity to stick it for as long as he did. This young man did valiantly; he refused to be shaken off. There were but two laps to go when Lermond was in third position, and if his pounding action told of tiredness, there remained much fight in him. Nurmi, hereabouts, gave signs that all was not well with him; every now and then, the while he kept trotting along a couple of yards behind Ritola, he would look round as if apprehensive of Wide. The common impression was that Nurmi was calculating when it would be best to increase his pace and, by so doing, not only rob Ritola of the lead but leave Wide hopelessly behind.

These three, when the last lap but one was entered upon, had left the brave Lermond far behind; the pace and distance were too much for him. When they were rounding the bend to come into the straight for home, it was not Nurmi who spurted, but Ritola. There was a great shout when it was seen that Nurmi could not catch him; it was as if he had become suddenly old; instead of racing as was expected, and running according to the schedule he is given to mapping out, he halted. It seemed as if some vital thing had snapped, and Ritola, at least twelve yards ahead, won. Wide had come up with a rattle, and almost gained second place. Nurmi, however, with all his wits about him, took a side glance at the little Swede, and found it possible to pull enough out of himself to follow Ritola. On all hands it was felt that the winner of the 10,000 metres could not have been himself; that he had not got over the effects of the shaking he suffered by his fall when negotiating the water jump in the steeplechase trials on Wednesday. But it would be wrong to disparage or belittle the conquest of Ritola, who ran the race of his life to beat probably the greatest long-distance runner the world has ever seen.

---

6 AUGUST 1928

NURMI BEATEN AGAIN

B. Bennison

AMSTERDAM, Sunday

The outstanding feature of the day was the 3,000 metres steeplechase, which brought Nurmi and Ritola in opposition again. Nurmi was among the first to make an appearance, and, dressed in a blue pull-over, he trotted along the track to the water jump, at which in the trial he came a cropper, and there he stood for several minutes so as to take full stock of the task exacted by that particular obstacle. Then, with a wag of his fair head, he ran along to jump the first hurdle and generally take a lung-opener, preparatory to stripping for the fray. Ritola was content to huddle up on a form in the arena with the rest of the competitors, oblivious, apparently, to the existence of his rival. It was plain to see that Nurmi and Ritola had pretty well fought themselves to a standstill on Friday in their grim war for victory in the 5,000 metres. Ritola was nowhere in the steeplechase. As a matter of fact, he dropped out several laps from the finish, and Nurmi, though all his heart was in the job, never looked like winning; he was a different, a strange, incredible Nurmi. For all that, it was Finland's race. Loukola was first, fully twenty-five yards in front of Nurmi, and Anderson third. Loukola ran in magnificent fashion, making all others, save Nurmi, appear cheap.

LOS ANGELES 1932

29 JULY 1932

FIFTY NATIONS IN SPORTING RIVALRY AT THE TENTH OLYMPIAD
TOMORROW'S GAMES & WORLD GOODWILL
Bevil Rudd
Winner of 400 metres, Olympic Games, 1920

At two o'clock tomorrow the tenth Olympiad will be opened by President Hoover in the gigantic stadium at Los Angeles. Nearly fifty nations are competing, and the pageantry of the opening parade will be almost as inspiring as the fierce competition that will rage daily until 14 August. America is on her mettle: not only to show that her comprehensive athletic organisation can produce world-beaters – gods from the machine – but also to demonstrate that her crowds are track-minded, critical of technique and appreciative of courage and sportsmanship. She would like to illumine the dream of Baron Pierre de Coubertin, to justify his vision of forty years ago, when he conceived the idea of, and carried out, the first of the modern Olympic Games.

When fifty nations rally their exuberant manhood in circumstances which make victory ecstatic and defeat acute it is not to be wondered at that occasional contretemps occur. It is, however, significant that those people who consider friendship and foreigners disloyal to Britain, are forced to remember that hardy annual of sporting reminiscence – the Halswelle incident of 1908 – or else to read the imaginative peevishness of journalists who have never witnessed nor certainly competed in an Olympiad – before they can arm themselves with anti-Olympic Games arguments.

Actually an Olympiad is the Cinderella hour for athletics. The stadium events predominate, and with an American crowd they will have more than their share of the magic wand. Detractors have called the Games 'gladiatorial', but Douglas Lowe could scarcely be styled a swashbuckler, and there is nothing about Lord Burghley to suggest that he could immolate himself to create a raucous Californian holiday.

Personally, I went to the Games in 1920 in a mood of scepticism, just as I had gone to run in the U.S.A. earlier that year with misgivings. I soon became a devoted supporter of the movement. In the 800 metres at Antwerp I was warned by several people that as there were four Americans in the final I should be prepared to meet with all sorts of tricks. What did happen was this: a Swede accidentally bumped an American, who collided with me at the beginning of the second lap. It was not the American's fault, and he could have taken advantage of the jostle. Instead he shot me a fleeting smile; and said 'Sorry, Bevil', and dropped back to let me regain the tactical position out of which he had unintentionally pushed me. Before this race was started a Hollander I knew, who had unexpectedly reached the final, came to me and said: 'I have already done more than my country ever expect of me. I have the final reached. Of course, I cannot win; but I would like you to win – South Africa is dear to Holland. Can I help you?'

In 1924, before the Paris Olympiad, I wrote with a certain defiance: 'In the Olympic Games there is pageantry without squalid contrast, excitement without hate, bravery without cruelty, victory without undue elation, defeat without chagrin, and, above all, effort that is not wasted.' I repeat that today with a sure confidence.

Tomorrow, when the multitude of pigeons – the original broadcasters – are released in compliance with ancient tradition, and the oath of amateurism is taken by the massed athletes, and the gay din proclaims the opening of the tenth Olympiad, in its gorgeous and mammoth setting, a renewed era of international goodwill and understanding will have begun. Los Angeles will become more effective than Lausanne. And while national animosities and suspicions are being disarmed, prodigious feats will be accomplished.

————————

4 AUGUST 1932

BRITISH RUNNER'S TRIUMPH AT OLYMPIC GAMES
T. HAMPSON SETS UP NEW WORLD RECORD IN THE 800 METRES
THRILLING RACE WON ON POST

T. Hampson, of the Achilles Club, gained a great triumph for Great Britain in the 800 metres race at the Olympic Games. After a thrilling finish Hampson won by six inches in the world's record time of one minute forty-nine and eight-tenths seconds. He beat the record held by Ben Eastman, of America, by one-fifth of a second, and broke D.G.A. Lowe's Olympic record of one minute fifty-one and eight-tenths seconds. Fifty thousand spectators saw Hampson win one of the greatest 800 metres in the history of athletics. In winning this event for Great Britain, he continued a 12-year-old sequence in the Olympic Games begun in 1920 by Albert Hill and continued at Paris and Amsterdam by Douglas Lowe. Of these four successive British victories, Hampson's was not only the finest, but by a long way the most thrilling.

It was anybody's race as the runners entered the home stretch. At this stage Alex Wilson, of Canada, held a slight lead over his team-mate, Phil Edwards, with Eddie Genung, the American champion, third, and Hampson fourth. As they tore down the final straight, Hampson put in an electrifying burst which carried him up to the leaders. It was not, however, until practically on the post that he succeeded in getting the better of Wilson, and by hurling himself at the tape Hampson gained the day. The official distance was given as six inches, with Edwards only a yard behind, third – a triumph for the British Empire. In spite of the fast pace cut out by Edwards and the three Americans – Genung, Hornbostel and Turner – Wilson and Hampson refused to be hurried, and they tucked themselves in behind the leaders. Hampson won not only because he was the best runner in the field, but because he timed his final burst to perfection.

---

5 AUGUST 1932

ANOTHER OLYMPIC TITLE FOR GREAT BRITAIN
T.W. GREEN WINS LONG-DISTANCE WALK

T.W. Green, the veteran Belgrave Harrier, won the newly inaugurated 50,000 metres walk yesterday, thus gaining the second Olympic title for Great Britain. Green, who is the hero of many London–Brighton walks, and the holder of the record for that journey, was up against the sternest Continental opposition. Among his rivals was another veteran, Ugo Frigerio, who was winning Olympic titles in 1920 at Antwerp. Only seven of the fifteen starters for this event finished, owing to the intense heat. Frigerio and his compatriot, Rivolta, were so distressed at the finish that they had to be carried to the dressing-room.

Green was always among the first half-dozen, but it was not until the half-distance that he took the lead from the Italian trio, Pretti, Frigerio, and Rivolta, these four being joined by the Latvian champion, J. Dalinsh. A terrific struggle ensued between Green, Frigerio, and Dalinsh over the last stages of the race. For a time Dalinsh and Frigerio held a slight lead, but the British veteran, walking with that determination that has scored him so many triumphs, passed them in the last mile, to win a notable victory. His time of four hours fifty minutes ten seconds was rather slow, but this was due to the heat.

---

16 AUGUST 1932

THAMES WIN OLYMPIC FOURS FOR BRITAIN
LEANDER EIGHT NARROWLY BEATEN IN THRILLING FINAL

G.C. Drinkwater

LONG BEACH (CALIFORNIA), Saturday

Leander were beaten in the final of the Olympic Games eight-oars here today, but the crew rowed a really good race and have no regrets. It was a magnificent struggle, three-quarters of a length covering the four crews at the finish. California beat Italy by six feet; Canada were half a length behind Italy, and Great Britain only six feet more.

As a set-off to this disappointment the Thames crew gained a splendid victory in the four-oars; so our record at the Regatta – two wins and two defeats – is quite satisfactory. Italy led soon after the start in the eights final, but by the 500-metre mark California were in front, with Canada and Great Britain a few feet behind. The leaders settled down to thirty-six, the British crew rowing at a slightly slower rate, and so they raced to the 1,000-metre mark. After that California and Italy drew away to half a length. At the 1,500-metre mark Luxton put in a fine spurt and gained a short lead on Canada; but, with Italy drawing nearer them, Leander were just thrown out of their stride in the row-in, and finished fourth. California's time was six minutes thirty-seven and three-fifths seconds and Leander's six minutes forty and four-fifths seconds. There was a cross-wind, slightly ahead, and the times show how slow the salt-water course was.

Thames, with H.R.A. Edwards at number three, beat Germany in the four-oars final by nearly five seconds, Italy by six, and U.S.A. by sixteen. They led practically all the way, Germany driving them half a length behind up to about twelve hundred and fifty metres, when the British four gradually drew away to win comfortably by a length and a half. Their time was six minutes fifty-eight and one-fifth seconds.

BERLIN 1936

I AUGUST 1936
LIKE A HUGE FILM STUDIO
INCESSANT DIN
Howard Marshall
BERLIN, Friday

Olympic excitement is blazing in Berlin. It blazed rather too realistically last night, when the storehouse of the State Opera House caught fire. Otherwise we are saving ourselves with an effort from spontaneous combustion. The last Olympic Games were held at Los Angeles. Something of the Hollywood atmosphere has passed on to Berlin. The city is like a

. gigantic film studio. Never did I see a whole town so carried away with enthusiasm. Cup final day in London is a trifle by comparison.

It is difficult to move in the streets, which are thronged with visitors and German provincials staring at the brilliant banners and streamers. The noise is prodigious. My hotel bedroom looks out over Unter den Linden, the Piccadilly of Berlin, so I speak with feeling. Traffic, crowds, aeroplanes, loudspeakers everywhere; the din is incessant. The Stadium itself is magnificent. When I arrived a dress rehearsal of the opening ceremony was in progress. Round the rim of the great grey granite bowl which encloses the arena are tall flagstaffs. At the base of each stood two sailors. The German talent for organisation is having full scope. Uniforms are everywhere – interpreters, sports controllers and dozens of telegraph girls in electric-blue blouses.

Walking round with cameras were members of various teams, men in their blazers, and here and there were groups of women athletes. These women in shorts were extremely picturesque. The Czechoslovak team wore orange trousers; very charming and brown and fit they look. Unter den Linden is thronged with sightseers. A great crowd stands silent and still before the war memorial, where a flame burns perpetually. The traffic is dense. The Lustgarten, the wide space before the Museum, is flanked by enormous scarlet banners, swastika-emblazoned. Across the road, in front of the ex-Kaiser's Palace, huge flags of every nation form a vivid background to the great bowl where fire will be kindled tomorrow from the sacred Flame which has been carried through Europe from Mount Olympus.

Tomorrow we start our excitements early. I have no chance of escaping them. At eight o'clock under my window the 'Ceremony of Awakening' begins, with music from military bands. From that hour onwards we have fanfares, processions, and the thunder of the great airships Hindenburg and Graf Zeppelin overhead. The crescendo works up to the final ceremony in the Stadium itself, when Herr Hitler opens the Games. I rather like the Hollywood tradition.

I hear that Herr Hitler has just issued a special order that fathers of ten or more children are to be given a one day's ticket for the Games. It is not yet certain whether all these worthy gentlemen are to parade together ceremonially on the same day, but the gesture is pleasing. The Crown Prince Umberto of Italy arrived by air this evening. He is staying for the Games.

3 AUGUST 1936

SUPERB PAGEANTRY AT OPENING
'HEIL HITLER' FROM 100,000 VOICES

Howard Marshall

BERLIN, Sunday

The scene here is amazing. Every seat in the great granite bowl is taken, and the massed banks of spectators sway and roar as the athletes pass in the arena below. The gay dresses of women and children against the grey stone move like flowers in the wind. A German victory is greeted with an ear-splitting yell of triumph. National feeling is strong beyond a doubt. We saw that yesterday during the opening ceremony, when the French team marching past saluted Herr Hitler with arms extended. The crowd cheered wildly. France, it thought, had given the Nazi salute; but it was wrong. The French extended their arms sideways, not forward, thus giving only the Olympic salute. A subtle distinction, but an important one, and Great Britain's 'eyes right' was met with significant silence.

Today we revelled in the proper excitements of the Games. Yesterday we were immersed in the pomp and circumstance of German ceremonial. As I took my seat at the stadium the great airship Hindenburg swung slowly overhead, with engines roaring, so low down that we could see the smiling faces of the crew peering from the gondolas. Suddenly one hundred thousand hands fluttered upwards in salute, a tremendous yell drowned the airship's thunder, and Herr Hitler stood on top of the towering steps which lead into the arena. He was sun-burnt and smiling as he walked slowly to his seat. A final salute, the sombre rhythm of the Horst Wessel song, a last prodigious 'Heil Hitler!' and the Greek athletes appeared in the dark archway to lead the grand march past.

From the high tower behind the stadium the deep tones of the Olympic bell came swinging, and the pageantry of the procession began. For three-quarters of an hour the athletes in their brilliant blazers wheeled and circled, wave upon wave of colour. Behind the blue-turbaned files of India came one man saluting alone, the solitary representative of Haiti. The intricate pattern spread and grew up in the grass until the centre of the arena glowed like a superb herbaceous border. So fifty nations waited for the supreme moment of the day. Through the loudspeakers came the voice of Baron de Coubertin, the Frenchman to whom the modern revival of the Games is due, delivering the fine words: 'It is not important to win but to take part. In life it is more important to play our part bravely than to conquer.'

The tension grew. Again the loudspeakers rang with an address of welcome, and then after a pause the strong metallic voice of Herr Hitler, brief, staccato, declaring the Games open. As his words died away a great rustling whisper rose from the crowd, and upon the steps we saw the slender figure of the last runner bearing the flaming Olympic torch. He was well chosen for the part, this runner. His golden hair streamed in the wind, and as he moved with swift and lovely grace sparks from the blazing torch fell in a golden cascade behind him. The cheering rose in a frenzied crescendo as he ran lightly up the steps again and halted before the immense bowl. There he stayed for a moment, a symbol of youth, and then with a sudden gesture he thrust the torch forward and a sheet of flame shot upwards, to burn throughout the Games. Guns roared, thousands of pigeons swept upwards and swung and circled in grey beauty against the sky, and slowly the Marathon winners of the 1896 Olympiad, dressed in Greek national costume, advanced to present an olive branch to Hitler. With this simple but significant gesture the opening ceremony ended. It had been strangely moving. It will remain in our memories as a background to the excitement of the days to come.

---

4 AUGUST 1936

HITLER SEES GERMAN TRIUMPH AT THE GAMES
HAMMER-THROWER BREAKS RECORD
OWENS'S GREAT SPRINT WIN

Howard Marshall

BERLIN, Monday

The Olympic Games continued today amid intense excitement. Unpleasant weather failed to damp the spirits of the enormous crowd. Herr Hitler arrived just in time to see Hein, a German hammer-thrower, break the Olympic record with a throw of 56.49 metres – sixty-one yards – amidst thunderous cheering. This has, indeed, been a great day for

German athletes, who have won many heats and events. Herr Hitler again received a great welcome when he took his place. There is no doubt of his tremendous personal popularity. When he drove back from the Stadium to Berlin hundreds of thousands of people lined the route to catch a glimpse of him. It was only a glimpse, for the German leaders drive fast. Yesterday the Crown Prince of Italy was present at the Stadium, and with him one of Signor Mussolini's sons. Today the spectator who, next to Herr Hitler, caused most excitement was Max Schmeling, the German heavyweight boxer, who recently defeated Joe Louis, the American.

The victory of Jesse Owens, the American sprinter, in the final of the 100 metres, provided the great moment of the day. His time was 10.3 seconds, equal to the world record. It has been decided that Owens's time of 10.2 in his heat yesterday cannot stand, as he had a strong wind behind him. No British runners reached the final. A.W. Sweeney and A. Pennington ran well, but not well enough, in the semi-finals. The final was a magnificent race and provided a great thrill for the spectators. Complete silence fell on the vast crowd as the runners took their places for the start. Owens and Metcalfe, another great American runner, bent over their marks. Osendarp, of Holland, fair-haired and thick-set, rubbed his hands nervously on his shorts. Wykoff, the slim American, waited quietly, and Borchmeyer, of Germany, and Strandberg, of Sweden, shifted in their footholes. A warning from the starter, a crack from the pistol, and they leapt from their marks like arrows. For thirty yards they bunched. Then Owens and Metcalfe, running with superb grace, drew away. 'Owens! Metcalfe! Osendarp!' The names were shouted by thousands of spectators as, by inches, Owens flashed first to the tape. What a race, and what a runner! Probably the greatest the world has ever seen. Owens is twenty-two, a student at Ohio State University. He is a delightful personality, modest and friendly. When congratulated on his triumph he shook his head, shrugged his shoulders and grinned immensely.

5 AUGUST 1936
OWENS SMASHES MORE RECORDS
LONG JUMP AND 200 METRES IN A DAY
Howard Marshall
BERLIN, Tuesday

This was another day of records in the Olympic Games. More world records have been beaten, subject to ratification, and six Olympic records have gone. Without a doubt Jesse Owens, the American, is the outstanding personality of this Olympiad. Having already equalled the world record for the 100 metres with a time of 10.3 seconds, he today broke two more records. His long jump of twenty-six feet six and a quarter inches beat the previous Olympic best by one foot one and a half inches. In two 200-metres heats, running well within himself, he beat the Olympic record of 21.2 seconds by one second. Owens is extremely popular with his fellow competitors, and his remarkable triumph has not in the least affected his modesty. Tall and perfectly built, he is one of the greatest athletes of history, and he may well break yet another world's record in the 200 metres final tomorrow.

The weather is turbulent and stormy, with the wind so strong that it threatens to blow out the Olympic fire. It succeeds, at any rate, in whirling paper, programmes and hats off all nationalities wantonly through the air. What with the wind, the constantly blaring loudspeakers and the cheering of the crowd, concentration is difficult. We are constantly standing up, moreover, as the victors take their places in the middle of the arena to be crowned with the Olympic laurels. This oft-repeated little ceremony is impressive. The first, second and third men in their events stand on a dais and are crowned by three girls dressed all in white. Then the victor's national anthem is played by a versatile band and his country's flag run up to the great masthead. Today the band has been playing *The Star Spangled Banner* almost exclusively, but one of these days there will be a Japanese winner and then these brave musicians really will be tested. Leni Riefenstahl, the German film star, has been in the arena all day producing the official film of the Games.

6 AUGUST 1936

BRITAIN'S FIRST OLYMPIC VICTORY
WHITLOCK SETS UP RECORD IN
50 KILOS. WALK
S.C. WOODERSON'S SURPRISING DEFEAT
IN 1,500 METRES

Bevil Rudd

BERLIN, Wednesday

H.H. Whitlock's magnificent win today in the 50-kilometres walk — Britain's first triumph in the eleventh Olympiad — was sharply counterbalanced by the failure of S.C. Wooderson to qualify for the final in a fast heat of the 1,500 metres. Wooderson was not himself, and, although his ankle did not appear to be bothering him, the consciousness of the trouble may have been distracting. He struggled gamely but his dash was lacking. One world's record was beaten today when Senorita Valli ran the 80-metres hurdles in 11.6 seconds and Jesse Owens again broke an Olympic record when he won the 200 metres. This was his third victory.

Owens's 200-metres final was absolutely masterly, and he ran the distance in 20.7 seconds, easily a new Olympic record. He drew the third lane, with Robinson just outside him. He had caught Robinson in the first few strides, and won by nearly three yards from Robinson who was that distance in front of the Dutchman, Osendarp.

Things seemed to be looking up for Great Britain's depressed team when the announcement was made that H.H. Whitlock, at halfway in the 50,000-metres walk, had moved up into third place behind Dalinsh, the Latvian, and Stork, of Czechoslovakia. A little while later the news arrived that he had passed Stork, and there was a sporadic cheer from the scattered British community in the arena. We next heard that at thirty-two kilometres Whitlock had taken the lead in the walk, and our spirits revived.

———

7 AUGUST 1936

J.E. LOVELOCK BREAKS WORLD RECORD
BRILLIANT WIN IN FINAL OF 1,500 METRES

Bevil Rudd

BERLIN, Thursday

Jack Lovelock has achieved his ambition and won the 1,500 metres. He ran a brilliant race and set up a new world's record of three minutes 47.8 seconds, which is roughly the equivalent of a four minute six and a half second mile. It was shortly after four o'clock when the 1,500 metres finalists – twelve of them – trickled slowly over to the start, and our hearts beat faster. Beccali had drawn the inside place, Cornes fourth and Lovelock eleventh. Edwards (Canada) was next to him and Venske and Cunningham, the American, just inside Edwards. Jack Lovelock was last to strip, and just before they lined up Herr Hitler arrived. The crowd rose and cheered, and the Olympic and German flags were hoisted. Thirty seconds later a shrill whistle brought a sudden hush. The runners lined up, and a moment later the starter's gun barked. Cornes ran into the lead, followed closely by Beccali, Bottcher (Germany) and Lovelock. Bottcher dashed in front after two hundred and fifty yards, but Cornes regained the lead before the first bend of the second lap. Later in this lap Cunningham, Bottcher and Lovelock passed Cornes, and then Ny, of Sweden, moved up. Cunningham led by three or four yards with eight hundred metres to go, and Ny was going very quickly and easily. He was quite content to run outside Cunningham on the bend of the third lap and, just before the bell, he went in front. The time for the first four hundred metres was 61.4 seconds and for the eight hundred metres two minutes five seconds.

Cunningham and Lovelock let Ny lead until the far straight and then made their efforts. It was Lovelock who took the initiative. He raced in front and, before Cunningham quite realised what had happened, Lovelock had a four yards' lead. Cunningham responded grimly, like the great runner he is, but all the way down the far straight he could not close the gap. Beccali meanwhile was challenging Cunningham, and the fierce speed of the race was tailing off the rest of the field. Could Lovelock keep the pace he himself had set? He took an imperceptible 'breather' as he began to swing round the final bend, and then just before the straight threw all his carefully husbanded resources decisively into the scale. Try as he might the sturdy Cunningham could not catch up those four precious yards. In fact, Lovelock added another in the run-in. Beccali was exerting every ounce of energy three yards behind Cunningham, but the positions were now static. San Romani made a belated rush and beat Edwards and Cornes for fourth place.

But the race was over. Lovelock had broken the tape in three minutes 47.8 seconds, an Olympic and world's record. Cunningham's time of three minutes 48.4 seconds was also two-fifths of a second inside W. Bonthron's world record time in 1934. Six of today's finalists had also been in the 1932 race. Then Beccali was first, Cornes second, Edwards third, Cunningham fourth, and Ny fifth. Lovelock ran, but was not in the first six. It speaks volumes for the merit of all these men that, after four years, they should continue to dominate the world at this distance.

---

10 AUGUST 1936

BRITAIN'S OLYMPIC RELAY TRIUMPH
RAMPLING'S BRILLIANT RUN
LEADS TO VICTORY
HARPER SECOND TO JAPANESE IN
MARATHON: BOTH BEAT RECORD

Bevil Rudd

BERLIN, Sunday

If Great Britain came into the eleventh Olympiad like a lamb, she went out like a lion. Our four quarter-milers brilliantly won the 1,600 metres relay from the Americans in three minutes nine seconds, less than a second outside the world's record. The hero of this race was Godfrey Rampling, who retrieved a desperate situation, and regained the lead by running his four hundred metres in a little over forty-six seconds.

The rumours of a sensational pair of Japanese marathon runners proved correct, and Sohn won in record time. But E. Harper was there to wrest second place from the other Japanese, and he, too, beat the record. The famous Finns could only get fourth and fifth places. D. McNab Robertson was seventh, between the South Africans, Coleman and Gibson.

Jesse Owens won his fourth Olympic medal when, as the first runner in the 400 metres relay team, he set up a lead that enabled the American team to create a world's record of 39.8 seconds. The world's record was inevitable. We had been well prepared for it on Saturday, when the American quartet of sprinters, including Owens, Metcalfe and Wykoff, the three 100-metre medallists, equalled the record of forty seconds for the 400 metres relay. Today they beat that time by two-tenths of a second. As a race it was all over after Owens had run the first distance. Metcalfe kept up the good work, and Draper raced into the straight to give Wykoff a ten yards' lead. Wykoff improved on this in the run-in. This extraordinary team had rounded off its superb running with some remarkably smooth baton changing.

3

LONDON 1948

22 JULY 1948

OLYMPIC GAMES TO OPEN WITH TRADITIONAL RITUAL
Lainson Wood

War-scarred Britain, with all her economic difficulties, is about to undertake the extremely delicate and intricate operation of presenting an Olympic festival at which the pick of the amateur athletes, boxers, wrestlers, footballers, swimmers, yachtsmen, oarsmen, horsemen and crack shots from sixty-two nations will compete. London's hotels are filling. Visitors from overseas are arriving hourly. Besides those taking an active part or an active interest in the Olympic Games there are many who are coming quite as much to have a look at Britain in these post-War years, to see how we are facing up to adversity, and to gauge for themselves the tempo of our recovery.

Visitors to the Olympic Games which, from next Thursday, Britain will present to the world in celebration of the XIVth Olympiad will not expect to see lavishness of production that marked the Berlin Games in 1936, when, regardless of the cost involved, a gigantic new stadium and a village to house the 800-odd competitors were built for the occasion. Britain has had to refurbish and utilise what she had already in existence. The main arena where the principal events of the Games will be held is the 26-year-old Empire Stadium at Wembley. The swimming, boxing and wrestling events will be staged in the Empire Pool, adjacent to the Stadium. The satellite arenas are Torbay (yachting), Henley (rowing), Aldershot (equestrian events), Harringay (wrestling and basketball) and Herne Hill (cycling).

But the Olympic events about which people will be talking in years to come are the track and field contests. Sprinters, quarter-milers, middle-distance runners, long-distance runners, hurdlers, jumpers, walkers, weight-putters, javelin, discus and hammer throwers, and all the rest of the army of athletic specialists, of every creed and colour, will vie for supremacy. Wembley Stadium will accommodate approximately one hundred thousand spectators at each session for these stirring contests. The Games will not be voted a success unless times in general are well up to Olympic standards and some new records are set up. There much depends on our fickle climate – and the track. The track has presented one of the major problems in the organisation of these Games. Though Wembley Stadium has been since its erection the traditional home of perhaps the biggest national sporting event in the English calendar, the Football Association Challenge Cup Final, it does not belong to the National Trust or any similar body. It is a private concern run for profit and leased to the British Olympic Committee.

Its maintenance is largely dependent on greyhound and speedway racing. It is only round the greyhound track perimeter that it is possible to lay the 400-metre circuit required for the Olympic Games. It has always been reckoned in athletic circles that it takes three years for a cinder track to settle and become desirably fast and weather-proof. To have bought Wembley off greyhound racing for three years would have cost a vast sum. There was one salvation. The clinker foundation for a running track, the thing which takes the time to settle, was laid when Wembley Stadium was built and has been there, buried under a strip of turf, these past twenty-six years. The problem was to hit on a top dressing solution that could be put down almost on the eve of the Games and as quickly removed when the last Olympic laurel has been carried off so as to cause the shortest possible suspension of the money-spinning 'dogs'.

Experiments were carried out in the laboratories of firms specialising in hard lawn tennis courts, running tracks and similar playing surfaces: strips of the different surfaces were laid on the Wembley foundations, and athletes were brought along to run on them and test them out. It was only last spring that one was found the cost of which was commensurate with the Olympic purse, which satisfied the athletes and which was scientifically warranted to stand up to the tremendous strain to be put on it and to all weathers. So a geological wonder has been created which made it possible for greyhounds to race at Wembley up to a quarter to ten on Saturday, 10 July, and for the world's premier athletes to run there from 30 July until 13 August. Within a week of the latter date greyhounds will be chasing the electric 'hare' round the re-turfed track again.

Another and seemingly ever-present problem in Britain was housing. Where are anything up to four thousand competitors to be put up for from three to six weeks? The building of a village was out of the question. Even had money and materials been available, what an outcry there would have been from people crying out for houses. Plans to build a village which, after the Games, could be handed over to families seeking homes were finally rejected. Investigations were begun to turn schools into temporary houses and some of the competitors will be accommodated there. The Royal Air Force brought the major relief when, with the approval of the Air Council, they offered to equip and hand over their finely appointed camps at Uxbridge and West Drayton, conveniently close to Wembley, for the period of the Games. Here approximately two thousand competitors will live in comfort if not luxury, the envy perhaps of the less fortunate who have been detailed to the less well appointed schools.

The training of the British team is another singularly fine achievement, for which all praise to that energetic and self-sacrificing enthusiast, Mr Jack Crump, the team manager. Nine months ago some two hundred men and women were listed as Olympic possibles to undergo special training and coaching. The team finally entered has been whittled down to sixty-two men and twenty women, and even though we can expect few first places, we have genuine hopes of Britain being represented in several finals, which is an achievement in worldwide competition. One of the biggest obstacles to training and preparing a representative British team has been rationing. A continuous supply of food parcels from generous donors in the Dominions and colonies has helped to overcome it. Our team will not fall far short of its rivals in the matter of physical fitness.

Whatever the Fates, or should I say the gods of Olympus, hold in store the stage is set for the opening ceremony next Thursday. It promises a carnival of unrivalled pageantry. The traditional ritual will be observed. The King will be there for the march past of the competing nations, the unfurling of the flags of sixty-two countries at a given signal, the simultaneous release of seven thousand carrier pigeons, the solemn taking of the Olympic oath, and the entry of the torchbearer. The torchbearer will circle the track before climbing to the summit of one of the Wembley towers, there to light the Olympic fire, which must burn throughout the duration of the Games. That moving ceremony will send us all home thinking gratefully of the French patriot and sportsman,

Baron Pierre de Coubertin, who conceived the idea of reviving in 1896 the ancient Greek Games, thus providing a modern focus of world friendship.

---

29 JULY 1948

LEADING ARTICLE
OLYMPIC GAMES

Today The King formally opens the Olympic Games, held for the second time in this country since they were revived in 1896. The sacred Flame, brought to Wembley by runners from the Temple of Zeus, two thousand miles away, symbolises the continuity of our civilisation with its ancient origins. It has travelled across a sadly distracted Continent, but comfort may be derived from the fact that all along the way there have been eager hands to pass it on.

Mr Attlee aptly recalled, in his broadcast speech last night, that in ancient Greece, when the Olympic Games were being held, States which happened to be at war made a truce for the occasion. In the two world wars of this century it was the Games which were suspended in favour of the fighting. What a sigh of relief would go up from all mankind if their resumption now were an earnest of enduring peace. Sport, as the Prime Minister said, 'oversteps all frontiers'. Though the world's present unhappy divisions have been reflected in absences from this year's Olympiad, the many who are present will be drawn closer together.

---

30 JULY 1948

EIGHTY THOUSAND WATCH THE KING OPEN OLYMPIC GAMES
Daily Telegraph Reporter

In a setting of brilliant colour on a glorious afternoon, The King yesterday declared open the Olympic Games at Wembley Stadium. The varied hues of the flags and blazers of the six thousand international competitors stood out in vivid contrast to the fresh green of the arena turf. For fifty minutes in broiling sunshine His Majesty had stood rigidly to attention, saluting continually as, headed by standard bearers and Scouts carrying name-cards, teams from fifty-nine nations marched past the Royal box. The King, in naval uniform, was accompanied by the Queen, Queen Mary and Princess Margaret. Seated near the Royal group were Prince Bernhard of the Netherlands, the Shah of Persia, the Duke and Duchess of Gloucester, and Earl and Countess Mountbatten.

The teams differed greatly in numbers, from the single competitor of Panama and the two from Singapore and Malta, to the 300-odd from the United States, marching six abreast. Massed bands of the Brigade of Guards, in scarlet and bearskin and some in Highland uniform, played for the procession as more than eighty thousand spectators cheered the entry of each team. The track circuited, the athletes paraded on the arena, forming a striking mosaic. The Danes had red blazers, the Indians bright blue, with blue turbans, and others were in green and brown. The British team, who as Olympic hosts marched last, wore dark blue blazers bearing a Union Jack badge.

The parade assembled, Lord Burghley, chairman of the Games Organising Committee, delivered the Olympic address. 'A visionary dream has become a glorious reality,' he said. 'In 1946 the clarion call went forth to the athletes of the world, bidding them gather in London in 1948 to celebrate the fourteenth Modern Olympiad. Here today is assembled the cream of the youth of the world, drawn from fifty-nine nations who have answered this call. Here is the proof of the inherent strength and vitality of the Olympic Movement.' They believed that The King would be kindling a torch the light from which would travel to the uttermost corners of the earth, 'a torch of that ageless, heartfelt prayer of mankind throughout the world for peace and goodwill'.

Through a microphone in the Royal box The King pronounced the traditional formula: 'I declare open the Olympic Games of London celebrating the fourteenth Olympiad of the modern era.' A fanfare was sounded by the trumpeters of the Household Cavalry, and seven thousand pigeons were released from baskets around the track, a symbol of ancient Greece when pigeons carried the news of the start of the Games. A Royal salute of twenty-one guns followed, then the torchbearer, the last of the relay of seventy-two runners from Dover, ran on to the track from the South Gate holding the flame above his head. He paused for a moment before circling the track, cheered every step of the way. Only then was his identity disclosed. He is John W.E. Mark, twenty-two, of Surbiton, a former president of Cambridge University Athletic Club, a six foot two inch fair-haired athlete, who is now a medical student at St Mary's

Hospital, Paddington. Back at the South Gate he mounted a platform and lit the beacon which will burn until the end of the Games.

––––––––

31 JULY 1948
AMAZING 10,000 METRES RACE
CZECH'S RECORD TRIUMPH
Lainson Wood
WEMBLEY, Friday

Emil Zatopek, 26-year-old Czechoslovakian engineer from Prague, stole all the thunder of the first day of the Olympic Games here today when he almost lapped the entire field in a brilliant victory in the 10,000 metres in the new Olympic record time of twenty-nine minutes 59.6 seconds. His nearest rival, Alain Mimoun-O'Kacha, a French Arab, was forty-eight seconds slower and nearly a lap behind. Some of the competitors Zatopek lapped twice.

It was an amazingly thrilling race, the last half of it cheered to the echo as, ignoring the fact that he had no one to press him, Zatopek crowded on the pace, fairly burning up the track. It was, too, a surprising race for though Zatopek clung to the heels of his great rival, Heino, he never looked to be running with the same ease and grace as the stylish Finn. They changed the order after half-a-dozen laps, but Heino did not look in the least worried at being headed. He ran snugly at Zatopek's heels for a lap and a half. Then Zatopek spurted. In another lap he had put twenty yards between himself and Heino, and then the Finn, to everyone's astonishment, ran off the track into the middle of the arena.

Heino's compatriot, Heinstrom, kept going doggedly. He, Mimoun, and the Swede, Albertsson, who, with Zatopek and Heino, had been a quintet out in front on their own almost from the start, stuck closely to one another, and the race developed into the spectacle of an ever-increasing gap between them and the untiring Zatopek. But in the last lap Heinstrom had obviously had enough. His stride grew shorter, his footsteps began to falter, and compatriots rushed over and dragged him off before he fell in his tracks. Meanwhile, another enthusiastic mob had invaded the track to congratulate Zatopek, and had to be hastily hustled off to allow the rest of the field to finish.

3 AUGUST 1948

CZECH MISSED A DOUBLE
ZATOPEK BEATEN BY ONE-FIFTH
OF A SECOND

Lainson Wood

WEMBLEY, Monday

Track events of the Olympic Games again ended on a thrilling note here today when Emil Zatopek, the Czech long-distance runner, failed by a fifth of a second to add the 5,000 metres to his 10,000-metres triumph of last Friday. Many of the huge Bank Holiday crowd had been driven away by the heavy rain that began to fall midway through the afternoon. They missed Zatopek's magnificent last-lap surge to catch the Belgian G. Reiff, which reduced a deficit of about thirty yards to one of barely three yards. Water lay on the track. The runners splashed their way through puddles with grim tenacity. Yet, despite the conditions both Reiff and Zatopek beat the previous best Olympic time for the event.

It was a strangely run race. Zatopek, as usual, jumped early into the lead. The Swedes, E. Nyberg and E. Ahlden, in turn took it from him. Clearly there was a team plan between the Swedes to jockey the lone Czech along. Reiff at this time was running steadily in second or third place with Slijkhuis, the Dutchman, at his heels. Nyberg was the first of the leaders to drop out and after five laps it was a four-man race. For the next four laps the order was Zatopek, Reiff, Slijkhuis, Ahlden, with a gap between them and the rest of the field which gradually widened. Then Reiff took over and, striding out easily, put at least thirty yards between himself and Zatopek. When in the last but one lap Slijkhuis overtook the Czech, it seemed that Zatopek was finished with, and when Reiff looked over his shoulder, starting on the last lap, he must have felt supremely confident that he could not be caught.

How nearly he was caught napping! With only three-quarters of a lap to go, Zatopek suddenly put on a spurt. He seemed to accelerate with every stride and when he reached the home stretch he was going like a sprinter and rapidly overhauling the Belgian. Could he catch up in time? The crowd were on their feet yelling as he thundered down the track. The roar warned Reiff. In time he, too, spurted to make it by a bare three yards. Slijkhuis was a bad third.

In the semi-finals of the women's 100 metres Britain suffered two disappointments when Mrs Jordan and Miss Batter both failed to qualify for the final. Only Miss Manley succeeded. Five of the last six were from the Empire, two from Canada, one from Australia, one from Jamaica and the home-born Miss Manley. In the final Miss Thompson, of Jamaica, was quickest away, but was soon caught by Mrs Blankers-Koen, of Holland, holder of the world record. Mrs Blankers-Koen went smoothly ahead yard by yard to win easily in 11.9 seconds. There was a spirited fight for second place between Britain's Miss Manley and Australia's Miss Strickland and the photo-finish showed Miss Manley to be just in front. The time of both girls was 12.2 seconds.

---

4 AUGUST 1948

SAD END TO A GREAT CAREER
FINLAY, FINALIST TWICE, NOW LAST
Lainson Wood

WEMBLEY, Tuesday

The story of the fallen stars is the saddest in the world. It was told again in the Olympic Games here today, when 40-year-old Wing Commander Donald Finlay, D.F.C., after leading to the last flight, finished up in a fallen heap a yard from the winning line in his heat of the 110-metres hurdles. Finlay was an Olympic hurdler in 1932; he looked an Olympic possible winner today, until he just touched the top in sailing over the last but one hurdle. It threw him out of his stride, and he hit the last fence hard. He checked, stumbled on, tried hard to keep his feet over the short run, was passed, tripped and sprawled on the track. The truth was he had not stayed the course at the cracking pace he set. *Anno Domini*, it is to be feared, had caught up on him.

It was a pathetic ending to a great career. In five Olympiads Finlay has run in two hurdles finals, being second at Los Angeles in 1932 and again second in Berlin in 1936. After two uncelebrated Olympiads he this time crawled over the line on his hands and knees – last. The crowd was not slow to appreciate a poignant situation. As Finlay got up, and, unhurt, began to sprint back across the turf, a round of applause started which increased in a huge crescendo as one of Britain's greatest ever athletes snatched up his tracksuit and ran out of the arena – perhaps for the last time.

Unluckiest man of these Olympics is the 30-year-old American H.N. Ewell. Second in the 100 metres' photo-finish final on Saturday, he again missed a winner's medal in another thrilling final – the 200 metres – in the last race tonight. The winner was Mel Patton, the beaten favourite in the 100 metres, and his time was 21.1 seconds. As Ewell was returned the same time he presumably was closer to the winner than when he thought he had broken the tape in the 100 metres. To have lost two Olympic finals by inches must seem to the aspiring athlete the last drop in the cup of disappointment. Patton ran a beautifully judged race and maintained the pace in a desperate finish with Ewell thundering along beside him. La Beach, of Panama, third in the 100 metres, gained a medal, beating the much-vaunted Herbert McKenley, of Jamaica, into fourth place.

---

5 AUGUST 1948
CROWD SINGS FOR THE QUEEN
BIRTHDAY VISIT TO OLYMPIC GAMES

The King and Queen, with the Duke of Edinburgh, were cheered by a crowd of eighty thousand when they arrived at Wembley Stadium yesterday to watch the Olympic Games. It was the Queen's forty-eighth birthday and she was given a particularly enthusiastic reception. The band played and the people sang *Happy Birthday To You.*

The Royal party arrived just too late to see the first big race of the afternoon, in which Miss Maureen Gardner, a 20-year-old Oxford dancing teacher, was narrowly beaten in the final of the 80-metres hurdles. The judges' stop watches could not separate her and the winner, Mrs F.E. Blankers-Koen, of Holland, and both were returned as having done 11.2 seconds, one tenth of a second faster than the world record set up by Signorina C. Testoni, of Italy, in 1939 and equalled by Mrs Blankers-Koen in 1942.

---

6 AUGUST 1948

WINT EQUALS RECORD
BRILLIANT RACE IN 400 METRES

Lainson Wood

WEMBLEY, Thursday

Arthur S. Wint, six foot four inch tall Jamaican, a former R.A.F. bomber pilot and now a student at St Bartholomew's Hospital, in London, stole all the thunder at the Olympic Games here today by winning the 400 metres and equalling the Olympic record of 46.2 seconds in the final. Second was Herbert McKenley, who went to the same school as Wint in Kingston, Jamaica, and from there to the United States for his university course. Third was M.G. Whitfield, the American 800-metres winner last Monday.

Wint, whose long, easy stride and perfect style has been the admiration of every athlete here this week, stepped up on his heat times in the semi-final and won with something to spare in 46.3 seconds. The fact that McKenley's time in winning the other semi-final was a full second slower signified nothing. The line-up for the final – Bolen (U.S.A.), in the inside lane, McKenley, Wint, Whitfield, Guida (U.S.A.), with young Morris Curotta, of Australia, on the outside – was as speculative as a race between the world's six best 'quarter-milers' could be.

They were off first time but Wint did not get a good start. Neither did he get quickly into his stride. McKenley, on the other hand, was off like a streak and he made the pace a cracker right up to the final bend. If he could have kept it up he would have smashed all records, but he faltered slightly coming into the straight and his speed began to flag. Meanwhile, Wint had settled down into his long, rhythmic stride and racing with him was Whitfield. Wint checked ever so slightly on the third bend and then lengthening and quickening his stride without losing any of his grace and easy movement he gradually began to bear down on his fellow countryman. Ten yards from the tape he drew abreast, another five yards and he was in front, and he went on to win a fine race by a couple of yards. Wint ran with rare courage. It took some pluck to go after a man as far ahead as McKenley was. Maybe he knew McKenley's weakness in finishing and had timed his effort right. It certainly made for a spectacular finish which brought the crowd to their feet yelling like mad.

So Wint, who has done most of his running in this country and in Britain's colours, is an Olympic champion, but not in his favourite 800 metres – he was second in that event. Now, if you please, he plans an attempt on the world's record before the season is out – the 800 metres record, not the 400. Wint's success caused the R.A.F. band to play *God Save The King* for the first time at an Olympic winning ceremony at these Games for Jamaica has no national anthem.

———

7 AUGUST 1948
DUTCH WOMAN'S THIRD TITLE
Lainson Wood
WEMBLEY, Friday

Mrs F. Blankers-Koen, Holland's brilliant woman runner, won her third Olympic track event gold medal here today – a feat bettered only by the immortal Finns, Hans Kolehmainen and Paavo Nurmi, who won four races in 1912 and 1924 respectively. Today Mrs Blankers-Koen streaked ahead of her rivals in the women's 200 metres to win by eight or nine yards. Her time on a track which held the water of a day's rain was 24.4 seconds   excellent in the conditions. Second to her was Miss Williamson, of Great Britain, a junior commander in the A.T.S. – Britain's only Army representative in the women's section – stationed at Cheltenham. As this is her first season in senior athletics it was a most praiseworthy performance.

As Mrs Blankers-Koen broke the tape a small child, appropriately garbed in oilskins, ran on to the track and presented her with a bouquet of carnations and mimosa. She was the daughter of an American friend. Mrs Blankers-Koen's own children, a son and a daughter, were in Holland listening in to their mother's world-beating performances, but her husband, who is an athletics coach, watched his wife's great feat.

———

7 AUGUST 1948
BOY OF 17 WINS DECATHLON BY ARC LIGHT
OLYMPIC ATHLETES' 12-HOUR DAY
Daily Telegraph Reporter

Athletic events in the Olympic Games went on at Wembley Stadium until 10.30 last night by the light of arc lamps. The handful of spectators who stayed on had to wait for a further twenty minutes to hear the announcement that R.B. Mathias, a 17-year-old schoolboy, had won the decathlon with a total of 7,139 points. His mother, brother and sister joined in the applause.

The stadium presented an eerie appearance at 10.30 p.m. when the events terminated. The area was lit by lamps some distance away from the running track. The centre of the ground was devoid of light. At the eastern end the Olympic Flame blazed in sharp contrast to the incandescent glow from the lamps. About two hundred spectators watched while thirty-seven athletes completed their 12-hour day. They were taking part in the decathlon contest, under conditions of which competitors must complete ten track and field events in two days. Midnight was the deadline.

At 10.30, in semi-darkness, Bob Mathias, from Tulake, California, sprinted second past the winning post in the final event, the 1,500 metres, to make him winner of the most fantastic decathlon of the modern Olympic Games. He had been on the track nearly twelve hours. At the finish he all but collapsed. Friends half-carried him to the verge of the track. E. Anderssen, Sweden, won the race barefooted and with his right leg bandaged.

---

9 AUGUST 1948
HOLLOW FIRST FOR BRITAIN
BELGIAN'S GREAT MARATHON BID
Lainson Wood

Four Rugby football wing-three-quarters took first place on the honours rostrum and the Union Jack was hauled to the masthead for the first time in the Wembley Stadium on Saturday, concluding day of the athletics part of the Olympic Games. Britain's sprinters, A. McCorquodale, J.A. Gregory, K.J. Hones and J. Archer, had won the 4 × 100 metres relay race but it was a somewhat hollow triumph. The American, Mel Patton, breasted the tape eight yards ahead of Archer, but his team were disqualified for a faulty first take-over. The brilliant sprinting of Harrison Dillard, the 100-metres champion, and Patton, 200-metres champion, in the final stages was all in vain.

The fact that Britain's representatives were all better known on the football and cricket field before Olympic training started, does, however, seem to symbolise the British attitude towards sport. As an excuse for lack of success in the Games that is, of course, both sloppy and feeble. We are, generally speaking, a long way behind the Americans in technique. Maybe we shall be, and there are many who prefer it that way. At the same time the cheer that went up from eighty-five thousand, mostly British, throats when a home success was at last announced will head the cavalcade of my memories of the greatest carnival of athletics this country will see for at least another forty years.

Another last-day memory is of Gailly, a little Belgian paratrooper, struggling up the slope from Wembley Way to the tunnel leading back into the Stadium at the end of the twenty-six miles 385 yards Marathon. It was Dorando Pietri of 1908 all over again. But no one, as was the case of Dorando, helped the gallant Gailly, who had led the field for nineteen of the twenty-six miles, had been overtaken and forged his way to the front again. I knew as I watched him swaying from side to side, his footsteps flagging, his head almost dropping, that he must be overtaken in that final punishing lap round the track.

While the Marathon runners were out in the country the Stadium spectators saw the first five in the 10,000 metres track walk break the previous Olympic record; Arthur Wint, the 400 metres champion, broke down with cramp to put Jamaica out of the 4 × 400 metres relay; and Mrs Blankers-Koen, the greatest-ever woman athlete, make up three or four yards in the last stretch of the women's relay to win her fourth gold medal.

There was still a dramatic 'curtain' to come. Not until 7.30 did Mrs Dorothy Tyler, Britain's woman high jumper, haul down her flag, beaten into second place, as at Berlin in 1936. Again she jumped the same height as the winner, Miss Alice Coachman, the American. But Miss Coachman did it at the first attempt, Mrs Tyler at the second.

---

9 AUGUST 1948

LEADING ARTICLE
OLYMPIC GAMES

With the end of the track and field events on Saturday the first stage of the Olympic Games closes with none of those dire consequences that the superstitious saw in the momentary failure of the Flame when it first touched English soil. There remains much to be striven for among the competing nations in the present week before the closing ceremony on

Saturday next. Yet already it may be written that the experiment of reviving the games within three years of a world convulsion, and of making London the host city, has fulfilled the hopes of those who greatly dared. The many thousands who have crowded the Wembley Stadium to capacity daily, and the lesser numbers who have watched the contests in other arenas, bear witness to that universal love of sport that makes for closer understanding between nations.

Though the large American team has already gained a supremacy that is not likely to be threatened, the women from Holland have shown that great populations are not necessary for the production of outstanding athletes. If Great Britain has so far recorded but one victory, and that, unhappily enough, by the disqualification of the United States team, various competitors in surpassing various previous records have shown that the misgivings with which we entered the arena were far from fully justified. A nation that has been the pioneer in many forms of athleticism can afford to applaud, as the crowds have done, the successes of those who have known how to better their instruction. We have no excuses to make. In furthering the revival of the Greek Olympiad, nearly fifty years ago, British pioneers had no thought but that of raising the standards of sport throughout the world. That they may claim to have done.

In one direction there is cause for pride. The organisation of the games has been excellent. 'No city has had greater experience of staging sporting occasions of the highest importance than London,' wrote Mr Jack Crump in his foreword to *The Daily Telegraph* guide to the Games. That confidence has been justified. If the ostentatious pageantry of Berlin in 1936 has not been emulated, the efficient management of the many events has attested the quality of many months of preliminary work. London as host may feel that it has done well.

———

10 AUGUST 1948

BRITAIN WINS TWO ROWING TITLES
EIGHT LOSES TO U.S. CREW

Kenneth Payne

HENLEY, Monday

Britain had a successful final day in the Olympic rowing here with two firsts and a second out of seven events, and Australia secured another first for the Empire. The British winners were W.G.M. Laurie and J.H.T. Wilson in the coxswainless pairs and R. Burnell and B.H.T. Bushnell in the double sculls, while in the eights the home crew was second. M.T. Wood, of Australia, secured the third Empire title by winning the single sculls.

Laurie and Wilson, who did not touch an oar for ten years and have had only just over two months to train, crowned a remarkable career when winning by nearly three seconds. They won the Silver Goblet at Henley in 1938 and equalled the record. Both went to the Sudan and spent ten years in a tropical climate. In May of this year they returned home on leave and set to work to train for the Goblets and with an eye on the Olympics. They won the Goblets for the second time and now, both at the age of thirty-three, have won an Olympic title.

The race was closely fought and their success was partly due to excellent steering. Switzerland went off fast, leading by half a length at two hundred and fifty metres, with Great Britain and Italy level. At seven hundred and fifty metres, Italy dropped back a length. Soon after the thousand metres Britain, rowing at thirty-one, had taken the lead which they increased to three-quarters of a length by fifteen hundred metres. Switzerland were not steering too well. Britain gradually worked their stroke up to thirty-five in the last four hundred metres and finished with something in hand.

The last race was the final of the eight-oared event. California University represented the United States in 1932 and were then successful. Mr K. Ebright, who coached both crews, thought this one was the superior of the two. It was beautifully drilled and perfectly together with a very powerful finish. The British crew was based on the Cambridge one of this year. At Henley, rowing as Leander Club, a slightly different crew had been beaten by Thames Rowing Club. Since then Barton had returned to the stroke position, and in the last two weeks the crew had made great strides and put up a magnificent performance. Barton started at forty-one in the first minute and gained half a length by two hundred and fifty metres. At four hundred metres they were rowing forty and had increased this lead to over three-quarters of a length. The Americans then began to reduce their lead. At the thousand metres the Americans showed ahead, and in spite of the determined efforts by the British eight continued to draw away slowly. At fifteen hundred metres the crews were a length apart. The United States, still slowly gaining, went on to win in the fast time of five minutes 56.7 seconds by about two and a half lengths. Barton never dropped below thirty-seven strokes to the minute and many must have been surprised at this performance.

I I AUGUST 1948
BOXING COMEDY OF ERRORS
CONFUSION OVER FOREIGN NAMES
Lainson Wood
WEMBLEY, Tuesday

Arnoldo Pares, Argentina's bantamweight, was the innocent instigator this morning of a 'comedy of errors' that developed throughout the day and nearly reduced the Olympic Games boxing to a farce. Scene of the first act was the weighing-in room. For nearly twenty minutes Pares stood weeping on the scales. He was overweight. They cut his hair almost to the roots, scrubbed the soles of his feet, blew the dust off the scales and used every manoeuvre that might get off an ounce or two. It was no good.

Then the first error crept in, one of pronunciation. D. Williams, the South African flyweight, who had to oppose another Argentine, P. Perez, was told he had a walkover. The Argentines, puzzled by their man's failure to make the weight, deposited £1, the fee required to lodge a protest with the Jury of Appeal. They protested that the scales were wrong. Weights and measures experts were sent for. They testified that the scales were infinitesimally inaccurate. Williams, whom it did not really concern, was asked if he minded if Perez, who was really Pares, weighed in again. With South African nonchalance Williams waived his right to the walkover that wasn't really his, and Pares, who had had an hour in which to run and boil and use every known method of weight reducing, this time beat the scales.

Boxing began, and in due course Williams was beaten – by Perez. He was watched by some Hungarians who, hastily scanning the programme, spotted the error. Their bantamweight, T. Csik, if he won his next round, would probably have to meet Pares. They promptly paid £1 and lodged a protest. While the harassed Jury of Appeal was trying to sort this one out, Pares fought an Australian, J.W. Carruthers. It was one of the best contests of this long day. Carruthers won, but received a cut eye which may compel him to withdraw. Pares, almost bald as the result of his fight with the scales, also suffered a damaged eye to bear testimony of his fight with Carruthers.

The Jury of Appeal, despite all these activities, continued to weed out judges and referees. More were told today that their services were no longer required. And judging by some of the decisions I saw it will be surprising if the panel is not considerably reduced by tomorrow morning.

_____

11 AUGUST 1948
FILM DECIDES OLYMPIC RACE
BRITISH TITLE GOES
Daily Telegraph Reporter

The biggest surprise of the Olympic Games occurred yesterday when the International Jury of Appeal, having seen a film of the baton change incident in Saturday's 400 metres relay, revoked the disqualification of the United States team and awarded them the race. The placings have been revised as follows: 1, United States; 2, Great Britain; 3, Italy. So Britain loses her only Olympic athletics title. The four relay runners must hand over their gold medals to the Americans and take the silver ones from the Italians. The Hungarians, who have already returned to their country, must forward the bronze third-place medals to Italy. I understand a new winning ceremony will take place on Saturday.

The film producers made enlargements of stills from the film and slow-motion stripes of the disputed baton change-over at the first bend between the Americans, Ewell and Wright. These showed that Wright took the baton from Ewell eight feet inside the change-over box. There may be wide repercussions from the jury's precedent. In effect, the referee's decision is no longer final.

Camera evidence has often before been used to decide disputed points. One case was the Newcastle–Arsenal Cup Final in 1932. Pictures showed the ball had gone over the line before it was hooked back for the winning goal to be scored for Newcastle. A cameraman from the unit making the official Olympic Games film assured me there was no camera directly commanding the baton change-over line. 'In my opinion,' he said, 'camera evidence is unreliable in a case of this kind. The camera at an angle can give an erroneous view.'

_____

13 AUGUST 1948
LETTERS TO THE EDITOR
PHOTO DECISIONS

Sir – The photo-finish decisions at the Olympic Games are deplorable and quite out of keeping with the true spirit of the Games. When Bradman and his team arrived from Australia he was asked about the photographs showing Lindwall dragging his foot over the bowling crease. He replied that they did not play cricket to a camera, but to umpires. That is how it should be with all games. Umpires, referees and judges are human, and are liable to err like the rest of us, but their decisions should be accepted. To abide by a decision one feels to be wrong is the test of the true sportsman.

This bickering and appealing about the result makes a mockery of the fine sporting spirit which is so proudly proclaimed in large letters at Wembley. 'The important thing in the Olympic Games is not in the winning but in the taking part ...'

P. Waddell
London SW1

———

13 AUGUST 1948
THIRD BRITISH OLYMPIC WIN
GOLD MEDAL FOR YACHTSMAN
Our Yachting Correspondent
TORQUAY, Thursday

Glorious sailing by Stewart Morris has won Britain's third gold medal of the Olympiad. Following two rowing victories at Henley last week, Britain today won the Swallow class yachting title in Torbay. Although Britain did not get medals in any of the other four yachting classes, she was fourth in the Dragon and Star events. In the 6-Metre she finished fifth, and the Firefly ninth. The United States appear among the first three in four classes, with wins in the 6-Metre and Star. Scandinavia took the two other firsts, Norway winning the Dragon and Denmark the Firefly.

Weather today was almost perfect, with a strong offshore wind from the north-west, increasing steadily from the start at 11 a.m. to rather over force five as the day wore on. Torbay scintillated in the sunshine, and the sea was flecked with white. The great battleships *Anson* and *King George V*, with the aircraft carrier *Victorious*, and British and foreign destroyers, formed an impressive background to a scene of intense activity in the day. I watched the start of the Firefly, where twenty-one nations came to the line. There was a good deal more wind than most of the helmsmen wanted in these 12-foot boats. Portugal capsized before the start but was baled out to finish eleventh, a fine effort. Eire was dismasted. The first nine or ten boats completed the race without upsetting. Some of the remainder finished after capsizing and baling out, but Austria, Eire, Finland, South Africa and Great Britain retired. Denmark, sailing under reef mainsail alone, finished first, and Holland, who nearly capsized when almost on the finishing line, struggled across into second place half full of water.

Crossing to the Star course I saw that some of the boats were not under control. *Gem II*, Great Britain (Durward Knowles), lost her mast when lying second, and later, having established a long lead, Italy was dismasted, putting Australia into first place, which she held to the finish, with Cuba, having sailed a fine race, second, and Portugal third. In the Star class six boats lost their masts and two dismasted in previous races did not start. Although making an excellent start in the Swallows, Britain's *Swift* (Stewart Morris, with David Bond as crew) dropped back to eleventh place, with Portugal, her only serious rival, in the lead, which she kept and increased. This meant Morris had to finish fourth to win. Eventually he got into fifth place, and then followed a period of desperate anxiety which lasted almost until the end, when, making use of his dinghy experience, he planed past the Brazilian on the final reach.

The Dragons made an excellent start, the first six remaining together. Argentina, when in the lead, carried away a crosstree and retired. Belgium tore her mainsail but continued. Denmark, Sweden, Britain (*Ceres II*, W.E. Strain) and Norway had a hard battle, and, although at one time second, *Ceres II* finished fourth, Sweden winning. The Sixes, too, seemed to have all the wind they wanted, and heeled over at an acute angle. *Llanoria*, the U.S. boat, led all the first round, with Norway, Argentina and Britain hard astern. Norway got into the lead in the second round, but lost it to Argentina and was afterward also passed by the U.S. Britain (*Johan*, J. Howder Hume) came fourth. The winning nations will be honoured at the closing ceremony at Torre Abbey, Torquay, tomorrow night, when the Flame will be extinguished.

---

16 AUGUST 1948

FAREWELL TO THE GAMES
GREAT SPORTING MEMORIES

Lainson Wood

The Olympic flag was lowered; the Flame went out. The Games of 1948, celebrations of the XIVth Olympiad, were over. Only the banner bearers of the fifty-eight competing nations gathered in a half-circle round the Tribune of Honour from which Mr Sigfrid Edstrom, of Sweden, president of the International Olympic Committee, in an address of thanks to London and the people of Britain, solemnly proclaimed: 'Ties of brotherhood and friendship have been made.' Most of the competitors had dispersed, but eighty-five thousand people who had watched entranced the equestrian competition for the Prix des Nations, over as difficult a course as was ever set man's best friend, stayed in their seats to join in the signing of the Olympic hymn and Sir Alan Herbert's cantata, *Let us be glad*, to the music of the *Londonderry Air*.

There was a note of sadness in the raising of the Greek, British and Finnish flags, symbolising the inspiration of the Games, the host country, and the celebration of the next Olympiad in Helsinki in 1952. Sadness at the thought that Londoners will not see this unique sporting carnival again for at least another forty years. Britain, as the organising nation, has much for which to congratulate herself. In competition with the world's greatest athletes few honours came the way of the home representatives. We expected few and we have no excuses to make. But the Games just ended were freer from unfriendly incidents than many of their predecessors; they were watched by approximately one and a half million people; the organisation in the main was all it ought to be; the spirit of competition throughout was keen and sporting.

Great tact was needed to keep it so with men and women of differing temperament, tongue and colour competing for the highest honours in the wide realm of sport, and living and messing together in encampments so well improvised that there was scarcely a grumble. The governing bodies of seventeen sports have carried out their tasks magnificently, and there should be a surplus of about £100,000 from the £500,000 take at the box offices to share among them for the furtherment of their activities when the final balance-sheet is drawn up.

LEADING ARTICLE
OLYMPIC LAURELS

On the athletic track, as on the cricket field, we have in these times to content ourselves with being good losers, taking what consolation we can from those Olympic trophies which we won last week on the river and the sea. But our recent visitors would, it is believed, willingly grant us laurels for the successful organisation of the Games and the way in which British resourcefulness overcame those obvious material difficulties which faced us as the hosts of more than fifty nations. It is only to be regretted that the Olympian deities who were once supposed to regulate the weather could not have deputed the control of this important element of the Games to the same friendly human hands.

Before the opening ceremony there were many in this country and abroad who supposed that financially the Games would show a loss. Difficulties of travel and fears for the disturbed state of Europe certainly robbed us of many who would have swelled the number of our foreign visitors. British spectators, however, flocked to seize the opportunity of viewing contests some of which were unfamiliar and many of which lacked the speed and excitement normally demanded by a vast crowd. Nor were they disappointed, for it was not simply record-breaking which they went to see, but the grace and skill and doggedness of men and women of many nations inspired by a common sporting ideal. There were times when the ideal of sport declines to the lesser ideal of victory, but such deviations were rare at the XIVth Olympiad. For this achievement, competitors, judges and spectators from all countries may well share the laurels.

4

THE FIFTIES AND SIXTIES

HELSINKI 1952

18 JULY 1952
LEADING ARTICLE
CROWN OF WILD OLIVES

Helsinki is now crowded with the competitors for the fifteenth Olympiad which formally begins tomorrow. When the Baron Pierre de Coubertin revived the Olympic Games fifty-six years ago, he produced something that was no more Greek than the Gothic Revival was Gothic. The spirit of the original Olympic Games was religious and exclusive. The Olympic religious ceremonies meant something because all the competitors and spectators shared a common faith, when they did not share a common scepticism. It was exclusive because all shared a common culture and inheritance. Barbarians were rigorously excluded along with women.

The modern Olympiads are marked by a hopeful internationalism that was more characteristic of the nineteenth century than it was of the twentieth. There were no barbarians for de Coubertin. All were welcome who came to the Games in a spirit of manly and strictly amateur emulation. That is why there is no national 'championship' of the games, and why the elaborate system of point scoring, now generally accepted, wins no official recognition. But the reality of national rivalry, sometimes friendly and sometimes not, has increased, while the reality of amateurism has diminished. Many of the competitors take the Olympic oath with considerable reservations that are generally understood. Much has been changed, and not altogether for the better, since the runners set off in

1896, on the first Marathon in history; for the event was an antiquarian invention, quite unknown to the ancient Greeks.

The extent of the change may be indicated by the fact that women are as free to participate in the modern Games as they are to watch and applaud. There are purists who shake their heads at this innovation, believing that female athletes deserve no more than the commendation which Dr Johnson gave to female preachers. There are other purists who regret the introduction of football, yachting, rowing, equestrian events and slalom, and, indeed, the track and field events are still of overwhelming importance, yielding the most generally accepted prestige.

What of the British team? Success in any Olympic event cannot be confidently forecast for any performer, however brilliant. In perhaps a third of the male events, our representatives have little or no chance, but the team includes some of the greatest athletes in the world who, if they cannot command success, will most certainly deserve it. If the ancient tradition could be fully revived, it would include a truce between warring States for the duration of the Games, something devoutly to be wished, but not by any means to be expected.

---

21 JULY 1952

ZATOPEK STORMS HOME IN OLYMPIC 10,000 METRES
SANDO FINISHES FIFTH: PIRIE SEVENTH

Lainson Wood

HELSINKI, Sunday

Wonder runner Emil Zatopek, of Czechoslovakia, approached his own best, slammed an Olympic record and doused the first of Great Britain's hopes here today when he won the 10,000 metres championship in twenty-nine minutes seventeen seconds. His time knocks 42.6 seconds off the record he set up at Wembley in 1948 and was only 14.4 seconds slower than his own world record made in Czechoslovakia two years ago. Whatever made us think that young Gordon Pirie would beat this superb distance runner? Because the long, lean and, we cherished the hope, inexhaustible young Surrey bank clerk has been in the 'twenty-nines' this season. Because Zatopek has already appeared to take so much out of himself with his rolling ungainly gait, we thought he might by now have burnt himself out. We bow to him, bow in deepest admiration for a man whose name will go down in the annals of athletics coupled with that of Paavo Nurmi, who yesterday, amid tremendous national enthusiasm, ran into the arena with the torch and lit the sacred Flame. Such must surely be the privilege one day of Emil Zatopek when in a more settled world it is given to Czechoslovakia to organise the Games.

What Zatopek actually did was to burn up young Pirie. He can only have been gratified when he discovered early in the race that Pirie's plan was to dog his footsteps. After running a couple of laps in the rear of the field Zatopek improved in the third to ninth place, with Pirie tenth. In the fourth lap the two moved up again to eighth and ninth. Along the back straight in the sixth lap Zatopek spurted to the front with Pirie on his heels, and on the bend Pirie forced his way in front of the remarkable Czech. For a moment the hopes of British spectators were roared to the skies.

Zatopek was swerving from side to side, wagging his head woefully and dropping his left hand to his side every now and then; Pirie was running with classic grace and inspiring ease. Alas! we forgot, in our, perhaps, justifiable elation, that that was ever Zatopek's way. Still swaying, still hanging his head, still evincing every sign of physical distress, Zatopek kept at it, ever increasing his already wonderful speed for such a long run. He was soon in front again and hereabouts Mimoun, the Frenchman, made his challenge to be sure of being with the leaders when the field began to spreadeagle and the inevitable gap appeared between the pacemakers and the best of the hangers-on. The first of the stragglers was lapped as early as the tenth circuit of the track.

Zatopek, Mimoun and Pirie continued in the fore, a couple of yards separating Mimoun from Zatopek and Pirie from Mimoun until in the thirteenth lap there was a definite gap between Pirie and the fourth, at that time Popov, the Russian. The margin gradually widened and Pirie, also to our alarm, let a distance elapse between himself and Mimoun. There was now so much lapping taking place that the order became a hopeless confusion. The only thing clear was that Zatopek and Mimoun were striding it out on their own. Pirie put in another consoling spurt to once more tag the leaders for half a lap but the effort seemed to cost him something. He was now breathing heavily and puffing his cheeks and the first quite definite signs of the strain the race was imposing on him began to show clearly. He lagged behind again. All this while his team-mates

Sando, who was able to run despite a sore throat, and Norris had never been out of the first ten. Norris spurted up to pass Pirie, now fifty yards behind the leaders, in an endeavour to spur his colleagues on, but it was no good. Pirie just could not accelerate. Zatopek went from strength to strength and positively waddled his last lap at almost quarter-mile speed.

Mimoun clung to second place, though well beaten at the finish, but Pirie dropped back and could finish only seventh. It was left to the plucky Sando to give Great Britain the consolation of points for fifth place. I doubt if anyone would have credited him with being capable of that in such exalted company before the race began. As an illustration of how the field was straggled in the end, Zatopek had been congratulated, still in his track suit, and had left the arena as Van Tram, from the Dutch East Indies, crossed the finishing line. A steward held up a card with the figure two on it, indicating that the never-say-die Van Tram still had two laps to run. He finished alone.

----

22 JULY 1952

MCDONALD BAILEY THIRD IN OLYMPIC PHOTO-FINISH
100 METRES FIRST FOUR CLOCK 10.4 SECONDS

Lainson Wood

HELSINKI, Monday

Four of the world's leading sprinters, including Britain's E. McDonald Bailey, were clocked to have finished the greatest, if not the fastest, Olympic 100 metres final in the same time – 10.4 – here today. The judges, who had earlier placed McDonald Bailey second in a semi-final heat he had clearly won and had reversed their decision after examining the evidence of the camera, this time waited for the photograph, and a highly excited crowd was kept on tenterhooks for ten minutes before the result was at last set out on the electric scoreboard. It made a remarkable feature:

1. Remigino (U.S.A.) 10.4 seconds
2. McKenley (Jamaica) 10.4
3. McDonald Bailey (G.B.) 10.4

4. Smith (U.S.A.) 10.4
5. Soukharev (U.S.S.R.) 10.5
6. Treloar (Australia) 10.5

Never before can a tenth of a second have split the entire field in so important a final as an Olympic event and McKenley, Bailey and Smith are to be sympathised with.

From where I sat, not half-a-dozen yards past the finishing line and close above it, it seemed that McKenley had broken the tape and, indeed, this seemed the general opinion of the competitors themselves. Remigino, looking rather rueful, walked over to the wildly excited McKenley, who was all smiles and waving to friends in the crowd. It must have been a bitter disappointment to him when the result was at last announced. Remigino is a remarkable runner. With his head sunk between huge hunched and curiously rounded shoulders he appears to be deformed. But there is no mistaking his class as a sprinter, nor the power of his thrusting, high-stepping stride.

This track is not a fast one for sprinters, and the nip and dampness of this afternoon did not make for good times, so that one-fifth of a second outside the world record by four finalists can be accounted tip-top running. Bailey, who had set his heart on winning this classic event, took his defeat philosophically. His placing within inches of Remigino, who ran between him and McKenley, at least brought the Union Jack to the honours masts for the first time.

---

25 JULY 1952

CHATAWAY CRACKS WITHIN SIGHT OF THE TAPE
FALLS AND FINISHES FIFTH TO ZATOPEK

Lainson Wood

HELSINKI, Thursday

Five thousands metres, at Olympic record pace, was just one hundred metres too far for Chris Chataway, the young Oxford student of philosophy. Coming into the straight for the last time in his gruelling battle with the indefatigable Emil Zatopek of Czechoslovakia, Mimoun of

France, and Schade, the German, probably the three most experienced distance runners in the world, Chataway tripped over the verge of the track and sprawled his length on the side. He picked himself up and ambled along the final stretch after Zatopek, Mimoun and Schade, who finished in that order. His face was ashen-grey and there was scarcely a flicker of breath left in him, but these symptoms were more of exhaustion than the effect of the fall. Right at the post Gordon Pirie, Chataway's team-mate, came pounding along to pip him for fourth place.

I do declare Zatopek, for one, was resigned to giving the young Englishman best until he saw him faltering. Then, wagging his head and swaying his body more furiously than ever, he took up the chase again with little Mimoun still full of running and in close attendance. Chataway had beaten Schade and but for his fall could, I think, have held Mimoun's challenge. But I am convinced he could not have resisted the final effort of the revitalised Zatopek who, highly elated, tore down the eighty metres of the home straight like a sprinter. Poor Chataway scrambled over the line half a yard behind Pirie, collapsed and had to receive attention from a doctor. Zatopek's time of fourteen minutes 6.6 seconds was an Olympic record.

---

28 JULY 1952

AMAZING ZATOPEK LANDS GREAT OLYMPIC TREBLE
ADDS MARATHON TO EARLIER TRIUMPHS

Lainson Wood

HELSINKI, Sunday

The curtain was rung down here tonight on the track and field athletics of the Games to celebrate the XVth Olympiad on the highest possible note. At the last but one victory celebration the man who this week has won the affection and esteem of the entire world stood proudly at the top of the rostrum. Emil Zatopek, the amazing Czech, followed his victories in the 5,000 and 10,000 metres races by winning the Marathon. No record stands for ever, but I predict it will be many years before another man takes home from the Olympic Games, wherever they may be held, these three long-distance gold medals. It would, indeed, have been an achievement to have completed the course in all three. The 5,000 metres, the race in which Britain's best effort of the week – by C.J. Chataway – came to an abrupt end one hundred yards from home, was the only event that presented any difficulties to the man who must now be acclaimed the greatest long-distance racer of all time.

Zatopek had received congratulations, kissed his wife at the side of the track, pulled on sweater and track suit and was chatting with friends when the next man, R. Corno, from Argentina, swung through the gates of the arena. That was one measure of his victory. Another was his time of two hours twenty-three minutes 3.2 seconds, easily a record and more than two and a half minutes better than Corno. Yet another was the fact that, supreme in the knowledge that he had the race to himself, and had sufficient in reserve to withstand any surprise challenge from behind, he ran the last few miles smiling and joking with cyclists and being patted on the back by police patrolling the roadside.

When this small, sandy-haired, balding little man, hands still held high and wagging his head in his inimitable style, ran on to the track the scene was unprecedented. He had three quarters of the track to cover to the tape. He ran it amid the most deafening cheers I have ever heard in a sports stadium, and that goes for Hampden Park when Scotland are a goal up on England. Seventy thousand people of all nationalities rose to their feet and yelled for the little man who had accomplished what all sane-thinking people imagined to be impossible.

Alas for Britain's hopes. J.H. Peters was drawn number one, and we had dared to hope it might be a lucky omen. Before the two laps of the track preliminary to taking to the broad highway had been covered Peters had taken the lead. There he stayed for the first fifteen kilometres with the Swede, Jansson, and Zatopek in ominously close attendance. After twenty kilometres Peters and Zatopek had changed places. The times recorded over the next ten kilometres showed that Peters was falling back and we heard no more of him until the race was over. He was the last in. We then learnt that five or six miles from the finish Peters had stopped and rested by the roadside. 'I've had it,' he gasped. 'Cramp has done me. The pace was too hot.' I cannot forbear to point out that he himself set it. Only one of the three British runners finished the course, G.L. Iden, who came ninth, just seven and a half minutes behind the winner. The first seven home all beat the previous Olympic record, suggesting a fairly easy course.

We leave this department of the Games with some bronze medals and one silver one – Sheila Lerwill was second in the women's high jump today – but there is no depression in this house. Our best men will, if they can afford the time, all have another Olympic chance. They are, thank goodness, all young enough to get better still.

––––––––––

4 AUGUST 1952

BRITAIN WIN FIRST GOLD MEDAL ON LAST DAY
FOXHUNTER HERO OF OLYMPIC TRIUMPH

Lainson Wood

HELSINKI, Sunday

By her final effort in the last competition of the Olympic Games Great Britain gained her only gold medal here today. It was won by a horse, and it went to the whole showjumping team, in which Britain was most appropriately represented by an Englishman, a Welshman and a Scotsman. By his perfect clear round of a very stiff course late in the afternoon of an August day which had blazed with steady sunshine and had brought to the stadium a capacity crowd, Foxhunter, ridden by Colonel H. Llewellyn, made characteristic amends for a most uncharacteristic performance in the morning.

When he came out for his second round the difference was magical, and he went like the champion he is to the emotional outburst of a crowd who had, in the morning, been struck dumb. White had another great round, with only one technical fault, and for the rest of the day stood second. In due course others joined him with a total of eight minus points, but had second place been decided on time values White would have got a silver medal. Instead, the five equal on this mark jumped off for the honour, and Nizefella then failed for the first time and left White fifth in the individual events.

Colonel Llewellyn has announced his retirement from the captaincy of the British showjumping team, although he will continue to compete on Foxhunter, who is still in his prime. He has closed an illustrious era of leadership with a spectacular success just when one great effort was needed to save Britain's fortunes at these Games from total eclipse. What deserves special comment, and commendation, is that the British team was a veteran one. Llewellyn is forty. White is forty-eight and Stuart thirty-eight. It has taken the Old Brigade, the men from the Shires, to bring down Helsinki's curtain on that great last act.

MELBOURNE 1956

15 JUNE 1956

BRITISH RIDERS ROMP AWAY WITH TOP PRIZE
WELDON GAINS BRONZE MEDAL

A Special Correspondent

STOCKHOLM, Thursday

Britain, as expected, won the three-day team event of the Equestrian Olympic Games, which finished here today. Germany were second, and Canada third. Lieutenant-Colonel Frank Weldon, on Kilbarry, best-placed Briton in the individual list, gained a bronze medal. He was third behind P. Kastenman, of Sweden, and A. Lütke-Westhues, a German. Once the three British horses had trotted out sound before the veterinary surgeons this morning a British victory in the team event was a foregone conclusion. The great issue was whether Weldon and Kilbarry could catch Kastenman and Iluster in the jumping phase. It was in the balance until the end.

The course of twelve jumps was one of the best I have seen. It made great demands on the horses' suppleness and obedience, especially the enclosed combination, numbers ten and eleven, which necessitated a quick turn round in front of a fence and a jump out on the same side as the entry. This caused surprisingly little trouble, although only a few, notably the German Otto Rothe with Sissi, accomplished it without a good deal of hard pulling on the bit. The sixth fence, parallel bars three feet nine inches and three feet eleven inches, a spread of four feet eight inches and no ground line, turned out to be a stiff one. It was knocked down by more than half the riders. A measure of the testing nature of the course – and of the severity of the preceding endurance phase – is the fact that out of thirty-eight starters, there was only one clear round – by K. Wagner and Prinzess, of Germany.

Major L. Rook and Wild Venture came in first for England and a rather awkward round brought ten faults (at number six) and 3.75 time faults. When his turn came A.E. Hill took Countryman very carefully and looked like doing a clear round, but he too was caught at number six and also had a quarter time fault. The two German horses, Sissi and Prinzess, had ten faults between them so the Olympic team gold was ours. But all thoughts were on the individual prize.

First came Kastenman and Iluster for Sweden, leading with 46.53 points. The first four jumps were faultless, then they blundered at the wall (number five); they recovered for number six and were clear to the enclosure where the horse lost all impulsion and had the exit fence down. Next to come were Lütke-Westhues and Trux von Kamax of Germany, second with 64.87. They, too, failed at number five, and then at the water (number nine) – again twenty faults, and the final score was 84.87.

At last came Colonel Weldon and Kilbarry with one of the greatest chances of an individual gold medal that he may ever have – but what a difficult one! The anxiety of the crowd could be felt as he started his round calmly enough. Fences one, two and three were clear; there was a slight awkwardness at number four but nothing touched; at five they were going beautifully; Kilbarry seemed to be easily over number six, but he hit the bar with his hind feet, lazily it fell and with it our hopes. But there was still a chance for a silver medal until unaccountably Kilbarry went into the water. His faults were twenty and his final score 85.48 and the situation remained unchanged. This was a great day for Britain, a fitting reward for the leadership and inspiration of Colonel Weldon and Kilbarry and the culmination of years of hard work and perseverance since 1952.

---

29 NOVEMBER 1956

SUPERMAN KUTS HUMBLES BRITAIN'S BEST CHATAWAY CRACKS UP IN 5,000 METRES: PIRIE, OUTPACED, FINISHES SECOND

Michael Melford

MELBOURNE, Wednesday

There was no doubt in the Olympic 5,000 metres this afternoon as to who was the master, just as there was no doubt in the 10,000 on Friday. Kuts, the tough, fair-haired, irrepressible Russian sailor, ran his three British rivals into the ground and bounded home alone, fresh and exuberant ninety yards ahead of the first of them. A mile from home Chris Chataway, Derek Ibbotson and Gordon Pirie were at Kuts's heels, running together like the Finns of old, fifty yards ahead of the rest of the world. It was a fine sight to British eyes even if Kuts looked ominously unflagging. His laps, around sixty-six seconds, had so far been fairly level. Now he spurted and suddenly the race was over.

Surprisingly, the most fancied of the other three, Chataway, who had only recently moved up to second place, cracked most completely, dropping back swiftly as Pirie did on Friday. Pirie and Ibbotson, who had been second and third for most of the race, passed him and for a lap strove to close a 15-yard gap. Kuts merely unleashed another spurt and they had to accept the inevitable. It is a measure of this remarkable man's ability that two and a half laps from home in an Olympic final the last doubt as to who would win had been removed. He went on remorselessly with a rolling shrug of his shoulders, broke the tape after a last lap of sixty-two seconds and once again jogged round his lap of triumph to a thunderous ovation. The Australians love a great runner as they love a great horse, and this one has a particularly cheerful, friendly personality. As someone said, he has something to be cheerful about. Pirie found a turn of foot in the straight which took him into second place in front of Ibbotson. Chataway, all the life gone from him, finished eleventh.

Kuts had led after the first one hundred yards, had reached the mile in four minutes twenty-five seconds and two miles in eight minutes forty-three seconds. He did not have to beat Pirie's world record, though on what he afterwards referred to as a slow track he was twenty-one seconds inside Zatopek's Olympic record. Such are the standards of distance running nowadays. Pirie was eighteen seconds outside his world record and obviously would have been nearer if he had not run in the 10,000 metres on Friday. But as Kuts has run at Melbourne it needed a superman to beat him.

---

30 NOVEMBER 1956

BRASHER WAITS THREE HOURS FOR GOLD MEDAL
APPEAL AGAINST DISQUALIFICATION UNANIMOUSLY UPHELD

Michael Melford

MELBOURNE, Thursday

Chris Brasher will stand on the winner's rostrum tomorrow as the first Briton to win an individual Olympic running event since 1932 and as one of the most remarkable Olympic winners of all time. Even without his disqualification for alleged interference with Ernst Larsen, of Norway, and the reinstatement which followed three agonising hours later, the story of his advance from third string to the world's best steeplechaser and Olympic record-holder is a classic of character and determination.

While the jury of appeal considered Brasher's protest against a decision which seemed grossly unjust at the time, and turned out later to be based on no solid ground at all, one had time to think over his long career. It reached a peak today at a time when those who ran under Brasher's presidency at Cambridge seven years ago have long put aside their running shoes. One thought of the resolute but far from brilliant runner who for years acted as friend and pace-maker to Bannister and Chataway, ran behind Disley and Shirley, scarcely ever won a race himself and had to work desperately hard to earn a place in the British team. Then one thought of the new, rather incredible hopes which were born of his race at Geelong two weeks ago and of his own confidence these last few days against all previous form.

It seemed the most brutal trick of Fate that any man should make this astonishing improvement at the age of twenty-eight, run the race of his life and then be disqualified. One felt the same awful pang of unbelief as when Devon Loch slipped up at Aintree last spring. However, as dusk fell, the Marquess of Exeter, chairman of the jury, which included another Briton Mr D.T.P. Pain, an Italian, a Russian and a Czech, came out of the jury room and announced that the appeal had been unanimously upheld. The jury decided that though Brasher and Larsen had come into contact this had not affected their running. All was well, and one regretted only that anyone should have to suffer such an unkind intrusion at this moment of triumph.

Some bumping in a field of ten is inevitable and the jostling in this event was nothing compared with that which knocked over a German and passed unpunished in a 1,500-metres heat half an hour later. The trouble occurred as Brasher made his effort approaching the third hurdle from home with three hundred and fifty yards to go. Earlier he had lain seventh behind Larsen, who at one time led the field by fifteen yards. He did not move up past Disley and Shirley into fourth place until three laps from home. Ten yards still covered the field when with six hundred to go the Russian, Rjichine, took up the running from Larsen, Rozsnyoi and Brasher. At the bell Shirley, after looking as comfortable as anyone, had gone and Disley was beginning to lose contact with the four leaders. Brasher at this point seemed itching to make his run and was going well enough to stir wild hopes in British minds, which have had their fill of disappointments since 1932.

As the four approached the third-last hurdle Brasher pulled out to pass Rozsnyoi. Larsen was on his outside and some mild scrimmaging took place from which nobody lost ground. Brasher has made himself into a highly competent hurdler and as he cleared the obstacle and started up the back straight he was in front. In a few strides he was eight yards up and still gaining. Over the next hurdle he went, over the water, over the last hurdle and then, every British heart racing with him, up the run-in. At last he was there, fifteen yards ahead of Rozsnyoi. As he pulled up the plugging stride became a stagger and he collapsed on the grass. There he was tended by Disley, who had pioneered Britain's advance in an event once the private property of the Scandinavians but who, when the great day came, was only sixth himself. The objection that followed came from an official standing by the hurdle, not from one of the other competitors. They, I believe, told Brasher that they were completely satisfied.

---

6 DECEMBER 1956

MISS GRINHAM WINS GOLD MEDAL BY A TOUCH
MISS EDWARDS THIRD, MISS HOYLE SIXTH IN BACKSTROKE FINAL
Ossian Goulding
MELBOURNE, Wednesday

The Duke of Edinburgh was among the crowd who watched 17-year-old Judy Grinham, of Neasden, win a gold medal in the women's 100 metres backstroke event in an Olympic record time of one minute 12.9 seconds here tonight. It was Britain's first Olympic swimming victory since Lucy Morton won the 200 metres breaststroke in Paris in 1924.

Britain's young team of girl swimmers, none of the three over seventeen, will never want a closer, more thrilling finish than this. Miss Grinham was clocked home in the same time as the silver medallist, 16-year-old Caren Cone, of the United States, and won by the length of her fingers while Margaret Edwards, of Heston, who won a bronze medal for Britain, was only one-tenth of a second behind the American girl. Britain's third contestant, Julie Hoyle, of Watford, taking part in her first international race, returned the fastest time of her life to take sixth place.

The electric time recorders in use at Melbourne's Olympic Pool showed that all eight finalists finished within one and one-tenth seconds of each other.

It was obvious from the very start of the race that Miss Grinham was nervous and unsettled, for she was left trailing a bad last for the first half-length of the 50-metre long pool. She and Miss Edwards gradually drew up to the leaders, but at the 50-metre mark it was Miss Hoyle who turned first. Miss Grinham always swims a much stronger second length and sure enough she came ahead after the turn with Miss Edwards and Miss Cone neck and neck behind her. Suddenly, fifteen metres from home her usual sustained finishing sprint faltered and it looked as though she was spent. But she came again with a second magnificent burst of speed, hurling herself at the end of the bath to win by a touch.

ROME 1960

26 AUGUST 1960
LEADING ARTICLE
INTERNATIONAL GAMES

Success in the Olympic Games is now judged not merely on a national but only too often on a *bloc* basis. A gold medal for Czechoslovakia is regarded in Russia as a victory for Communism. A gold medal for Britain or Canada is regarded in the United States as a victory for the free world. The time may come when a gold medal for an athlete from an uncommitted country will be regarded as a medal for neutralism. Aggregate national or *bloc* success is calculated by an arbitrary system of points which is totally foreign to the intended purpose of the Games, and is devoid of all athletic realism. All these things may be inevitable in international games, but they have their regrettable side.

All is not lost, though the original purpose of the Games is thus unfulfilled. We can recognise, for example, that in Olympic competition some gold medals are much more equal than others. The nation which wins the 1,500 metres, the sprints or the Marathon has gained enormously more prestige than the nation which wins at clay-pigeon shooting or equestrianism. There may be no entirely logical reason why there should be such a clearly marked scale of values in the huge variety of Olympic events, and due credit must be given to competitors who do well in the less important events. There are, perhaps, too many events. Nevertheless, though the Games may not be an occasion for the unqualified spreading of sweetness and light, they are the culmination of immense national and individual effort and still contain the possibility of doing more good than harm. It would be ungracious not to wish all competitors well – and especially our own contingent.

---

29 AUGUST 1960

MISS LONSBROUGH KEEPS STRICTLY TO PLAN

Michael Melford

ROME, Sunday

Anita Lonsbrough's gold medal in the 200 metres breaststroke last night was won after the sort of race which has normally unexcitable middle-aged citizens on their feet shouting like schoolboys. As a tonic and example to others who are to follow, it was priceless, as indeed was Elizabeth Ferris's bronze medal in the springboard diving. Success here is very much a matter of producing your best at the right moment. Miss Lonsbrough not only broke the world record but carried out with wonderful composure and self-discipline what cannot have been an easy plan.

In the previous round on Friday, Wiltrud Urselmann went off at a great pace but, even to an inexpert eye, seemed of somewhat suspect stamina over the later stages. Nevertheless, she was nearly a second and a half faster than the English girl and, with Ada den Haan of Holland, had the added morale advantage of having relieved Miss Lonsbrough of the 200 metres and 220 yards world records which she set up last year. It must have needed great patience and restraint to let the German build up an apparently unassailable lead, but Miss Lonsbrough bided her time and swam her out of it over the second one hundred metres.

The new champion, only the second British Olympic swimming champion (after Judy Grinham) that Britain has produced in thirty-six years, is nineteen and is a Huddersfield Corporation clerk in the motor taxation department. She was not in the best of health earlier in the season but has been in great form in recent weeks. Like most of the English girls here she did not get the best of starts. The German was as fast away as she was on Friday and was a yard ahead at twenty-five yards. Halfway down the second of the four lengths she must have been three yards ahead of Miss Lonsbrough and Miss den Haan, who were level, but at halfway the English girl was clearly in second place.

On the third length the race changed completely. Anita Lonsbrough almost closed the gap and turned no more than two feet behind the German who must have been suffering all the agonies of the fugitive as the hunt draws close. Halfway down the final length they were level until the English girl was nearly a yard ahead with a beautifully-judged race surely won. In the last ten strokes, however, the German fought back and there was an awful moment when it seemed that the British girl's hard-earned victory might be going to slip away at the last moment. But she held on and was clearly the winner.

---

8 SEPTEMBER 1960

THOMPSON GAINS SECOND GOLD FOR BRITAIN
VICTORY BY SIXTY YARDS IN 50-KILOMETRE WALK: 1948 WINNER FINISHES SECOND

Michael Melford

ROME, Wednesday

Shortly after seven o'clock this evening, Donald Thompson came into the floodlit Stadio Olimpico weary, but triumphant, at the end of the 50-kilometre walk. He completed a lap of the track and Britain had won their second gold medal of the 1960 Games. Thompson had taken the lead just before halfway, but for the next two hours he could not shake off the gallant Swede Ljunggren, winner at Wembley in 1948, third in Melbourne in 1956 and now nearly forty-one years old. Only in the last five kilometres along the road beside the grey Tiber did he open up a slight lead. He won in the end by sixty yards in four hours twenty-five minutes thirty seconds which beats the eight-year-old Olympic record by some two and a half minutes.

Thompson, a 27-year-old fire insurance clerk from Cranford, Middlesex, who was turned down from National Service because of sinus trouble, had recorded the fastest time in the world this year, but little was known about the form of the Russians. Most people therefore seem to have considered that Matthews, in the 20-kilometre walk, was a more hopeful proposition than Thompson. In fact, the only Russian in the first six was fourth. The 50-kilometre walk is an event in which Britain has a record second to none, having now won three times out of six. When it was first included in the Games of 1932, T.W. Green won it. In 1936 the winner was Harold Whitlock, who was chief judge today.

As they passed under the walls of Castel St Angelo after five kilometres and skirted the Vatican, two Sikhs were leading with Thompson third, thirteen seconds behind, and Read fourth. At ten kilometres Read had dropped back but the first three were the same. By fifteen kilometres the Sikh previously second had taken the lead, fifteen seconds ahead of his compatriot and Thompson who were together. At this point a minute covered the first seven and the Russian Klimov had begun to move up. Before the twentieth kilometre there was some reshuffling and the leading group of four included the Sikh, two Australians, Crawford and Freeman, and Klimov. Thompson was still nine seconds behind them, but by the time they turned at halfway he had not only gone to the front but opened up a gap of a minute over all but Ljunggren.

At one time during the next ten kilometres Thompson had a lead of over half a minute and hopes rose very high, but the Swede came back at him and at thirty-five kilometres was actually some few yards ahead. The first Russian Stcherbina was third, over a minute behind. The warm afternoon had given way to a cool evening by the time they reached forty kilometres where Thompson led again, though only by six seconds. It was now almost certain that, barring disqualification or retirement, one of them must win, for the Italian Pamich, lying third, was two minutes back. Passing the Vatican again with five kilometres to go Ljunggren was at Thompson's shoulder still, but now Thompson, walking with great resolution, made his final effort. In the next two kilometres he gained eighteen seconds on the Swede, roughly the amount by which he won.

The wait until he came into a stadium still holding some thirty-five thousand seemed interminable, but at last he appeared through the tunnel, a short, slight figure in glasses wearing a peaked cap with a flap over the back of the neck. Mercifully he was walking strongly enough to make the appearance of Ljunggren behind him no serious threat. As he walked round the track Union Jacks appeared in all parts of the stadium and they waved again five minutes later when Misson came in fifth. Half an hour later Thompson limped to the rostrum between two opponents each a head taller to receive the gold medal from the Marquess of Exeter, and the Union Jack, floodlit in the night sky, flew for the first time from the centre masthead.

TOKYO 1964

15 OCTOBER 1964

WORLD RECORD & GOLD MEDAL FOR MRS RAND

James Coote

TOKYO, Wednesday

With one precious gold medal in her pocket and her confidence at its peak, Mary Rand, the greatest woman long-jumper the world has seen, is convinced she can now bring off a unique Olympic double. For seven anxious minutes she sat in the drizzle in the centre of the huge floodlit National Stadium here tonight before knowing that her world record-breaking leap of twenty-two feet two inches had made her the first woman athlete to earn for Britain the supreme Olympic award. Celebrations had to be restricted to a glass of Champagne. On Friday, Mrs Rand, twenty-four, a Henley housewife, begins her gruelling five-event campaign in the pentathlon.

All day in the rain Mrs Rand never put a foot wrong. From her first qualifying jump this morning of twenty-one feet four and three-quarter inches she led the field at such a pace that no one could keep up. Her greatest rival, Tatyana Shchelkanova, of Russia, the former world record holder, crumpled under the strain. It was left to the young, slim, Polish girl, Irene Kirszenstein, to keep up the pressure until the last second. Mrs Rand confessed afterwards that she was worried until the result of Miss Kirszenstein's final jump was flashed on the electric signboard.

For four years Mrs Rand, under the tutelage of John Le Masurier, the national coach, has improved so steadily that for two years she has been spoken of as the possible Olympic champion. That she has come through to take the world title is a great achievement when one remembers that after the last Olympic Games she was written off as a failure, and even at one point threatened to quit. She is a different character to the one who failed in Rome. She has a young daughter, Alison, and has matured immeasurably since those days. The real test of this maturity came this morning after she had led the qualifiers, as she had done in the last Olympics. The thought in everyone's mind was: would she crack again?

After three rounds only the leading six performers qualified. Mrs Rand improved to twenty-one feet nine inches, then decided to make a special jump for her daughter and sped down the track to her world record and became the first woman to clear twenty-two feet. Still the Pole did not give up. She pulled out a jump of twenty-one feet seven and three-quarter inches, eight and a quarter inches better than she has done before. Mrs Rand 'warmed down' with a final twenty-one feet eight inches to record the greatest long-jump series seen in an athletics arena. Miss Shchelkanova, whose world record was until today twenty-one feet eleven and three-quarter inches, could manage no better than twenty-one feet and three-quarters of an inch.

———

16 OCTOBER 1964

MATTHEWS TAKES GOLD IN 20-KILOMETRE WALK

James Coote

TOKYO, Thursday

A gold medal and an Olympic record for Ken Matthews in the 20-kilometres walk was the climax of the most encouraging day's athletics Britain have had in an Olympic Games since before the War. Already, after two days' athletics, Britain have won two gold medals, and it is necessary to go back to 1936 to find when Britain have done so well. Yet on a day in which the standard of performances was astounding there was no greater event for Britain than the 20-kilometres walk. Matthews's victory for the small British contingent here in the National Stadium overshadowed even Bob Hayes's classic 100-metres victory, Al Oerter's third successive gold medal in the discus and the high-jumping of Iolanda Balas that brought her another gold medal. At too irregular intervals news was posted on the electronic signboard at one end of the stadium of Matthews's progress. At the five-kilometre mark he was only one second ahead of Ronald Zinn, of the United States, who had set a cracking pace. So fast was it that Matthews later said that he wondered briefly if he would flag at the end. But he need not have worried. He went out ahead and none of the opposition dared stay up for risk of being 'pulled' for lifting. By halfway Dieter Lindner, of Germany, had moved into second place, a position he was to keep until the finish, and was twenty-four seconds behind. By fifteen kilometres Matthews's back had retreated further into the evening haze and Lindner could only concentrate on the second-place medal which he acquired fairly comfortably. This was a procession led by Matthews whose feet, shod with the dirty old black shoes that he wore to win his European gold medal in Belgrade, pattered a regular rhythm on the Tokyo streets.

The barriers were erected at the main entrance of the stadium where the walkers would come in to make sure they went the right way and although everyone knew how far ahead Matthews was we did not dare say anything just in case something disastrous had happened. We could only keep our fingers crossed. The wait seemed immeasurable, but then in came Matthews as relaxed as if he had been on a Sunday afternoon stroll. Round the track he strode, completing the last four hundred metres blowing kisses and waving to the cheering crowd. He crossed the line and, laughing with joy, clasped his hands above his head like a fighter who has just won a world title. As he went over to the place where most of the British contingent were standing his wife, Sheila, dashed out on to the track and hugged him. To get on to the track was in itself no mean feat for she had to take down no-entry signs and move aside two heavy steel barriers, but she had come all the way from Britain with money raised by her husband's work-mates, and nothing was going to stop her now. It was an emotional moment as they embraced before being escorted off.

---

19 OCTOBER 1964

DAVIES OUTJUMPS THEM ALL TO LAND GOLD

James Coote

TOKYO, Sunday

Lynn Davies, whose first sporting steps were taken among the slag heaps of Nantymoel, spent the longest twenty seconds of his life seated, with eyes closed, on a damp bench in the National Stadium here tonight before learning he had won a coveted gold medal. On a wet, miserable day Davies outjumped the 1960 Olympic champion, Ralph Boston, from the United States, and Igor Ter-Ovanesyan, of Russia, who have monopolised the world rankings these past four years, and in so doing set a British record.

It is, I think, fair to say that Davies's victory over two jumpers who have frequently cleared greater distances, is the outstanding athletics achievement of the Games so far. Although he came with the chance of a bronze medal it was impossible to give him much more than that, because he is still only twenty-two and lacks the experience of many of his rivals. How, then, could this young Welshman, who only just qualified with his last jump this morning after he had found he placed his run-up mark two feet short, beat the world? Because he was the strongest of them all and because the conditions we experienced here today suited him down to the very tips of his spikes.

Under the aegis of Ron Pickering, national coach for Wales, to whom Davies gave much of the credit, he has been lifting an immense poundage to increase the power of his thighs. How this paid off became apparent today when on a soft run in Boston and Ter-Ovanesyan could never reach the 27-foot plus marks to which they are accustomed. The Russian held the lead with twenty-five feet six and a quarter inches after the opening round, with Boston second on twenty-four feet nine and a half inches and Davies third on twenty-four feet five and a quarter inches. Boston improved to take the lead with twenty-five feet nine inches in the second round, but there was no change until the final three rounds, in which the last six competitors fought out the battle for the medals. All improved in the fourth round, Boston to twenty-five feet ten and a quarter inches, Ter-Ovanesyan to twenty-five feet seven inches and Davies to twenty-five feet six and a half inches.

Then came the crucial fifth round. Davies stood in the rain waiting for the head wind to drop, knowing that this would be the big one. Boston had just no-jumped and, carefully, Davies checked his run-up mark. Then down the run-up he went, faster and faster until he hit the take-off board at precisely the right point. As he got out of the pit with a broad grin on his face the officials took over. It was obvious he was in the lead. But by how much? A great shout from the British contingent in the stands near the long-jump pit and a 'whoopee' from Davies coincided with the revolving indicator board in the centre of the stadium lighting up the figures 8.07 metres – twenty-six feet five and a half inches, one inch more than his recently set British mark.

The Russian followed with a too-close twenty-six feet two and a half inches, and then came the final agonising jumps. Boston, who could not get going in the cold, spun out to twenty-six feet four and a quarter inches. Davies had a lowish one and then sat waiting for Ter-Ovanesyan to let fly. 'It was agony,' he said later. 'I did not dare to look. I could only wait and wait.' But the Russian was nowhere near and Davies had won the first men's field events gold medal for Britain since Timothy Ahearne was successful in the triple jump in 1908.

---

21 OCTOBER 1964

ANN PACKER INSPIRED BY FIANCÉ'S DEFEAT
GOLD MEDAL AND WORLD RECORD
IN LAST RACE

James Coote

TOKYO, Tuesday

The defeat of Robbie Brightwell in the 400 metres yesterday inspired Ann Packer, his fiancée, to win a gold medal and set a world record in the 800 metres at the National Stadium here today. At 3.50 p.m. yesterday, immediately after Brightwell had finished fourth, Miss Packer, already the silver medallist in the women's 400 metres, vowed that she would win the 800 metres. Until that moment Miss Packer had been prepared to run as well as she could in this event. She qualified only at the last minute and was selected on condition that she did not let it interfere with her 400 metres training.

She had no idea of tactics, of pace-setting or how to avoid getting boxed in. She had run her first two-lap race at Leyton in May. This final was only the seventh time she had covered a competitive 800 metres ... and it would be her last individual race. Though Miss Packer came here with a fair time she lacked until yesterday the motive that is necessary to win a gold medal. Today, just before going on the track, she was overjoyed to see Brightwell cross the line first in a 4 × 400 metres relay semi-final. She went to the start ready to win but not knowing how fast she would need to travel. Marise Chamberlain, of New Zealand, who finished third, had no such inhibitions. Runner-up to Dixie Willis when she set a world record of two minutes 1.2 seconds in 1962, she knew it would take a world record, but thought that Maryvonne Dupureur, the French champion, would be the one to do it.

Miss Dupurer and Nagy Szabo, of Hungary, were the front-runners by the time the first one hundred and twenty metres had been covered. Antje Gleichfeld, a German, strode confidently behind in their wake and in sixth and seventh positions were Miss Packer and Anne Smith, the other British competitor. The French girl had a fractional lead at the end of the first lap which she covered in an amazing 58.6 seconds. Miss Packer was half a second behind and looking easy, but Miss Smith was out of the running. Soon after entering the back straight Miss Dupurer attempted to break away but gained little advantage. Behind, the action was becoming really live. Miss Chamberlain, who wanted to delay her finish, was just to the outside of Miss Packer, who tried every way to get through. Finally, in desperation, she slackened her pace, swung out and then, to the delight of the British crowd, moved steadily through the field.

From sixth, to fifth, to fourth, on she travelled, accelerating all the while. The unfortunate French girl, her head wobbling from side to side in fatigue, could not hold on and to her despair had to watch Miss Packer striding nearer and nearer the finish and the gold medal that she had thought would be her own. Miss Packer's time of two minutes 1.1 seconds beat Miss Willis's record by a tenth of a second and is 4.2 seconds faster than she has done before. Sin Kim Dan, of North Korea, who did not compete here because of political squabbles, has covered the same distance in one minute 59.1 seconds, but this mark has not been accepted because it was set at an unratified meeting. What a pity that Miss Packer will never be seen in action again after this trip. I am convinced she could bring the time lower than the ultimate of one minute fifty-seven seconds she forecast for this race.

---

22 OCTOBER 1964
BRIGHTWELL SIGNS OFF WITH BURST FOR RELAY SILVER
James Coote
TOKYO, Wednesday

What a fairybook way for Britain's athletes to finish their greatest Olympic Games! On a final day during which the action seldom flagged, they added two silver medals and one bronze to their already inspiring collection of four gold and five silver. Not only did Basil Heatley finish second in the Marathon, but the 4 × 400-metre team came through to take the silver in a time well within the existing world record. Not to be outshone, the women's sprint squad also finished inside the old world mark, yet had to be satisfied with a bronze, so high was the standard. The much-maligned men sprinters also broke the United Kingdom record by one-tenth when finishing last of eight in the final, and finally Alan Simpson was pipped for a medal in the 1,500 metres which gave Peter Snell of New Zealand his second title of the Games. He had already won the 800 metres.

It was fitting that Robbie Brightwell should run his greatest race in his last international competition, but less predictable was the way he came through to take the British team into second place in the finest display of his international career, which started back in 1958 with the Cardiff Empire Games. He insisted that not all the credit should go to him. 'I could not have run this last leg but for the effort of the three before. It was a team effort, symbolic of the unity of this British team.' Tim Graham, Adrian Metcalfe and John Cooper and Brightwell knew that they had to run better than ever if Britain were to stand a chance.

Metcalfe said: 'When I took over I knew I would have to go flat out from the start to avoid the rush when the field left their lanes.' He was so successful that he was able to cut right across the eight lanes with a clear advantage. As he entered the home straight Mike Larrabee, the United States 400-metre champion, accelerated past, followed by Trinidad's Kent Bernard. But their lead was not large and Metcalfe could hand over to Cooper, having run his leg in 45.1 seconds, secure in the thought that he had not failed Britain. To say merely that Cooper ran the slowest leg is unfair. Although not as fast as the others he more than held his own and managed to keep the American world record holder, Ulis Williams, Trinidad's Edwin Roberts and Jamaica's Mel Spence within striking distance. Cooper, the 400 metres hurdles silver medallist, covered his stint in 45.7 seconds. The team captain seized the baton, 'trampling' on the unfortunate Pole, Andresz Badenski, in the process, he said afterwards, and settled down behind Harry Carr, of the United States, Wendell Mottley, Trinidad's silver medallist in the 400 metres, and George Kerr, of Jamaica.

Carr, the 200-metre gold medallist, in only his fourth one-lap race of the year, loped along easily. When Kerr and Mottley challenged he moved away so gracefully that it would have been a joy to watch but for the fact that he was leading. Brightwell made his expected challenge in the home straight, warding off a couple of elbows from Trinidad and Jamaica to finish second – and flat on his face. He had covered the final four hundred metres in 44.9 seconds, only three-tenths slower than Carr's time. Britain's time of three minutes 1.6 seconds was sixth-tenths inside the old world record time set by the American team when they won the same title at Rome, an indication of the rise in standards. The winners here came within eight-tenths of breaking the three-minute barrier.

By winning the bronze medal with the women's sprint relay squad Mrs Mary Rand became only the second athlete in the history of the Games, and the first woman, to strike gold, silver and bronze in the same Olympics. The late Bevil Rudd, of South Africa, formerly athletics correspondent of *The Daily Telegraph*, picked up the same collection in 1920 (400 metres gold, 4 × 400 silver, and 800 bronze).

MEXICO CITY 1968

4 OCTOBER 1968
OLYMPICS GO ON DESPITE GUN BATTLES
FORTY DIE AS 'CIVIL WAR' HITS MEXICO
Henry Miller
MEXICO CITY, Thursday

The Olympic Games will open in Mexico City on Saturday week despite last night's vicious gun battle in the city, during which at least forty people were killed and hundreds injured. Tonight a massive force of troops equipped with heavy armour held the battle area in a state of siege. Mr Avery Brundage, eighty-one, president of the International Olympic Committee, said the Mexico authorities assured him nothing would interfere with the Games. He added: 'As guests of Mexico we have full confidence that the Mexican people, universally known for their sportsmanship and great hospitality, will join the participants and spectators in celebrating the Games, a veritable oasis in a troubled world.'

But last night as I crouched for five hours behind a Mexican Army lorry in the city and saw troops and well-armed guerrilla bands fight a gun battle, there was all the appearance of a full-scale civil war. The fighting was among the worst known in the capital since the 1920s. At the Olympic Village today it was agreed training would continue normally, but athletes would be allowed into the city by day only in groups. Mr Sandy Duncan, the British team chief, announced this after meeting the different team managers. After 6 p.m. only organised groups going to specified places with the approval of the British headquarters would be allowed into the city.

I had arrived at the plaza just as snipers started shooting. They aimed at police and troops equipped with tanks and armoured cars who had formed a solid ring around the area in anticipation of major disorders. Three thousand students had assembled for a protest rally in the square and were planning to march two miles to the National Polytechnic at Santo Tomas to try and force out troops who have occupied the buildings for the past two weeks. But when the shooting started it appeared that groups other than students were involved. Bullets soon flew all over the square. Students who tried to flee found no escape and spent hours on their stomachs or hiding inside entrances to buildings.

After leaving the scene temporarily to call London, I returned to find troops and the opposing gunmen engaged in a full-scale battle. Rifles, machine-guns, Bren guns and hand grenades were soon creating conditions more appropriate to Vietnam. Tracer bullets streaked across the rooftops and stray shots sped in every direction. Several times I was forced to change my position because of stray shots. But I was allowed to remain with troops along the Avenue San Juan de Lefran in what became a front-line for the next five hours.

As the fighting intensified, it seemed unbelievable that this conflict would be taking place so close to the Presidential Palace and to the heart of a city gaily decorated for the Olympic Games. Then the shooting subsided, and scores of ambulances were sent in to bring out the dead and wounded. Squads of troops evacuated some of the innocent people trapped in the square. But the snipers were regrouping expertly in other positions among the darkened blocks of flats and behind the Foreign Ministry building. Suddenly the whole area was again a battlefield. Thousands of rounds were exchanged as a green Verey light, fired by the Army, signalled a final drive on the gunmen, still shooting from the buildings.

At this point more than twenty were already reported dead. From the intensity of the ensuing fight it seemed likely that there must be many more casualties. Shortly before midnight the gunmen were silenced, and more soldiers moved cautiously into the plaza on clean-up operations.

Horrified crowds of civilians filled the streets behind the lines of troops and watched convoys of ambulances go in for casualties.

———————

16 OCTOBER 1968

DAVID HEMERY STREAKS TO WORLD RECORD SHERWOOD GRABS BRONZE IN LAST-YARD DIVE

James Coote

MEXICO CITY, Tuesday

David Hemery, twenty-four, shattered the world record when he won Britain's first gold medal of the Olympics in the 400 metres hurdles here tonight. He flew around the track in a blistering 48.1 seconds. His time is exactly one second faster than the listed record of the South African Gert Potgieter, but a month ago this was lowered by one of the men in this race, Geoff Vanderstock, to 48.8 seconds.

The blond Briton had no doubt he would win. He has reduced this event to one of theory and practice, and has a notebook in which every performance and every time between hurdles of his rivals is noted. His father lived in America and in England. Hemery was born in the West Country, but most of his education has been received in the United States. Primarily he used to be a high hurdler, and won the Commonwealth Games 120 yards hurdles title in 1966 in Kingston, but because of repeated injury switched to the intermediates with immediate success. Such fast times had been set in the previous rounds of this race that it seemed impossible the improvement could be so great. Before he left the States he had recorded 49.8 seconds, which in itself was considered remarkable. He improved this to 49.6 seconds before leaving for Mexico and in his heat of the Games reduced this to 49.3 seconds.

Heavy rain had left the air cool, but the track was not affected. Hemery was drawn in lane six with his main rival, Ron Whitney, in lane seven and the second Briton, John Sherwood, in lane eight. The starting gun fired. There seemed the fraction of an interval before Hemery clicked into gear. Then it was so smooth it was if there were no obstacles at all. Within two flights he had overtaken Whitney. It seemed impossible that he could keep on increasing his lead. But he did. He came off the last flight so far ahead that he could scarcely believe it. The remainder of the world's finest hurdlers looked 'scrubbers'. Hemery crossed the line.

We screamed our pleasure, but failed to see that Sherwood had bravely thrown himself across the line to seize the bronze medal in forty-nine seconds dead, behind the German, Gerhard Hennige, and ahead of the man who had lost the world record, Vanderstock. So Sherwood joins his wife Sheila [silver medallist in the long jump] in becoming the first British husband and wife partnership to win medals in the same Games.

18 OCTOBER 1968

BLACK POWER PROTEST MARS OLYMPICS MEDAL CEREMONY

A Black Power protest was made on the Olympic rostrum by two American sprinters after they had received their medals. Tommie Smith, who won the 200 metres in a world record time of 19.8 seconds, and John Carlos, who came third, gave Nazi-style salutes with black-gloved fists as their national anthem was played. They refused to look up as the Stars and Stripes were hoisted. Spectators greeted their action with cat-calls.

19 OCTOBER 1968

THREE ATHLETES WEAR BLACK BERETS
Donald Saunders
MEXICO CITY, Friday

Three American athletes, who took the three medals in the 400 metres tonight, made a protest at the victory ceremony when they appeared wearing black berets and making the Black Power salute. Lee Evans, gold medallist and one of the leading advocates of the Black Power movement among the American athletes, Larry James and Ron Freeman removed their berets during the playing of *The Star Spangled Banner*. They had been warned that 'the strictest disciplinary action' would be taken against them if they staged any political or racial demonstration.

Earlier Tommie Smith and John Carlos, the American sprinters who gave the Black Power salute when receiving their medals on Wednesday, were given forty-eight hours to leave Mexico by the United States Olympic Committee. The two athletes, who finished first and third in the 200 metres, were suspended from the American team and ordered to remove themselves from the Olympic Village. They will be sent home today. Smith and Carlos both wore black scarves and each raised a black-gloved fist as the anthem was played on Wednesday.

Carlos said at a press conference later: 'We are great American athletes for 19.8 seconds, then we are animals as far as our country is concerned.' As Carlos left the village with his wife today, after paying a brief visit, he was applauded and given the 'V' sign by a small band of competitors. There is no question of Smith or Carlos being deprived of their medals. The only way an Olympic medal can be forfeited is if a competitor is guilty of professionalism at the time of competing.

Mr Avery Brundage, president of the International Olympic Committee, criticised the violation by American athletes of the Olympic 'no politics' principle. 'The United States Olympic Committee carries the responsibility for its competitors.' This has given rise to unconfirmed reports here today that the Americans have been told their entire Olympic team will be thrown out of the Games if they do not control their competitors.

---

19 OCTOBER 1968

BEAMON CLEARS TWENTY-NINE FEET IN LONG JUMP

James Coote

MEXICO CITY, Friday

The most important world record to go this afternoon from Britain's point of view was in the long jump. The long-legged American Bob Beamon shattered the world record and won the gold medal with a fantastic twenty-nine feet two and a half inches. Beamon, who takes off from either foot, is no stylist, and has no knowledge of the finer points of jumping. But he has the spring of a kangaroo and the longest legs imaginable. 'They almost come under his chin,' Ron Pickering, Lynn Davies's coach, once told me.

Beamon's leap left Davies, the reigning Olympic champion and British record holder with twenty-seven feet, with an almost impossible deficit to recover. Davies's first leap was only twenty-one feet one and a quarter inches — just about a foot less than the women's champion achieved. Then confusion reigned. After three jumps it appeared that Davies had not qualified for the final pool, but his name appeared on the board as one of the qualifiers. He did not, though, jump in the final. What was clear was that Klaus Beer, of East Germany, was second with twenty-six feet ten and a half inches, and Ralph Boston, United States, third with twenty-six feet nine and a quarter inches.

Beamon was wearing the longest black socks, up to his knees, of any of the Black Power supporters. Another black sock wearer, though only ankle length, was Lee Evans, who cut a fifth of a second off the world's fastest 400 metres time despite a morning of mental and physical anguish. His time was 43.8 seconds. At one point Evans, the premier advocate of the Black Power movement among the athletes, was led from the American team headquarters in tears and on the point of collapse. Americans filled one, two and three positions, but none of them wore Black Power buttons. The second and third men, Larry James (43.9) and Roland Freeman (44.4), also broke the ratified world record.

———

21 OCTOBER 1968
FOSBURY IS NO FLOP
James Coote
MEXICO CITY, Sunday

Dick Fosbury took the high jump title back to the United States after a long absence with his unique style, the Fosbury flop, in which he pivots on his right foot as he goes over the bar. He pulls his knees up and lands on his back facing the way he came. Fosbury won with seven feet four and a quarter inches, a height beaten only by the world record holder, Valeriy Brumel, of Russia, and Ni Chih-Chin, of China.

———

22 OCTOBER 1968

SUPERDOCIOUS TRIUMPHS ON TRAFALGAR DAY AISHER COLLECTS BRONZE

A Special Correspondent

ACAPULCO, Monday

Rodney Pattisson and Iain Macdonald-Smith, in *Superdocious*, finished second behind Brazil in the final Flying Dutchman race here today to win the gold medal for Britain, and Robin Aisher pulled off a splendid third in the 5.5 metres to collect a bronze. And what could be more fitting than for Pattisson, a submarine lieutenant, to win his gold on Trafalgar Day. Pattisson and Macdonald-Smith finished first in the first six races and despite their disqualification on the first day, needed only to finish better than twenty-fourth in the concluding race today.

Starting alone out of harm's way at the wrong end of the line, they headed inshore and let the rest of the fleet go out. The wind, which had veered before the start, backed twenty degrees in the first beat and they suffered badly in consequence, rounding the weather mark about tenth. The second and third beats were still biased. The wind, though fresher than yesterday, was still full of holes and they were unable to catch the Brazilian crew. The *Superdocious* crew will have to wait now for their medals until tomorrow evening, as the presentation ceremony has been postponed in case of protests.

Pattisson, twenty-five, blond, good-looking, lives in Poole and is five feet nine inches and ten and a half stone, and has been on almost continuous leave from the Royal Navy since February. He was brought up on sailing and crewed for his sisters until he was old enough to helm himself to victory in the 1960 Cadet championship. From the Cadet he went to a 12-foot Firefly, and then made the large jump to the 20-foot Flying Dutchman, buying the ancient *No. 20* in time to sail in the 1964 Olympic trials and finish about eighth.

Superdocious has a conventional centre-board because of the rejection of the trailing-edge flap and a fixed rudder, which saves a useful six pounds over the normal lifting one. Pattisson and Macdonald-Smith are thorough in every detail. Every morning they check the entire boat, careen her, inspect the bottom and wash it free of dust. They hoist the mainsail by hand and shackle it at the head – no halyards to add weight or break. The success of Pattisson and Macdonald-Smith gave Britain her first yachting gold medal since Stuart Morris won in the Swallow class in 1948.

JONES CLINCHES TEAM PRIZE FOR BRITAIN
A Special Correspondent
AVANDARO, Monday

The British team won the three-day equestrian event gold medal here this evening, with Major Derek Allhusen, fifty-four, the captain, taking the individual silver on Lochinvar. It was a remarkably fine all-round performance. Only sixth after the dressage, the British team went into the lead in yesterday's cross-country event, when they were one of the few to surmount the terrible conditions which followed torrential rain. They started today's showjumping with a lead of forty-nine points over the United States, and maintained this advantage to the end. Showjumping has always been considered Allhusen and Lochinvar's weakest point, but the veteran Norfolk farmer and his ten-year-old went round the course, still deep in mud, without fault.

Richard Meade, who had led at Tokyo up to the showjumping phase, rode his new mount, Cornishman. They had two fences down for a total of twenty faults, and Staff-Sergeant Ben Jones, with The Poacher, needed a clear round to clinch the gold medal. Jones had the crowd on their toes, but he is too experienced a horseman to be rattled in any situation, and he took The Poacher, who he was riding competitively for the first time here in Mexico, round without a semblance of a fault.

This is the first time Britain have won an Olympic three-day event medal since taking the gold at Helsinki in 1952. The fourth member of the British team in Mexico, student nurse Jane Bullen, twenty, had the bad luck to slip up twice on the flat on her diminutive Our Nobby in the cross-country, and so finished out of the prizes.

The hard-luck story of this treacherous three-day trial belongs to the Russian team. In third place this morning, they seemed certain to win the bronze. But their leading horseman, Pavel Deev, took the wrong turning halfway through the showjumping course, and the judges ruled him out of the contest. This meant, in fact, the elimination of the Russian team, who were already without one rider, whose horse was drowned in yesterday's terrible storms. Deev, who was third in the individual event this morning, only nine points behind Guyon, was on the way to gold when he made his mistake. Four more jumps and the medal would have been his. Deev broke down and cried when he realised he had made an error.

---

28 OCTOBER 1968

FINNEGAN EARNS BRITAIN'S FIRST GOLD AT BOXING SINCE 1956
LATE OFFENSIVE DECISIVE

Donald Saunders

MEXICO CITY, Sunday

Chris Finnegan, twenty-four, of Iver, in Buckinghamshire, finds himself in the strange position today of being the amateur middleweight champion of the world, but not the holder of the British title. An eye injury suffered in the divisional qualifying competition ended his chances of appearing in last spring's A.B.A. Championships, but fortunately the selectors still decided to include him in the British Olympic team. At the Arena Mexico last night, he upset odds that would have been around 100–1 a fortnight ago by outpointing Alexei Kiselov, of the Soviet Union, to win Britain's first boxing gold medal since 1956.

As he sat in the dressing-room afterwards, Finnegan remarked: 'Well, it's better than being just a silly old bricklayer.' He knew he could not match the punching power of Kiselov, who was the light-heavyweight silver medallist in Tokyo and probably enjoyed an advantage of half-a-stone during last night's bout, the limit for which was eleven stones eleven pounds. 'My plan was to keep away from him, make the best possible use of my right jab, and put some real beef behind it,' Finnegan explained.

But during the first three minutes it did seem to me that Finnegan was rather overdoing things. He made few positive moves and I began to wonder if his only aim was to last the distance. David James, the British coach, was obviously worried, too. 'He gave me a right telling off during the interval,' admitted Finnegan, 'and I deserved it.' Those few sharp words did the trick. During the second round Finnegan began to work his way into the fight. He jabbed away effectively with his right against his fellow southpaw, tied him up inside and on my card earned a share of the points.

There was still some leeway to make up in the last three minutes. Finnegan closed the gap and just edged in front before the final bell by forcing the pace for the first time. Kiselov was clearly surprised by the Briton's sudden switch to the offensive. The Russian found himself being hooked solidly to the chin and punished about the body. He tried to hit back, but simply had not the strength left to gain control. The Mexican, Spanish and Cuban judges each gave Finnegan the nod by one point; the Thailand and Indian officials thought Kiselov had clinched it by a similar margin. The crowd had no doubt. They warmly applauded and cheered the fair-headed Englishman as he climbed on to the winner's rostrum.

---

29 OCTOBER 1968

GAMES FINISH, BUT THE CONTROVERSY RAGES ON
ALTITUDE PLAYS SMALLER PART THAN PREDICTED

Donald Saunders

MEXICO CITY, Monday

The Olympic Flame burns no more. The flag has been carefully stowed away. The Village is emptying. The stadiums, arenas, tracks, pools and lakes are silent. The conquerors and the vanquished are winging their way home. But though the nineteenth Games, easily the most controversial of the modern era, are over the debate continues. Perhaps it will never end while men are prepared to argue about sport. Was it as mistake to hold the Olympics here in Mexico City? You would quickly find one thousand volunteers to answer that question. But few would be in complete agreement.

Perhaps the fairest reply is that the nineteenth Games were better than most of us expected, but not as good as they might have been elsewhere. The spectre of altitude haunted these Olympics for six years before they began. It has never been far away from the track, pool, rowing lake or football pitch during the past two weeks. World-class long-distance runners collapsed, experienced oarsmen broke down, healthy young swimmers fainted and football teams like Czechoslovakia 'died'. Medical evidence has shown that none suffered more than temporary physical distress. I suspect, however, that more than one man has gone home with a broken heart, after failing, in the thin air of this city, to reach peaks of achievement he was sure he would have scaled at sea level.

Despite one more gold medal than gained in Tokyo, Britain has been left trailing and is unlikely to catch up in 1972. Lack of application, inadequate or ill-advised preparation and wrong mental approach have all been given as reasons. But, after a month of studying the cream of the world's sporting talent, and noting the relative failure of Western Europe in major events, I am left to wonder whether the more sophisticated a nation becomes the less successful they will be on the international playing field.

Behind the Iron Curtain, sporting achievement can raise a man or woman almost to the status of an astronaut, scientist or ballerina. In Britain, a lad may achieve fame and fortune as a professional footballer or heavyweight boxer. As an amateur sportsman, he will be briefly lauded, then forgotten. Consequently, there is not the same compulsion to succeed, and I, for one, am glad there is not. Amateur sport, especially, in the Olympic Games, was not meant to encourage competition at the expense of all enjoyment. It is fast approaching that stage of unhealthy development in the United States and Russia. Surely, it is better that we concentrate our efforts on enabling and encouraging more of our youth to enjoy playing games, even if it does mean that we lie a long way down the medals table, with which statisticians would turn rivalry between individuals into a worldwide battle of nations.

5

MUNICH 1972

26 AUGUST 1972

MUNICH'S SWINGING CITY GIVES REAL OLYMPIC MESSAGE

Donald Saunders in Munich

The twentieth Olympiad, the seventeenth Games to be held in the modern era, will be opened at the Olympic Stadium in Munich today by Dr Gustav Heinemann, President of the Federal Republic of Germany, with the emphasis placed quite clearly on the sweet innocence of youth. More than three thousand schoolchildren, aged between ten and fourteen, will welcome the competing nations with bows woven by themselves and with bunches of flowers. As the girls, dressed in bright yellow, and the boys, wearing green, play their feature role in sport's biggest extravaganza since the 'Mariachis' stole the limelight in Mexico City four years ago, a boys' choir will sing a thirteenth-century English canon.

All this, of course, is much more in keeping with the Olympic ideals than the opening of the 1936 Games, conducted in Berlin by Hitler against a background of strutting militarism. The Olympics are supposed to be all about youth, a fact that sometimes is overlooked when older men entrusted with the welfare of a noble and ancient idea spend their time, in the committee rooms, fighting political battles.

Indeed, it was with relief that I turned my back yesterday on the Bavarian State Parliament building in Munich, after the final session of the International Olympic Committee's congress and went to see how the youngsters who really matter are living. To describe their home as a village would scarcely be accurate. Here, for a few weeks, is the world's most swinging city. Long-haired, bearded youths and track-suited young misses, stroll, sometimes run, through the maze of tower blocks past boutiques, cafés and a discotheque, and sit on gaily coloured benches or grey concrete walls. They talk, they laugh, they argue, to the accompaniment of music – their music. To me, their city, like their music, is brash, noisy and bewildering. Yet, I left there more optimistic about the future of the Olympics, and of sport, than I had been at any time since returning from the Mexico Games in 1968.

When the last strident note of national anthems has died, and the flags have been tucked away for another four years, ninety per cent of those who parade round the stadium this afternoon will go home with no medal to show for their efforts. All will remember the 1972 Olympics as one of the greatest moments of their lives. That, perhaps, justifies the political manoeuvring and financial extravagance that now, inevitably, precede each celebration of an Olympiad.

---

27 AUGUST 1972
SUNSHINE OPENING TO THE OLYMPIC GAMES
David Miller in Munich

The opening ceremony of the twentieth Olympic Games began in Munich in bright sunshine today with the arrival of President Gustav Heinemann of West Germany. Athletes of one hundred and twenty-two nations paraded into the stadium before a crowd of eighty thousand spectators. A blond German runner carried in the Olympic torch, accompanied by four other runners. One of the first official sounds was the mellow baritone of eight Alpine horns, the signal to start the parade. This was followed later by the rattle of old blunderbusses.

The Games opened with the uppermost thought in the minds of many being, not for the first time, 'Can they survive?' The next two weeks will show us whether they are even worth preserving. Mr Avery Brundage, making his last welcoming address after twenty years as president of the I.O.C., said solemnly: 'Our German friends have done their best to stage this festival of youth with dignity.' The implication, that it was not their fault that the preliminaries at least have been marred by political intrigue, was unmistakable. Thirty-six years after the Olympics in Nazi Berlin, with their sombre tones of racialism and rampant martial ambition, Herr Willi Daume, president of the German committee, pleaded yesterday: 'May we all recognise the Games as a festival of hope for humanity.'

In a message to the I.O.C., Mr Kosygin, the Soviet Prime Minister, says: 'The Olympic Games should also serve this noble cause … the Leninist principles of peaceful co-existence.' The Games should demonstrate 'co-operation and solidarity between young people'. This solidarity, as we have seen, can mean the expulsion of those athletes from any state with whose policies a particular minority happen to disagree. The banning of Rhodesia has established a precedent which can ultimately destroy the Games.

―――――

I SEPTEMBER 1972
SPITZ AGAIN SHOWS WORLD RECORD FORM
Pat Besford

Two more world record-breaking performances by Mark Spitz, of the United States, last night brought the young dental student an Olympic Pool record for most gold medals won in a single Games. Spitz now has five, with the prospect of winning two more. His tally of three individual golds equals the achievement of his countryman Debbie Meyer at Mexico City in 1968. And by adding two relay golds, Spitz bettered the four medals in one Games record of another American, Don Schollander, in 1964.

Spitz, from Modesta, California, last night won the 100 metres butterfly in 54.3 seconds to trim three-tenths off the world time he set earlier this month in Chicago. Thirty minutes later, he swam in the 4 × 200 metres freestyle relay, won by the United States in a world record time of seven minutes 35.8 seconds – seven and a half seconds better than any four men have managed before. Earlier this week, Spitz won the 200 metres freestyle and butterfly, and the 4 × 100 metres freestyle relay gold. Still to come are the 100 metres freestyle and the medley relay – and who can doubt but that the dark-haired American will make it seven golds?

―――――

I SEPTEMBER 1972
SEVEN MEDALS FOR RUSSIA

Karin Janz, an East German medical student, and Olga Korbut, seventeen, of Russia, each won two gold medals when the women's gymnastics reached the halfway stage yesterday. Affairs were held up for five minutes when Miss Korbut was given a 9.8 marking for the horizontal bar – too low for the packed Sportshalle's liking. Miss Janz, twenty, as a result needed only a moderate score to clinch her second gold. In the event she scored 9.9 points, the highest of the series. The individual events provided a shower of medals for Russia and East Germany. Russia took seven in all – two gold, three silver and two bronze.

_____

2 SEPTEMBER 1972
TWO GOLDS FOR LITTLE OLGA

Russia and East Germany each landed two individual gold medals in women's gymnastics. Olga Korbut, the tiny Russian, won the balance beam and floor exercise events, and Karin Janz took the golds for the uneven bars and the horse vault. She also took a bronze in the balance beam to add to her silver in the all-round individual. The all-round title and gold medal went to Russia's Ludmila Tourischeva, and the Russians emerged as the top team.

_____

2 SEPTEMBER 1972
BRITAIN'S TWO IN A ROW FIRST SINCE AMSTERDAM 1928
Alan Smith in Riem

Richard Meade and Laurieston won Britain's first individual equestrian Olympic gold medal, and clinched the team title, too, yesterday with a clear showjumping round that brought the capacity crowd to its feet with wild, generous applause. It is forty-four years since a team last won two successive Olympic three-day events, but Britain's quartet kept a tight hold on the lead they had struggled so hard for across country the day before.

Right from the start they put everything into the fight. All too often three days of grinding effort have been thrown away in the showjumping phase, but that was not going to happen here. Mary Gordon-Watson and Cornishman, first of the four to face the twelve solid fences, came into the ring with determination etched all over them. Days before the event even started Mary had said she wondered how Cornishman would react to this huge stadium, and yesterday with twenty-five thousand people it was an awesome sight. But if this was a new experience for them both they did not win their World title two years ago for lacking courage. Settling straight down to business Cornishman strode magnificently round save only for one nerve-shattering moment. At the third fence from home he came in on a completely wrong stride, but Miss Gordon-Watson kept her head and her grip on Cornishman, survived without fault to the end and missed the bronze medal by just one place.

The horses faced an additional hazard at two of the fences, running from grass to the outside sand track which could easily throw them out of gear. It was at one of these that Bridget Parker and Cornish Gold made their only mistake, cracking round at a great pace. Mark Phillips and Great Ovation, who lost their chance with their disastrous round across country, still persevered in raising the team's morale and they, too, went clear. Could Meade and Laurieston do it as well? Richard said afterwards that memories of what had happened in the past were never far from his mind as he waited to go in. How Russia's Pavel Deev had thrown away team and individual medals in Mexico by taking the wrong course, how Jim Wofford had slipped up on the flat there, and how he himself had been in the lead in Tokyo only to lose it showjumping. But the 32-year-old Welshman is single-minded in his pursuit of victory and when he rode Laurieston into the ring all he was thinking about was jumping clear.

Apart from a sharp tap at the second they never looked likely to fail. Meade said that he thought the tap had made Laurieston keep his mind on the job and pick his feet up over the other fences. Whatever did it, it was a heroic effort. The eight-year-old sailed round safe and sound as if determined to give his owner, Major Derek Allhusen, the gold that he, as both owner and rider of Lochinvar, had so narrowly missed four years ago. Allhusen bred both Laurieston and his dam and no man has put more effort and enthusiasm into the sport. He had his reward yesterday.

————————

4 SEPTEMBER 1972
SPITZ SWIMS TO PLACE IN OLYMPIC HISTORY
Pat Besford

Mark Spitz set an Olympic record for the most individual gold medals won in a single games in Munich last night by taking his sixth title, the 100 metres freestyle. Like his victories last week in the 200 metres freestyle and two butterfly events, Spitz took the title with a world record-breaking performance – 51.2 seconds, three-tenths faster than the mark he set in Chicago last month. Despite ricking his back in the Olympic Village two days ago, Spitz proved he is in a class of his own. He led from the gun and stayed there. He touched two feet ahead of his team-mate Jerry Heidenreich with Russia's Vladimir Bure third in a European record of 51.8 seconds.

David Wilkie, eighteen, of Edinburgh, won Britain's lone pool medal, a silver, in the 200 metres breaststroke on Saturday after a fighting and courageous swim. His time of two minutes 23.7 seconds behind America's John Hencken, is a European, Commonwealth and British record and the third fastest time of all time. After his unexpected success, two American team coaches indicated they would like to see Britain's star on their university squads. Wilkie is thinking about it, but says he is very keen to go.

----

4 SEPTEMBER 1972
MARY PETERS TAKES PENTATHLON WITH WORLD RECORD
James Coote

Mary Peters, of Britain, at thirty-three the 'doyen' of the pentathlon, capped an amazing career to win the Olympic gold medal in Munich yesterday by the slenderest of margins, ten points, in a world record-breaking total of 4,801. This is a 26-point improvement on the previous record, held by Burglinde Pollak, of East Germany, who could not match the Belfast secretary's amazing two days and finished third with 4,768. The runner-up was Heide Rosendhal, of West Germany, European champion in the event last year and winner, on the first day of the athletics in the Munich Olympic Stadium, of the long jump.

This was the third Olympics for Miss Peters, who has had fourteen years of international competition. She was fourth in Tokyo behind the silver medallist Mary Rand, who was in the Stadium yesterday to see her former team colleague win the gold. In 1968 Miss Peters finished ninth. The best she has attained in a European championship is fifth in 1962.

So close was yesterday's event that everything hinged on the 200 metres, the final event. Although in the lead, Miss Peters could afford to lose to Miss Pollak by no more than four-tenths of a second and to Miss Rosendhal by no more than 1.3 seconds. Working on the basis that Mary would clock about 24.1 seconds, Miss Rosendhal had to run faster than 22.9 seconds while Miss Pollak had to beat 23.6 seconds. Miss Peters made a perfect start and held her own against the faster girls for the first one hundred and twenty metres. Then the sprinters came through. But Mary struggled on to finish fourth and no one dared guess whether she had won. At last the scoreboard flashed this message – 'Peters, Mary, 24.08'. We knew then that Britain had won the Olympic pentathlon for the first time, and that Mary had become only the third British girl to win an athletics Olympic gold.

Miss Peters, a five feet eight inch blonde, who works as secretary-assistant and general factotum to her coach Buster McShane in his health studios, started with a superb hurdles of 13.29 seconds to gain a 33-point advantage over Miss Pollak. Then, with fifty-three feet one and three-quarters inches in the shot putt, she increased her lead by another six points. But the real eye-opener came in the high jump. Using the Fosbury flop, Miss Peters finally cleared the bar at five feet eleven and three-quarter inches – a height bettered among British girls only by Barbara Inkpen.

In the long jump Miss Rosendhal took back one hundred and eighty points with a twenty-two feet five inch leap, and Miss Pollak recovered fifty points with twenty feet four and a half inches. Miss Peters narrowly avoided a no-jump to return nineteen feet seven and a half inches. Then came the 200 metres and an overall improvement of one hundred and seventy-one points on her previous British record. To complete a great day for Miss Peters she was reunited with her father shortly after the race. Unknown to her he had travelled from Australia, where he has been living for the past two years.

––––––––

5 SEPTEMBER 1972

SPITZ CLAIMS RECORD SEVENTH GOLD

Pat Besford in Munich

Mark Spitz of the United States made history in Munich last night by winning his seventh gold medal of the twentieth Olympics – a unique achievement in the seventy-six years of the modern Games. All his victories – four individual (100 and 200 metres freestyle and butterfly) and three relays – were gained in world record time, culminating in the storming American first place in the 4 × 100 metres medley relay in two minutes 48.2 seconds.

———

6 SEPTEMBER 1972

HOSTAGES KILLED IN GUN BATTLE
ARAB GUNMEN MURDER ISRAELIS
FOUR TERRORISTS DIE IN AMBUSH
AT AIRPORT

James Coote, David Shears and David Miller in Munich

Nine Israeli athletes and officials who had been held hostage in the Olympic Village for fifteen hours by Arab guerrillas were killed last night during a gun battle at a military airport twenty-five miles from Munich. The battle started when West German police ambushed the guerrillas and their hostages. Four Arabs were killed, three captured and one not accounted for. One policeman died in the battle.

The hostages were seized in a dawn raid on the Israeli headquarters at the Olympic Village by terrorists of the extremist Arab 'Black September' group. Two members of the Israeli team were shot dead by the Arabs in the initial attack. The Olympic Games were suspended until this afternoon. After hours of negotiations, directed by the West German Chancellor, Herr Brandt, the guerrillas were told that they and their hostages would be flown to an Arab country. The guerrillas and their captives were taken by helicopter from the Olympic Village to the Fürstenfeldbrück military airport. A Lufthansa Boeing 727 was at the airfield when they arrived. But Herr Ahlers, Bonn Government spokesman, said in a television interview later that there had been no intention of putting the guerrillas and the hostages aboard the plane.

As the hostages and the guerrillas walked towards the airliner, sharpshooters hidden in the darkness behind the plane opened fire. The guerrillas fired back, and the exchange of fire continued for several minutes before police fired flares to light up the scene. Before the shooting broke out, two of the guerrillas had left the helicopters and inspected the airliner. They returned to the helicopters, brought out the hostages and began marching them towards the airliner. It was at this point that police hidden behind the Boeing jet opened up with machine pistols.

The guerrillas and their hostages had been taken to three helicopters in the Olympic Village by bus. But the first bus provided by the Germans was not big enough and the terrorist leader sent it back demanding a bigger one so that he could supervise the prisoners more easily. When the second bus came, a khaki army vehicle, it had barred windows and was at least a 30-seater. When the hostages and their captors emerged it could be seen that some of the Israelis had been blindfolded and that others had their hands tied.

In their early negotiations with the West German authorities the guerrillas said they would start shooting their Israeli hostages at noon unless the Israeli Government released two hundred and thirty Arab political prisoners. These prisoners include Kozo Okamoto, the Japanese guerrilla sentenced to life imprisonment for his part in the Lydda airport massacre in May. The terrorists also demanded safe conduct from the Village and a plane to fly them out of Munich. If these demands were not met, they said, one hostage would be shot every hour from noon. But the noon deadline passed without further killings. Munich's police chief, Herr Schreiber and the Interior Minister, Herr Genescher, went into the building to negotiate with the terrorists. They returned at 1 p.m. refusing to talk. Shortly afterwards six armoured cars moved into position around the building.

The deadline for the shootings was extended hour by hour throughout the afternoon and evening. Police and troops cordoned off the Olympic Village and only athletes and officials were allowed in. Journalists and even many of the Village workers were forbidden to enter. As the negotiations went on one of the gunmen sat on the balcony on the first floor, his machine gun cradled between his legs. Sometimes he waved to athletes in the distance. The other four guerrillas stayed with the hostages out of sight. There was a completely unreal atmosphere about the whole affair. For while the nine Israeli hostages wondered whether they would be shot dead, athletes were strolling about or sunbathing only a few yards away. Police, camouflaged in tracksuits, but wearing ordinary black shoes, took up positions around the besieged building. There were fifteen to twenty groups of police, all equipped either with revolvers or 40-shot automatic machine pistols. There were also three marksmen waiting discreetly in the background.

One senior police officer told me as he munched his lunch of a dry roll and lemonade that they had no intention of going in. 'It is much too dangerous to attack with the hostages' lives at stake. We are prepared to sit things out.' Athletes I spoke to could not grasp the reality of the situation. Most were desperately worried that this might delay or even halt the Games – fears which proved to be true later on.

At 2.45 the guerrillas called for food. This on the orders of Herr Schreiber, was laced with a soporific drug in the hopes that the gunmen would eat the food and fall asleep. Unfortunately the trick rebounded, for the gunmen ordered the Israelis to eat the food and then sat back and waited for the dope to take effect.

An announcement that the Games were being interrupted came from Herr Hans Klein, chief press spokesman of the Olympic organising committee, at a packed press conference at 3.45 p.m. He read this statement from Mr Avery Brundage, president of the International Olympic Committee, and Herr Willi Daume, president of the Olympic organising committee: 'The Olympic peace has been broken by an act of assassination by criminal terrorists. The whole civilised world condemns this barbaric crime, this horror. With deep respect for the victims and as a sign of sympathy with the hostages not yet released this afternoon's sports events are being cancelled. The I.O.C. and O.O.C. will hold services in commemoration of the victims in a ceremony which will take place tomorrow, 6 September, 1972, at 10 a.m. in the Olympic Stadium. This ceremony will demonstrate that the Olympic Idea is stronger than terror or violence.'

---

6 SEPTEMBER 1972

PATTISSON AND DAVIES MAKE SURE WITH FOURTH VICTORY

Tony Fairchild at Kiel

Although it was uncertain late last night how the tragic events of Munich would affect the yachting Olympics at Kiel, Rodney Pattisson was already sure of becoming the first British yachtsman to win gold medals in successive Games. Before the announcement that the Games would be suspended, Pattisson and his crew, Chris Davies, made sure of overall victory in the Flying Dutchman series by winning yesterday's sixth race in *Superdoso*. *Superdoso*'s win was her fourth of the series and, since the 5.7-points total of Pattisson and Davies cannot be beaten, they do not need to sail in the remaining race of the seven-heat series – if it is run.

Games officials stated in Kiel last night that they hoped to continue the yachting today and were waiting a decision on this from Munich. If the yachting should be cancelled, then the International Yacht Racing Union rules relating to cancelled races will apply at Kiel: 'If there are not the scheduled seven races, then five out of six will count; if six races have not been sailed the results of all five count.'

Pattisson, who won his first gold medal in the 1968 Olympics in Mexico, when he was partnered by Iain Macdonald-Smith, had an easy victory. The north-north-westerly of between Force 2-3 remained reasonably steady for the Dutchmen, who shared the same course as the Tempests and Stars. The Dutchmen raced first and, although Pattisson and Davies lay fourth at the end of the first beat, the French Pajot brothers, the only real threat to the Britons, were twenty-third and out of the reckoning. After the first 1.4-mile reach *Superdoso* was ahead, however, and although she lost her lead just briefly on the second reach of the Olympic triangle, Pattisson quickly regained control of the front and remained there to the finish.

Never fond of being in the public eye or eager to talk about his sailing or his successes, Pattisson was thronged by admirers after his victory. He will have to get used to the idea that he has taken over from the Dane, Paul Elvstrom, the winner of four golds, as the world's top Olympic helmsman. Chris Davies, who is to be married in a fortnight's time, will not be crewing for Pattisson after the Games. He is to build a 12-foot National and sail it with his wife.

————

7 SEPTEMBER 1972

FURY AT GAMES MASSACRE
KILLERS TOOK JOBS IN OLYMPIC VILLAGE
ATHLETES MOURN ELEVEN DEAD ISRAELIS

Amid worldwide condemnation at the murder of eleven Israeli Olympic hostages by Arab guerrillas, West German authorities opened an inquiry last night into their ambush rescue plan that ended in disaster. German police admitted firing first after the terrorists and nine hostages touched down in helicopters at Fürstenfeldbrück airbase. Police marksmen failed to kill all the terrorists in their opening burst and in the battle that followed nine hostages, a policeman and five gunmen died.

As detectives questioned the three Arabs who were captured after the battle and bitter recrimination raged over fixing the blame for the airport disaster, it was claimed that the marksmen fired at the order of an unidentified police captain. He gave the order after two of the terrorists had left the helicopters to inspect the Boeing 727 airliner which they had demanded should fly them to Cairo. One of the terrorists was shot dead. Another was wounded. As he fell he fired his Russian-made submachine gun, killing a policeman. The other guerrillas promptly killed the hostages.

A second storm raged around West German ministers and officials because of the long delay in admitting that the hostages had been killed. Herr Conrad Ahlers, the Bonn Government spokesman, said that the original statement that the hostages were safe was based on information from the police. When it was realised forty-five minutes later that they were dead, it was 'too late' to issue a correction on television. The mistake went uncorrected for four hours, and newspapers, including those in West Germany, were misled.

The captured Arabs, Ibrahim Badran, twenty, Abd es Kadir el Dnawy and Samar Mohamed Abdulah, twenty-two, said they were students. Their nationalities are not known but they said they last lived in Jordan and Syria. Their location is being kept secret to guard against rescue attempts. Police are investigating how the ringleader of the massacre was able to work as an engineer on the Olympic building site. Two of the terrorists also worked as a gardener and a cook in the Olympic Village where two Israelis were killed at the start of Tuesday's siege. Mr Eban, Israel's Foreign Minister, said that the responsibility for the murder rested on countries who gave terrorists refuge. He reaffirmed his country's view that the Olympics should not continue.

But the Games were resumed yesterday after a memorial service which filled the Olympic Stadium. Tunisia was the only Arab country to attend. Some athletes followed the lead of Israeli and Egyptian teams in withdrawing, but the mood of many was summed up by David Hemery, the bronze medallist, who said: 'If something that is basically awful stops what is basically good, that makes two wrongs. And two wrongs do not make a right.'

7 SEPTEMBER 1972

JUST A MOMENT'S SILENCE IN CITY OF TRAGEDY

Donald Saunders in Munich

The show must go on, no matter what. That clearly is the view of the International Olympic Committee, who yesterday ordered the resumption of the Munich Games, despite the murder of eleven members of the Israeli team by Arab terrorists. Possibly, one day, that attitude will be seen to have been realistic, not callous. I doubt, however, whether the decision to restart this festival of sport with indecent haste, will ever be successfully defended.

Avery Brundage, retiring president of the I.O.C., solemnly announced a day of mourning at a memorial service attended by eighty thousand people at the Olympic Stadium yesterday morning. Within a few hours, fellow villagers of the slain Israelis were playing basketball, volleyball, handball and football; wrestling, boxing and fencing for Olympic medals. The official explanation was that the 24-hour mourning period had begun at 4 p.m. on Tuesday – when nine of the eleven victims of the terrorist attack were still alive.

Obviously, the need to make up the time lost by Tuesday evening's inconvenient suspension of the Games was considered so pressing that only a brief pause could be allowed to remember those who died at Munich's military airport. Perhaps that is why some of us now living in this city, which has endured more than its share of tragedies during the past forty years, believe the Games, far from being suspended for twenty-four hours, should have been abandoned. Sport was offered a great opportunity yesterday to demonstrate its disgust at the intrusion of political violence into the very heart of its world. Instead it shook its head sadly, then quickly looked the other way.

Consequently, the I.O.C. have left themselves wide open to accusations of submitting to commercial pressure. Already, I have heard it suggested that the Games would have been called off if bookings for the remaining days had not been so good. Amid the cynicism there may be a grain of truth. I suspect, however, that the I.O.C. decided on resumption because they feared abandonment would be interpreted as a victory for political terrorism.

I have yet to meet anyone over the age of thirty-five, and not engrossed in Olympic competition, administration, organisation or training, who agrees with the decision to carry on. A German of my acquaintance aptly summed up the attitude of many of his compatriots to the I.O.C.'s decision, shortly after it was announced: 'When you give a party in your home and some of your guests are murdered, you do not remove the bodies, then carry on celebrating,' he suggested.

————

I I SEPTEMBER I972

BRITISH RELAY MEN SO NEAR GLORY ON FINNS' GOLDEN DAY

James Coote in Munich

In a wonderful final day's athletics at the Munich Olympics, when Finland found gold in the 1,500 and 5,000 metres, Britain doubled her final medal tally with silver in the 4 × 400 metres relay and a bronze in the 5,000 metres.

With the United States, who had been firm favourites, unable to stand because of the absence of Wayne Collett and Vince Matthews, Britain's relay runners seized their chance. It was essential that Martin Reynolds, Alan Pascoe and David Hemery kept Britain in contention to give the powerful David Jenkins a chance on the final leg. Strong though Jenkins is, no one can close a ten-yard gap on Karl Honz, West Germany's European record holder, Julius Sang, bronze medallist in the 400 metres, or indeed Jan Werner, the Pole. Reynolds started with a steady 46.3 seconds, handing over to Pascoe behind Kenya, Finland and Poland – but not that far back. Pascoe, whose transition from hurdles to flat relay racing has been a revelation, was unable to stop West Germany and Sweden going ahead, but he still ran his leg in a personal best 45.1 seconds to finish a close-up fifth. Hemery, already the winner of a bronze in the 400 metres hurdles, snatched the baton and, within forty yards, had moved up with the leaders. He was able to hand over to Jenkins for the crucial last leg a mere yard behind the West German leader, Honz, having covered his stretch in 44.9 seconds.

Jenkins did not let anyone down. He closed up to Sang, who in turn took care of the German with two hundred metres to go, and then, arms flailing in that now familiar action, attempted to achieve the impossible and overtake the Kenyan. That he could not is no disgrace. Instead, he must be given great credit for a run timed at 44.2 seconds – a tremendous performance surpassed only by Sang's 43.6. It took Britain to an overall time of three minutes 0.5 seconds, the best ever by a British team, and a share in the European record held jointly by Poland and West Germany. Kenya's winning time of two minutes 59.8 seconds was slower than their second-place time in 1968, reflecting no doubt the absence of the American favourites.

Ian Stewart, the Birmingham gunsmith who has worked only part-time for the past four years so that he could prepare for the Olympic 5,000 metres, was rewarded with the bronze medal. Stewart, and many others in the 14-man field, were thrown off balance because no one would set the pace. David Bedford, the European record holder, looked lethargic and never offered a serious challenge. So it was a painfully slow first 3,000 metres, with first Ian McCafferty, of Britain, going ahead and then Nikolai Sviridov, of Russia. Then Lasse Viren, already winner of the 10,000 metres, decided to take action. With seven-and-a-half laps to go Bedford showed briefly. Then it was the turn of Steve Prefontaine, of the United States. McCafferty took over again a lap later before he allowed Frank Eisenberg, of East Germany, to lead. Prefontaine pushed the pace even further, but the reigning champion, Mohamed Gammoudi, of Tunisia, always looked ready to pounce.

The last lap came with Stewart, who has a good sprint finish, well in contention but, as so often in these Games, British hopes were premature. Stewart could not raise his pace and at one point looked as if he would do no better than fourth behind Viren, Gammoudi and Prefontaine. However, the American tired and Stewart just forced his way past for third place in thirteen minutes 27.6 seconds. Viren's time of thirteen minutes 26.4 seconds was an Olympic record but, more important, he became the first man since Emil Zatopek in 1952 and Vladimir Kuts, in 1956, to do the 5,000-10,000 metres double.

Then, when his team colleague Pekka Vasala won the 1,500 metres, it marked the best Olympics Finland have enjoyed since 1936 when they dominated the 5,000 and 10,000 metres and the steeplechase. Vasala took the opportunity to overtake a tired Kip Keino. Brendan Foster, from Gateshead, who equalled the British record in the heats, ran with spirit. He set the pace for the first six hundred metres and, though he was overtaken, he fought back bravely to finish fifth.

I I SEPTEMBER 1972

McCAFFERTY RAN LIKE DONKEY, SAYS WIFE

Mrs Betty McCafferty, twenty-six, watched the television broadcast of her husband Ian finishing eleventh in the Olympic 5,000 metres yesterday and then commented: 'He ran like a flaming donkey.' She said at Carluke, Lanarkshire: 'He is hanging up his spikes for ever. I can't take any more of this. My nerves are shattered by it all. I am waiting in for him no longer.' Mrs McCafferty, who on Tuesday told her husband she was expecting their first child, added: 'It should have been a walkover for him. I feel awful. Those months of staying in while he trained have all been in vain.'

---

12 SEPTEMBER 1972

LEADING ARTICLE
AFTER THE OLYMPICS

Munich's gas-powered Olympic Flame was extinguished last night, and there will be many people around the world who will greet that with a great sigh of relief. Leaving aside for the moment individual achievements, of which there were many fine ones, and records set, which were astonishingly numerous, this has been a horrible, hag-ridden Games. The veteran Avery Brundage, who now retires after twenty years as president, deserved a better end to his presidency than this.

Far overshadowing everything else, came last Tuesday's murder by Palestinian terrorists of eleven members of the Israeli team. The massacre was nationalism at its most rampant and rabid – and by and large it was nationalism in its varied forms which contributed most, at Munich as at Mexico City and Tokyo, to spoiling the atmosphere of the Games. If the Games are to continue, as they surely will, means must be found to curb it.

The I.O.C. should concentrate on this aspect between now and 1976, when the Games are due to be held in Montreal. The aim should be to emphasise individuals as opposed to countries. A first step towards this could well be to cut out the flag-raising and playing of national anthems at the medal presentations and reducing the martial processions of national teams in their national uniforms. In addition, the sheer bulk of the events should be reduced, possibly by eliminating many team sports. Spontaneous sporting patriotism can introduce quite enough nationalism without all this formal exaggeration. One of the rules says the Games are intended to 'create international respect and good will, and help to construct a better and more peaceful world.' Munich has done the opposite.

6

MONTREAL 1976

17 JULY 1976

AS THE BICKERING SUBSIDES MONTREAL FINDS ITS TRUE ROLE

Donald Saunders in Montreal

The most expensive festival in the long, extravagant history of sport will begin on time, this afternoon, at its originally specified venue, Montreal, when The Queen opens the twenty-first Olympic Games of the modern era. That in itself is an achievement of major significance by a city that has been obliged to live for the last three years under the constant threat of cancellation, and the ignominy such a disaster would bring in its wake.

Since the organising committee (Cojo) first realised, around 1972, the magnitude of the task they had eagerly, and so naively, undertaken two years earlier, Montreal has been shaken to its foundations by financial scandals, political warfare and industrial strife. This afternoon it will haul itself off the floor, battle-scarred, weary but still unbowed, to demonstrate to the world that sport has not yet fallen entirely into the clutches of politics and commerce. During the next fortnight, the now notorious unfinished tower that should have looked down majestically on proceedings, the bitter complaints of taxpayers who will foot the mammoth bill for Cojo's gross misjudgments and the racial debates that have raged in the Olympic committee rooms this past week will all be forgotten. Even those of us who detest the infiltration of commerce into amateur sport will temporarily turn a blind eye to the steady stream of athletes flowing through the plush offices of boot, shoe, shirt and tracksuit manufacturers.

We have to accept that this is an imperfect world and sport increasingly reflects its greed, corruption, dishonesty, intolerance, lust for power, nationalism, and willingness to resort to blackmail and violence with little thought for the consequences. Fortunately, most of the young men and women who will march self-consciously into the stadium this afternoon will not be tarnished by these human failings. There will be no medals, no glory, no illegal contracts for them. Their only reward will be the privilege of being present at amateur sport's most exclusive assembly. They may well treasure happier memories of their visit to Canada than more successful competitors who abuse their bodies and torture their minds in the relentless pursuit of success.

Nor are the Games any longer simply a jamboree for a few thousand athletes and a spectacle for a few thousand fans. Since 1964, television cameras and communication satellites have transformed the Olympics into a festival in which much of the world can participate. Millions, seated before their screens, will share the joy or the tears of their idols. Millions more will be delighted by the rise from obscurity to stardom of an unknown boy or girl, be he or she black, white, brown or yellow.

Let us hope that, sometime during the next fortnight, another minority sport will give birth to a star who will transform it into a worldwide pastime. That would be handsome compensation for the tedious repetition on the world's television screens of solemn national anthems that will re-emphasise the continued domination of the Olympics by the huge battalions of track and field athletes from the United States, the Soviet Union and East Germany.

---

20 JULY 1976

TOUCHÉ: RUSSIAN WITH A BUGGED BLADE BANNED

James Coote in Montreal

A Russian champion fencer was barred from the Montreal Games yesterday for blatant cheating by fighting two British opponents with a 'bugged' épée wired electrically to register hits illegally. An immediate inquiry by officials at the modern pentathlon revealed two bared wires in the épée which caused a short circuit when crossed with another piece of wire carried secretly in the weapon's handle. The cheating by Boris

Onischenko, silver medallist at the Mexico City and Munich Olympics and a gold medallist in the 1969, 1973 and 1974 world team championships, has ruined the Russian team's chances of repeating their Munich gold medal win.

In the competition, both opponents are wired to a control box on the judges' table. Any hit is registered by a bell-push type of device on the tip of the electric épée, which sets a light flashing on the control box. What Onischenko was doing was completing the circuit inside the bell-push by using the rigged wiring. Mr Carl Schwende, chief of discipline in charge of fencing, himself a former international fencer, said the rigging had been hidden in the handle. 'There was a tight skin over the handle so you could not detect the extent of the wiring,' he said. Colonel Wille Grut, secretary-general of the International Union of Modern Pentathlon and Biathlon, said officials were absolutely convinced it was a case of blatant cheating.

In the first bout of the morning between Britain and Russia, Onischenko faced Adrian Parker, the British number two, and the light went on as if he had hit Parker. The Briton protested, but as the recording equipment was found to be functioning correctly the hit stood. The next fight was with Jim Fox, who is competing in his fourth Olympics, and is possibly the most experienced pentathlete in the world. As Onischenko advanced towards Fox the registering equipment lit and the Russian said immediately: 'It is a mistake', and tried to change his weapon. Reporting the incident, Moscow Radio said Onischenko 'was fencing with a sword that did not meet the requirements of international rules. So a disappointing mistake has occurred'.

---

21 JULY 1976

WILKIE WINS SILVER MEDAL FOR BRITAIN
Pat Besford in Montreal

David Wilkie won Britain's first medal of the twenty-first Olympic Games in Montreal last night — a silver in the 100 metres breaststroke behind John Hencken of the United States, to add to the silver he gained in the 200 metres breaststroke, also behind Hencken, in Munich in 1972. The American clocked a world and Olympic record of one minute 3.11 seconds. Wilkie was a forearm behind in one minute 3.43 seconds, a European and Commonwealth record, and also inside the old world record.

The short, powerful, fair-haired Hencken, from California, held a one-second lead over the tall, slim, white-capped Briton as they touched at fifty metres, with Wilkie, at this stage, in sixth place. After the turn Wilkie powered up the pool, closing all the time on his great rival. But, with ten metres to go, Hencken held his place to win his second gold. This tremendous performance by Wilkie, who, like Hencken, is twenty-two, improved his previous best time by nearly a second to give great promise for success in the 200 metres breaststroke, his better distance, on Sunday. Duncan Goodhew, nineteen, from Yapton, Sussex, finished seventh in an exciting final.

---

23 JULY 1976
CAPTIVATING NADIA HERALDS NEW ERA
James Coote in Montreal

She is the epitome of perfection in her chosen sport – the tiny teenager no one in Montreal can fail to love; a gymnast captivating all who watch her. Not Olga Korbut, but Romania's Nadia Comaneci. Nadia is a young queen heralding a new era in a sport which is developing faster than most. Where Olga conquered the world with her tiny, fragile form and her delicate waif-like smile in that now immortal routine in the floor exercises in Munich, Nadia's aura surrounds her whatever she accomplishes on the floor and off the mat. Miss Korbut, from the Soviet Union, lost her innocence and fragility directly she finished her routine. Nadia, from a country where the smile has not been forgotten, is more natural a person. To see her spontaneous delight after she had scored the first-ever maximum ten points in an Olympic exercise made one realise that despite the last eight years' training up to five hours a day, she is still a normal 14-year-old schoolgirl.

Do not imagine that Nadia's Olympic and European gold medal are isolated flukes from a backward gymnastic nation. Along with her equally captivating team-mates, who won the team silver medal, especially the lovely Teodora Ungureanu, they are the peak of a broad-based pinnacle. It is the culmination of a 16-year climb which started, two years before Nadia was born, as the result of crushing defeats in the 1960 Olympics in Rome. Gymnastic teachers and coaches were sent by the government around the schools, scouring for all the available talent, the best of which was sent to special gymnastic colleges, four for boys, five for girls.

Bela Karoly, a Hungarian living in Romania, discovered Nadia in the town of Gheorghe Gheorghiu-Dej. Even at the age of six she possessed a special talent which, if handled properly, could become a world-beating factor. Nadia was taken to the gymnast school at Onesti. Her parents went along, too, and were given special social benefits, in the form of money and kind, which enabled them to give Nadia a stable and trouble-free home-life.

Nadia's training was progressive. Until the age of ten she trained, first one, then two, three and finally four hours daily in addition to her normal scholastic classes. From the start she was given special exercises to make her body supple and she was taught to appreciate and understand music, which is so essential to the potential gymnast. She received instruction in acrobatics and classical dance, with an emphasis on making both a pleasure – never a mental or physical strain.

During this time no set work is given to the pupils on the asymmetrical bars, beams or horse, although the equipment is used during their normal class work and they are encouraged to become completely familiar and never to feel frightened using them. By the age of ten they are ready to become gymnasts. They graduate from the playschool to the hard reality of exercising five hours daily. And this is where Nadia really showed. With so many potentially good gymnasts in her classes, Nadia had to work hard. Yet she progressed, through monthly exams, local Spartakiades, regional championships, making her international debut in 1971 at the age of ten. When not even fourteen, she became the youngest European overall champion, presenting exercises of such high difficulty that they have been homologated by the international gymnastics federation in her name. Thus, when she came to Montreal, much was expected. Yet her conquest of the 'invincible' Russians surprised the most knowledgeable experts.

---

23 JULY 1976

BRITAIN TAKE TEAM GOLD IN MODERN PENTATHLON

James Coote in Montreal

The modern pentathletes won Britain's first gold medal of the twenty-first Olympic Games in Montreal yesterday when after three magnificent runs, they came through to win from their overnight fifth position. Overnight Britain were one hundred and fifty points behind the leaders Czechoslovakia, but three inspired cross-country runs by Adrian Parker, Danny Nightingale and Jim Fox put them so far ahead that they were able to win the overall team competition by more than one hundred points. Britain totalled 15,559 points compared with runners-up Czechoslovakia's 15,451, with Hungary third on 15,395.

This was Britain's first medal in the event in an Olympic Games and was no doubt inspired by Fox, the veteran of the team, competing in his fourth and last Olympics. Last year Fox won a bronze medal in the world championships and his example has inspired a new breed of modern pentathletes. There was quiet hope before the team came to Montreal that an overall medal was possible. However after the unfortunate disqualification of the Russian Boris Onischenko, the world team champion gold medallist, Fox lost concentration and it seemed with it the team's medal hopes. Fox was so shocked by the action of his old sporting comrade that he lost valuable points in the fencing, which with running, swimming, shooting and riding make up the competition. Surprisingly it was his young colleagues who steadied him, though they did no more than hold their own in the shooting.

Going into the final day Britain on 11,608 points were one hundred and thirty-one behind the United States, one hundred and fifty behind Poland, two hundred and twenty-three behind Hungary and five hundred and thirty-seven behind Czechoslovakia. Ron Bright, the team coach, and Mike Proudfoot, the team manager, knew that they could beat the Hungarians and the Americans. What no one knew was the strength of the Czechoslovaks who had been going excellently this year and the Poles, for whom Janusz Pyciak-Peciak won the individual competition.

As it happened, Parker, drawn first of the entire field of forty-six, set a fantastic pace of twelve minutes nine seconds, which no one else was able to approach. This gave him the remarkable total of 1,378 points (putting him just outside the individual medal lists). He was followed by Nightingale, who ran twelve minutes thirty-two seconds for 1,309 points, and finally Fox who, in the bravest run of his career on an undulating course which was a killer for big men such as he, came home in twelve minutes forty-seven seconds for 1,264 points. This gave the team a massive 3,951 points, 370-odd points ahead of the second-best nation, Poland.

---

25 JULY 1976

GOLD – AND WORLD RECORD FOR WILKIE

Anita Lonsbrough

David Wilkie fulfilled his lifelong ambition to become an Olympic champion in tremendous style in Montreal last night. This was the moment not only the tall Scot had waited for, but something all British swimming supporters have awaited for over fifty years. Britain's first male gold medal winner and the first time our national anthem has been played in an Olympic swimming pool for sixteen years.

Wilkie, looking fit and tanned, won his gold in tremendous style and in the best way possible – in a world record. He led at the first fifty metres, which must have surprised even his arch-rival John Hencken, of the United States. But Hencken was not going to give up without a fight and he drew level and went into a slight lead, but Wilkie was right at his shoulder. As the eight swimmers went up the pool for the second time, Wilkie changed into top gear and started to move ahead. Once he was in the lead, there was just no catching this American-trained Scot.

After his great swim in the 100 metres, where he collected a silver, Wilkie started to relax because he knew his form was good, he knew what he was capable of, and he surpassed his own wildest dreams. He admitted before the Games started that he would go around two minutes 15.8 seconds, but he went even faster. With his gold medal round his neck, Wilkie said: 'I took the first hundred metres slower than I intended and had so much left at the last length. But I swam the race exactly as I had intended and I think Hencken swam his the only way possible. I thought all the year I could break two minutes sixteen seconds, but until today I had never put it all together. This is my last race and it is great to go out as Olympic champion.'

––––––––

27 JULY 1976

FOSTER STRUGGLES TO BRONZE BEHIND VIREN AND LOPES

James Coote in Montreal

Brendan Foster became only the second man in Olympic history to win a 10,000 metres medal for Great Britain when he finished third in Montreal last night. The title went to Lasse Viren, of Finland, who became the second man to retain his 10,000 metres title since the Games began, and the silver medal went to a gallant little Portuguese, Carlos Lopes, who cut out the pace that cracked the entire field, with the exception of Viren.

Lopes first made his name when he won the international cross-country championship in Chepstow in March – and he will never be forgotten after the way he tried to run everyone into the ground last night. After eight laps, with seventeen to go, he took the lead and held it until that last four hundred and fifty metres, occasionally glancing back to see what was happening. Just after the 5,000-metre mark, reached in fourteen minutes 8.9 seconds – compared with thirteen minutes 39.4 seconds in Dave Bedford's world record race of twenty-seven minutes 30.8 seconds – Foster looked to be set for one of his famous breaks. But it did not happen. With ten laps left, Mark Smet, who had fallen over just like Viren in the 1972 final, moved up behind Lopes, with Foster fourth and Viren third. Already a gap had opened, Simmons being some way behind in fifth place.

With eight-and-a-half laps remaining, Lopes made a little burst, looked around, and knew that the gold medal was between himself and Viren. Foster was too far behind to make an impression. Viren was obviously wanting to spring, but he held on as late as he dared. Then, when he went, there was a sudden display of Finnish flags throughout the stadium. Foster wearily hauled his body round the final lap and Simmons almost caught him with a brave last sprint.

---

27 JULY 1976

LEADING ARTICLE
MONTREAL'S PROFESSIONALS

What about those East Germans, then, eh? Much smaller population than Britain; already got ten times as many gold medals as us: poor old Britain, always making excuses. And so on. From the average saloon bar all the way down to the average plateglass senior common room, that sort of thing is, no doubt, the standard patter about Montreal from Britain's sophisticates – many of them bores of Olympic calibre. Furthermore – and this variation is especially popular among television critics short of a joke – it is considered side-splitting every time a BBC commentator observes that some British Fiona or Linda may have lost, but was true to the Olympic ideal. All of which just goes to show how stupid clever people can be.

For – and at the risk of providing a few further guffaws – Olympic athletes are supposed to be *amateurs*. Is it imagined that the undeniably formidable but manifestly full-time, obviously professional, specially-fed, frequently grotesque representatives of Communist civilisation sent to Montreal show us up in a bad light? Is it assumed that Britain would be incapable of producing such specimens? Of course we could. All that is needed is a totalitarian system of government – that is, a system which politicises and organises the nation's sport as it does the nation's everything else.

So it is true that, after the seventh day at Montreal, six countries which have smaller populations than Britain were above us in the medals table. All six were Communist dictatorships. Compared with her fellow open societies of comparable size, Britain was not doing too badly. We have had only two gold medals, and West Germany is likely to win several times fewer gold medals than East Germany. Yet, from other indices of well-being, the world does not get the impression that the West Germans are pathetic or incompetent people. Next time, the Olympics will be held in Moscow. It will be interesting to see how many Western competitors defect.

---

28 JULY 1976
WHITE AND OSBORN TAKE GOLD MEDAL: PATTISSON SILVER
Tony Fairchild in Kingston, Ontario

Reg White and John Osborn, Britain's brothers-in-law Tornado crew, made sure of a gold medal with a race to spare in the Olympic yachting regatta at Kingston, on Lake Ontario, yesterday. They led all the way in the sixth race to notch their fourth victory – the best record of the one hundred and thirty crews from forty-one nations – and do not need to compete in today's final heat. Rodney Pattisson, a sad victim of the shifty conditions apparent for most of the seven races, failed in his quest for a hat-trick of Flying Dutchman gold medals. He was beaten by Joerg and Eckhart Diesch, of West Germany, and had to settle for a silver medal.

Pattisson, crewed in his *Superdoso* by Julian Brooke-Houghton, was expected to meet tough resistance from the talented Germans. He still has a magnificent record and has served his country well in three Olympics. Pattisson had to beat the Dieschs convincingly in the last race to retain a hope of a gold medal, and it was clear from a bad start that he had little chance of so doing, except perhaps for one of his spectacular charges. He lay fifteenth at the first mark, three behind the Germans. The Dieschs finished fifth and Pattisson eleventh – though at one stage he was in danger of finishing in a bronze-medal position. White and Osborn, though acknowledging the tough opposition, were never seriously troubled throughout the regatta, let alone in their last race.

---

31 JULY 1976

VIREN MAKES IT A GREAT DOUBLE AS FOSTER FALTERS

James Coote in Montreal

Lasse Viren, of Finland, became the first man in Olympic history to complete a 5,000-10,000 metres double in successive Games at the Olympic Stadium in Montreal yesterday. Second in yesterday's 5,000 metres was Dick Quax, of New Zealand, with the West German, Klaus-Peter Hildenbrand, throwing himself over the line to take the bronze medal ahead of the second New Zealander, Rod Dixon. Brendan Foster, Britain's 10,000 metres bronze medallist, tried to dictate the race early on, but he was unable to match the finishing sprint of his rivals and came fifth, with the second Briton in the race, Ian Stewart, seventh.

Viren dictated the race. Early on, he allowed Foster to open up the field and to wear himself out, but he was always ready if the Briton made one of his breaks. In fact, this did not happen until the third kilometre, reached in eight minutes 16.2 seconds – seven seconds slower than the 10,000 metres earlier in the week. Foster broke, but the combination of his stomach bug and the tension of knowing that the New Zealander and Viren were always close turned what should have been a long, sustained challenge into a brief, not-too-successful sortie.

With four laps to go, Hildenbrand, who had been making little impact, took the lead, followed by the Norwegian, Knut Kvalheim, and Foster. Half a lap later, Dixon decided he, too, would have an attempt at breaking up the field, but the tummy bug that put him on his back for three days early in the week, again made him too weak. Viren, the master, then made his challenge. With three laps left, he led, repeatedly putting his head down and accelerating away. Though his rivals closed the gap, it was obvious that he was weakening them far more than himself. With two laps to go, it was still Viren, but with any one of six runners capable of winning, including Foster, though he does not have the finishing power of his rivals.

The last lap was a sustained sprint, with Viren always dominant despite Quax making a challenge for the gold medal. Somehow, Viren held on, with the traditions of Finnish running to help him. His winning time of thirteen minutes 24.76 seconds was fractionally slower than in Munich, with Foster recording thirteen minutes 26.19 seconds. Foster said: 'When Viren went past me, I had to compose myself to try again. I thought I had a chance two hundred yards out. I had had four hard races out here, and I think that I ran better today than in the 10,000 metres.' Stewart said: 'I would have helped Brendan if it had been any other race, but this, after all, was an Olympic final.'

---

3 AUGUST 1976

YOUNGSTERS GIVE OLYMPIC MOVEMENT HOPE FOR FUTURE

Donald Saunders in Montreal

As the chaos begins to clear at Montreal's Mirabel and Dorval airports, and the elite of the world's amateur sportsmen and women start the long journey home, the Olympic Movement can sit back and sigh with relief. Yet again it has struggled through to victory over politics, racism, commercialism, corruption, nationalism and plain stupidity. For that small mercy, sport must thank not the old men who argue in committee rooms but the youngsters who have striven for glory, honour or simple satisfaction on the tracks and fields and in the pools, lakes and arenas these past two weeks.

Flying home from Munich in September 1972, I vowed that never again would I visit the Olympic Games – if, indeed, the Movement lasted long enough for them to be staged even once more. Now, as thousands of us prepare to leave Montreal, I am so glad I changed my mind. Three weeks in Quebec have changed abject pessimism at least into limited optimism.

Having shrugged off the effect of a wholesale walkout by black Africa, its newest, most troublesome and potentially its most dangerous political bloc, the Olympic Movement surely can live on. Circumstances, for once, should aid survival. The next Games are scheduled for Moscow, so though Peking may wield some influence here and there, another large-scale boycott is unlikely. In any case, the likes of Kenya and Tanzania, who have lost so much by absenting themselves from the athletics track, and Nigeria and Ghana, potential powers in the boxing ring, now know they are not indispensable.

The twenty-first Games have achieved a high standard of sport without black Africa, especially on the main stadium's track and field and in the swimming pool. No one who visited these venues, or sat before their television screen, is likely to forget the achievement of Lasse Viren, the thin, bearded Finnish long-distance runner. As he crossed the line – first in the 10,000 metres, then in the five – hands reaching for the sky, his gesture of triumph surely must have uplifted even the most acutely depressed spirit, if only momentarily.

But before the Games of the twenty-first Olympiad have become faded entries in the yellowing pages of old record books, one picture surely will still be firmly fixed in the minds of all who watched them. Without any shadow of doubt the star of the once almost cancelled, sometimes chaotic, often brilliant and rarely dull Montreal show has been Nadia Comaneci, that wide-eyed waif from Romania. She has completed the transformation of gymnastics from sport to art.

7

MOSCOW 1980

8 SEPTEMBER 1979

LETTERS TO THE EDITOR
ORWELLIAN SLIP

Sir — I believe the International Olympic Committee made a grave mistake in awarding the 1980 Games to Moscow. It would surely have been more appropriate to have held the 1984 Games there.

L. Brown
Swindon
Wiltshire

---

19 FEBRUARY 1980

SPORTSMEN, GO TO MOSCOW!
Denis Howell, M.P., Labour's sports spokesman, puts the case against an Olympic boycott

If the sporting ignorance of some politicians is allowed to triumph, then the Olympic Games of the XXII Olympiad may well be the last occasion when the world will enjoy them. Suddenly, sport has been discovered. Its political importance has been realised by those who very properly seek means of confronting the outrageous Russian aggression in Afghanistan. Regrettably, some of these governments are now so anxious to use sport as an arm of foreign policy that they care not whether they destroy international sport in the process.

Sportsmen should care. For, with all its problems and deficiencies, sport is one of the very few opportunities for men to draw together and express pride in the excellence of their personal achievements and in their association with their fellow men and women. It is as absurd to suggest that participation in this summer's Olympics is an endorsement of Russian policy as it is to suggest that our presence at Lake Placid automatically endorses American policy. Thankfully, our own Government understands that in a free society our citizens cannot be ordered not to leave the country. It is, therefore, very odd to read that Colonel Sir Harry Llewellyn and his British Equestrian Federation are asking the British Olympic Association to 'support any Government-directed boycott' of the Moscow Games. If the British Government issued any such 'directions' we should know that we were in Moscow already!

This leads directly to one of the principal matters of concern for the International Olympic Committee. Far too many national Olympic committees seem to be acting as agencies of their governments. The I.O.C. should have addressed itself to this issue before now and cannot ignore it any longer. I am glad to say that the twenty-three Ministers of the Council of Europe did in fact address themselves to it during my term of office as Minister of Sport. The occasion was a proposal before U.N.E.S.C.O., initiated by the then French Minister and the Afro-Asian countries, that the Olympic Games should be made the responsibility of U.N.E.S.C.O. In leading the opposition to this move, which was gathering momentum at considerable pace, I obtained the support of all my fellow European Sports Ministers. We had the full support of the U.S. Government. Such a hard-won victory must not be surrendered lightly.

If half the world does not go to Moscow this year then it is difficult to see the other half attending the Los Angeles Games in 1984. Inevitably, the world championships of forty or more sports will not escape the consequences of this catastrophe. The Olympic Movement is the pinnacle of a very complicated structure. Here in Europe, where sport is much more regionalised than in America, those European competitions, such as the European Cup, which we hold every year, would be the first to suffer. The Government would have no alternative but to ask Liverpool, Nottingham Forest and others not to proceed abroad when drawn against Russian teams.

British influence in world sport would be put seriously at risk. The British are the founding fathers of world sport. We have over one hundred of our senior administrators serving on the various international governing bodies. The attempt to supplant them has been going on for years with a degree of success. I feel that we may well end up handing over, on a plate, the position and influence which Britain has gained by generations of leadership and endeavour. Sport may well support the proposal, as I do, that the Games should have a permanent home, probably in Greece, and an international status such as that of the Red Cross, but if we have destroyed the Olympic Movement this year there can be no future inheritance for Greece or anywhere else.

I once told my Russian counterparts that the reason why I supported the decision to award the Games to Moscow is that Moscow would never be the same again. The influence of twenty-five thousand sportsmen and women expressing their freedom in that city would be one of the most significant events of our time. I believe that sportsmen still appreciate that truth and we have a duty to sustain it against all opposition.

---

22 FEBRUARY 1980
LEADING ARTICLE
OLYMPIC DILEMMAS

Many of our readers have asked us whether, if the Olympic Games take place in Moscow, we will report them. Mr Douglas Hurd of the Foreign Office is said to be on the point of putting the same question to the broadcasting authorities in Britain and even to be contemplating offering them some advice. Our own answer is simple: we shall certainly give any international sports meeting which takes place in Moscow the precise degree of coverage which its news value dictates. Even a diminished Olympic Games would have considerable interest to the readers of this newspaper, and it is their curiosity which our news coverage is intended to gratify.

This does not alter our conviction, shared with the British Government, that the Games ought not to take place in Moscow. Just as the Government recognises that it has no right to further that wish by forbidding British athletes to leave the country, so we recognise that we have no right to express it by depriving our readers of information which many of them want to have. The broadcasting institutions, which are supposed to have no editorial opinions, must surely take precisely the same view. If Mr Hurd should offer them any counsel, he should confine himself to discussing the manner in which this controversial occasion should be presented.

No one in the business of news reporting should take the view that he is free to get and disseminate news in any way which is within the limits of the law. We have more than once pointed out, for instance, that reporters and cameramen in Ulster are not absolved from the ordinary civic duty of passing on valuable information to the security forces even if the result is to spoil a good story. The BBC and the ITV should certainly not allow themselves to become mere vehicles of Soviet propaganda. But this clearly should not prevent them from giving the Olympics whatever attention their value as a sporting occasion may turn out to merit.

---

21 JULY 1980

CEREMONY BOYCOTT SHOWS THROUGH MOSCOW PAGEANTRY

Nigel Wade and Roger Heywood in Moscow

Spectacular pageantry failed to disguise the impact of the Afghanistan crisis on the opening of the Moscow Olympic Games, though Russian television tried to hide it from millions of ordinary Russians. Seven of the eighty-one countries taking part in the Games took no part in the opening parade. In each case a Russian girl in a red cape carried the team's name-board, followed by a Russian man in red jacket and white trousers holding the Olympic flag. These teams, who had demanded to be represented in this way, were those of Belgium, France, Italy, Luxembourg, the Netherlands, San Marino and Switzerland. Britain, Ireland and Portugal were each represented by one of their own officials carrying the Olympic flag.

Tanzanian team members jerked into 'a ragged' goose-step as they gave President Brezhnev the eyes-right. Russian soldiers dressed as civilians also goose-stepped down the track, clutching twenty-two white doves symbolising peace. The *Soviet Military Review,* published on the opening day, repeated Russia's claim that 'the decision to give Moscow the nod to host the Games was recognition of the Soviet Union's merits in the struggle for peace as well as its contribution to the world Olympic Movement'.

Lord Killanin, president of the International Olympic Committee, again contradicted this in his opening remarks beside the Olympic track.

'I must repeat,' he said, 'that these Games belong to the International Olympic Committee and they are allocated purely on the ability of the host city to organise them.' He thanked the participating athletes and officials for the 'independence' they had shown 'despite many pressures placed upon them'. President Brezhnev was greeted by massed buglers. An announcer read excerpts from his writings and speeches. He wore a grey suit and showed little emotion as he read out the formal words of opening. Chariots, Russian girls dressed as Grecian maidens, and thousands of dancers wearing Soviet national minority costumes took part in the lavish celebrations. Hundreds of soldiers out of uniform made fast-changing mosaics with coloured placards and held up white boards to make a human staircase for the most spectacular torch-lighting ceremony ever seen.

Mr Dick Palmer, general secretary of the British Olympic Association, was Britain's sole marcher. He carried the International Olympic flag with style and good humour, often smiling and slightly nodding his head at the non-plussed crowd, many of whom obviously did not understand why there was no team behind him. 'I felt very lonely out there,' he said, 'but it had to be done. It was Britain's protest against nationalism in the Games. Let's hope there is less of it in future.'

---

23 JULY 1980

DUNCAN GOODHEW'S GOLD GETS FLAG FLYING FOR BRITAIN

Pat Besford in Moscow

The Union Flag flew proudly at the Olympic swimming pool in Moscow last night when Duncan Goodhew won Britain's first gold medal of the 1980 summer Games. It could not be raised alongside the Russian and Australian flags as Goodhew stood on the victory rostrum after receiving his gold medal as the 100 metres breaststroke champion. But as the Olympic hymn was played instead of *God Save The Queen*, a spectator in the front of the grandstand waved the British national flag, then dipped it in salute at Goodhew's achievement.

Goodhew, twenty-three, from Yapton, Sussex, was two-hundredths of a second down on Russia's Aleksandr Fedorowski at the 50-metre turn. But he surged to the front and held his place in the closing stages to win by a metre in one minute 3.34 seconds from Arsen Miskarov, of the Soviet Union, and Australia's Peter Evans. Still unable to grasp that he had followed Britain's David Wilkie to an Olympic breaststroke title, Goodhew took me through the race as television, radio, security and medical control people crowded round, sometimes almost pushing him back into the pool.

'I didn't know I was second at the turn and I won't believe I've won until I hold that medal in my hand. I let my mind wander three-quarters of the way down the first length and came out of the turn too hard and had to ease a bit on the way back. What encouraged me was the British support and hearing people call "Duncan, Duncan" as I walked to the start in my special red-white-and-blue bathrobe.'

---

26 JULY 1980
WELLS SPRINTS TO GOLD
Ken Mays in Moscow

Allan Wells, the Scot from Edinburgh, brought glory back to British sprinting after a gap of fifty-six years when he overcame the difficulties of a dreadful lane draw to win the Olympic 100 metres gold medal in Moscow last night. It was in 1924, in Paris, that Harold Abrahams won the only gold Britain had collected at this distance, but Wells equalled his achievement magnificently.

He knew he had won and so did the hundreds of Britons in the eighty thousand crowd, but so close was the finish that they were all kept waiting for more than ten minutes. Then came the verdict. Wells had won from Cuban Silvio Leonard, with Petar Petrov, of Bulgaria, collecting the bronze. Wells had the same time of 10.25 seconds as Leonard, who had looked a winner until the Scot burst through to catch him just before the line. The time was slower than the British record Wells set on Thursday – but times meant nothing, only victory mattered. Such was the agony of the wait for the verdict that Margo, Wells's sprinter wife who missed team selection but came to Moscow to watch, dashed to the TV room to try to see a replay of the race. After the Scot had done a lap of honour, before he knew the verdict, the only thing missing when he stepped on the winner's rostrum were the National Anthem and the Union Flag. The Olympic hymn was played; the Olympic flag raised.

Wells, handicapped by running in the second round with three other heat winners, and then finding himself on the outside lane for the final, shook off all the difficulties. With great rivals such as Hasely Crawford, the reigning champion, Don Quarrie, silver medallist in Montreal, and European champion, Pietro Mennea, all falling by the wayside early on, Wells's biggest danger, apart from Leonard, was Poland's Marian Woronin. Leonard played his part superbly, but it was not just good enough, while the Pole was left in the wake of the big Scot as he powered through the field, after being well down at the 40-metre mark, to win in a devastating finish.

---

27 JULY 1980

NO-GO COE AS OVETT TAKES 800 METRES GOLD

Peter Hildreth

Gold and silver medals went to British runners in the 800 metres final in Moscow yesterday. The winner was Steve Ovett, who captured Britain's second athletics gold medal of the Olympic Games, comfortably beating the world record holder Sebastian Coe. Ovett's winning time of one minute 45.4 seconds was nearly two seconds outside the Olympic record and exactly three seconds slower than Coe's world record established last year.

Ovett re-confirmed his constitutional capacity to win the big ones however they are run. This particular race started slowly, with the Brazilian Agberto Guimaraes pulling the field through the first lap in 54.5 seconds. Coe seemed to lack lustre as he lay at the back of the field up to three hundred metres from home. After the race Coe's coach and father, Peter, admitted that his son had made a tactical error. Ovett moved off the last turn with all his familiar drive and was never troubled as he coasted to the tape completely unextended. Coe, on the other hand, left it all much too late and only overhauled the Russian Nikolai Kirov about thirty metres out.

The race was not the sensational duel that it had promised to be. Coe looked almost off colour and I do not accept that tactical error was a sufficient explanation for his weak performance. Coe was afterwards: 'I went into the race feeling I could cover everything thrown at me, but I didn't cover what was going on up front. I don't remember too much about the race. Some days you run well, some days you don't. Today I didn't.'

---

28 JULY 1980

THOMPSON AIMS TO RECAPTURE HIS WORLD RECORD

Ken Mays

Daley Thompson, who gained Britain's third gold medal of the Games, is certain to defend it in Los Angeles in 1984, determined to prove to everyone that he is the best all-round athlete in the world. Thompson said yesterday: 'I told everyone five years ago that I would win the gold in Moscow, but not everyone believed me. Some day I will get my world record back and then win in America just to prove I am the best.'

Thompson had gone from strength to strength through the ten events, starting by winning the 100 metres by twenty metres on Friday; and from that moment on there was never any real doubt as to the outcome. He shook off one challenge after another to finish with several personal bests and a total of 8,549 points, one hundred and sixty-four ahead of his Russian rival, Yuri Kutsenko, but well short of the absent Guido Kratschmer's record, an attempt on which he abandoned early on because of the wet weather. 'I decided not to go after that when I slipped over while practising for the 110 metres hurdles,' said Thompson. 'Most of the others couldn't cope with the weather.'

But Thompson does not really care what happens from now on. 'There is only one pinnacle and that is the Olympic Games, and I would not really care if I did not win another competition,' he said. Thompson, who said he became more confident that he was going to win over the two days, finished last in only the 1,500 metres, the final race on the programme, but by then it did not matter.

While the Olympic flag was raised and the Olympic hymn played, he stood on the victory rostrum, with the gold medal around his neck, conducting the singing of the National Anthem by the two hundred and sixty supporters in the crowd. Thompson did keep one man waiting – the dope-testing doctor – and it was way past midnight and a ride back to the Village before he finally gave the sample.

28 JULY 1980

COX IS HERO OF BRITISH EIGHT'S SILVER MEDAL

The eight-oared crew capped a magnificent day for British rowing at the Olympic Regatta in Moscow yesterday by beating Russia to the silver medal to add to the bronzes won in the coxless fours and pairs. The eight produced a remarkable finish to move from fourth at the halfway stage to second behind the East Germans – despite breaking a rudder string with seven hundred and fifty metres to go. Colin Moynihan, the cox, reacted so swiftly in seizing the rudder bar that his crew were not even aware of the danger.

From the start, the eight moved so smoothly into top gear that they covered the first five hundred metres in one minute 21.7 seconds to lead the field. The brisk cross-wind was not boisterous enough to disturb them and, thankfully, the temperature was several degrees lower than it had been for Thursday's semi-finals. Eights rowing demands such harmony and produces such power that, at its best, it is not only the crown of its own sport, but one of the jewels of all Olympic activities. There will be few sights in these Games more satisfying to a Briton than that of the eight in overdrive, cutting a path without fuss in pursuit of the German boat and holding off the challenge from a Soviet crew that was at least half a stone per man heavier. The British eight were Duncan McDougall (bow), Allan Whitwell, Henry Clay, Chris Mahoney, Andrew Justice, John Pritchard, Malcolm McGowan, Richard Stanhope (stroke) and Moynihan (cox).

29 JULY 1980

WELLS LOSES GOLD TO ITALIAN BY FIFTIETH OF A SECOND
Ken Mays in Moscow

Allan Wells failed by the smallest of fractions to bring the double Olympic sprint gold medals back to Britain last night. He was beaten in the final of the 200 metres by his arch-rival Pietro Mennea, of Italy, in the Lenin Stadium. Wells, who had won the 100 metres title on Friday, was beaten by a superb burst over the final twenty metres by Mennea to finish with the silver medal. As the pair crossed the lines in lanes seven and eight Wells had to suffer a long wait for the photo-finish camera to decide. Unlike last week, he lost out this time.

He was beaten by two hundredths of a second by the Italian, with reigning champion Don Quarrie of Jamaica, third. Although his time of 20.21 seconds was easily a British record for Wells, Mennea, nicknamed the 'Blue Flash' had gained his revenge. In the Europa Cup final in Turin almost a year ago to the day Wells had hurled his massive frame around the track to outpace Mennea – last night it was a different story. Wells made a brilliant start from the blocks and looked every inch the winner. He was well ahead at the halfway mark and seemed to be increasing his speed. But, then, despite his strength, he could not maintain it as the slim Mennea surged alongside him and then just managed to edge him out of the gold at the line. This time Wells looked at the television replay screen above the athletes' tunnel and walked away while Mennea went on a lap of honour to celebrate.

It was the eighth race of the Games for Wells, a marine engineer, for earlier in the day he had to go through the qualifying round in which he had no trouble cruising home in fourth place, good enough and without too much exertion. 'I don't want to take anything away from Mennea, but the 100 metres is the blue riband and I'm quite happy to go home with gold and silver,' said Wells.

---

2 AUGUST 1980

COE ANSWERS CRITICS WITH 1,500 METRES GOLD

Ken Mays in Moscow

Sebastian Coe, the gentleman of British athletics, proved that the nice guys and champions can come back when he turned the tables on Steve Ovett, his great rival, by winning the 1,500 metres gold medal at the Olympic Games in Moscow yesterday. Coe, twenty-three, ran a superbly controlled, tactically correct race to win in three minutes 38.4 seconds, with the Germany Jurgen Straub depriving Ovett, twenty-four, of the silver as he finished between the two Britons.

Coe, so disappointing when taking the silver medal behind Ovett last Saturday in the 800 metres – an event at which he is the world record holder – climbed up off the floor, so to speak, to deprive Ovett of the glory of double gold. The London-born Loughborough student, who now lives in Sheffield, had not looked at all good in the qualifying rounds, especially on Thursday night when he climbed out of a sick bed to win the semi-final. But yesterday against the brash young man from Brighton, Coe reached the summit of his personal Everest. Despite his year of record-breaking glory he could not afford to lose face once more – and he made sure with the help of Straub, who ran just the kind of race Coe likes and wanted.

When the runners had stepped on to the track, even those who wanted Coe to win could not have had the absolute faith in him as they did before they set out on the trip to Russia – but he proved their doubts were groundless. Coe stayed at the front all the way, almost alongside Straub, with Ovett tracking him like a hawk, ready to pounce on his prey. As they passed the first lap, covered in sixty-two seconds, Ovett was still in third place with Steve Cram, the other young Englishman in the field, fourth. They covered the next lap in just on sixty-four seconds and though Cram was dropping back, Ovett still had the slim-line Coe well within his grasp.

The situation remained the same approaching the final bend when Straub increased his stride but found it difficult to shake off the two determined Britons. Ovett closed the gap slightly on Coe and the battle was really on when they headed into the straight and Coe accelerated away like a Formula One racing car. It was too much for Ovett. He could not match such devastating pace and though he tried to get at least a silver, he was a spent force as Straub held on to second place with Cram way back in seventh. As Coe crossed the line the one-and-three-quarter minutes of disaster six days before were forgotten. He threw his arms up in a victory salute and then collapsed on his knees. Coe soon recovered to go on the usual lap of honour cheered by the one hundred thousand crowd, among whom were three hundred and sixty wildly celebrating Britons who had travelled to the Russian capital to see two races that will live in everyone's mind for many years to come.

Ovett had been beaten. It was the end of his fantastic run of forty-five one-mile and 1,500-metres victories that had been compiled over three years of worldwide racing. The greatest middle-distance men in the world have levelled the scores in two races that promoters would have paid thousands of pounds to stage in the not-too-distant future of professional racing and it was ironic that they should take place behind the Iron Curtain. When the decider will be — and that must be over the mile — is difficult to foresee for it looks as though they will now go on avoiding each other over the next few months in races as far apart as Budapest, Brussels, Tokyo and Peking. 'All the time I have put into the sport with training has become worthwhile,' said Coe. 'It is a great feeling and I hope that all being well in four years' time I am able to defend the title in Los Angeles.'

---

4 AUGUST 1980

OLYMPICS 1980: SAD, CYNICAL AND LOCKED IN SECURITY

Donald Saunders in Moscow

There is always a certain sadness about the extinguishing of the Olympic Flame for those of us who spend our lives closely involved with sport, if only because, nowadays, we never can be sure it will ever burn brightly again. But as the Flame died atop the Lenin Stadium in Moscow last night, regret was tinged with relief that the most controversial Games of all time had reached its conclusion.

No doubt, the White House and Kremlin are now closely studying the effects of the American boycott and the Russian exploitation of this past fortnight's celebration of the twenty-second Olympiad of the modern era. In truth, sport has been cruelly abused by both camps. But somehow it has tottered, weary yet still defiant, over the finishing line. Whether it can return, fresh and willing in Los Angeles four years hence, is another matter. Much will depend on whether the International Olympic Committee, national Olympic associations and the international sports federations concerned take firm enough steps to combat political interference.

From a purely personal viewpoint, the Moscow Olympics were as depressing as the Munich Games. Despite the decision of most Western European nations to banish flags and anthems, nationalism still raised its ugly head every day, at every possible opportunity. Moreover, this time, excessive and often offensive security measures took much of the fun out of the Games for spectators and competitors. Yet, even here, there have been moments to treasure, glimpses of hopes for the future. By the end of the Games, guards who had stared poker-faced or scowled at our identity cards a fortnight earlier, had begun to smile, nod and express the wish that God go with us. A minor step forward, perhaps, but an indication that given time – a long time – sport could help spread a little tolerance and understanding.

The triumphs of Coe, Ovett and Yifter were in no way devalued by the United States boycott. But in the swimming pool and the boxing ring, the Americans were sadly missed. The American men would surely have taken home a clutch of swimming medals, and at least two of their boxers would have collected gold. Yet, strangely, once the Games got under way it was easy to forget the boycott. Long after the political and nationalistic bias of the refereeing and judging has been forgotten, I shall remember the huge grin on the face of Gomez, the Cuban middleweight boxer, when he lovingly fingered the gold medal he now has to place alongside his world championship. This is what sport is supposed to be about – happiness, satisfaction, achievement – not politics and chauvinism. And how good it is to be there when it occasionally shines through the murk.

Yet, alas, whenever I look back on the 1980 Olympics, I fear my most vivid memory will be the platoons of soldiers lining the route from the sports complex to the nearby Metro station, and the total absence of children from inside and outside the venues. The sinister military presence emphasises the grave problems with which international sport must grapple if it is to survive as something worth playing or watching. The refusal to allow the children to witness any part of this great festival, or mingle with those of us who had come to take some part in it, makes me despair of a solution ever being found.

8

LOS ANGELES 1984

23 JULY 1984

OLYMPIC MOVEMENT POWERLESS
TO RESIST POLITICIANS

Donald Saunders in Los Angeles

The 1984 summer Olympics, which open at the Coliseum in Los Angeles next Saturday, will be as different from the 1980 Games as Sunset Boulevard in high summer is from Gorky Street on a February dawn. Though it remains to be seen whether the Americans can stage as superbly efficient a show as the Russians did, those of us privileged to be in California will surely enjoy ourselves rather more than we did in Moscow. True, there are problems for the Olympic visitor. Travelling around Moscow's antiseptically clean, ornate Metro was decidedly less difficult than one finds navigating a hired car through the undergrowth of the largest urban jungle in the West. There are contradictions, too. Though our buxom, smiling airport hostess welcomed us enthusiastically into the bosom of the 'Olympic Family', we shall be allowed little casual contact with athletes in their villages. Yet, one can walk past bored-looking policemen and stroll freely round the corridors of the International Olympic Committee's hotel, taking due note of the room numbers of some of the most important figures in the world of sport.

I wish the I.O.C. had been sensible with an application by journalists from the Argus group of newspapers in South Africa to report the Los Angeles Games. These men and women have long waged a brave battle against the racist policies of their government and are more anti-apartheid than many of the journalists who will sit in the press boxes at these Olympics. Yet, the international committee, hiding behind a technicality, have rejected their application. 'Press accreditation has to be approved by national Olympic committees,' explained Madame Monique Berlioux, director of the I.O.C. 'South Africa are deemed not to have a national Olympic committee.' This, like the boycott of this year's Games by the Eastern bloc and the refusal of the United States to participate in 1980, emphasises just how powerless the Olympic Movement is to resist the politicians – whether they come from the Kremlin, the White House or Black Africa.

———

30 JULY 1984

OPENING SCENE HAS HALLMARK OF HOLLYWOOD

Donald Saunders in Los Angeles

The Olympic Movement, kicked around like a football by politics and big business for the last four years, is now back in the hands of the athletes, at least until Sunday week. The 1984 summer Games, opened by President Reagan at the Coliseum in Los Angeles in the longest, most spectacular and most moving ceremony in recent history, seems set fair for two weeks of high entertainment.

The Los Angeles organising committee wisely resisted the temptation to turn this festival into a stridently jingoistic exercise. From the moment a rocket man jetted noisily into the centre of the field to the departure of the one hundred and forty competing nations, this was three hours of what might best be described as good humoured, all-American razzmatazz. The scene was set for the memorable climax with a look at the old pioneer days, a dance through Dixieland, a brief visit to Broadway and a large slice of Hollywood with, as the movie-makers used to say, 'a cast of thousands'. Most important of all, the show eventually was handed over to the people who matter most in the Olympic Movement – the young men and women competing against each other during the coming fortnight.

There have been persistent rumours in this city of the Angels that the Olympic Flame would be ignited by Nadia Comeneci, the elf-like Romanian who helped turn gymnastics into a worldwide best seller in Montreal eight years ago. The organising committee sensibly ignored the opportunity to take so obvious a swipe at the Eastern bloc for boycotting the Games. Their reward was a tumultuous reception for the Romanian team, whose national Olympic committee had refused to follow the example of big brother from next door. Instead of marrying the climax of this ceremony with a political gesture, the Los Angeles committee chose Rafer Johnson, decathlon gold medallist in 1960 and one of the greatest all-round athletes in history, as the final torchbearer.

So Johnson, now fifty and struggling a little up the ninety-nine steps of an electronically-raised stairway, became the first black man to light the Olympic Flame – just as he had once been the first of his race to carry the American flag. He received the torch inside the stadium from Gina Hemphill, granddaughter of the late Jesse Owens, another outstanding black athlete whose four gold medals at the Berlin Games in 1936 remain the peak of Olympian achievement. This was an afternoon not only for remembering great feats but for adjusting old injustices and correcting past mistakes. The late Jim Thorpe, forced to return the decathlon gold medal he won in 1912 because he had played baseball professionally, surely would have smiled with pleasure had he been there to see his grandson among the Olympic flag escorts. And as China joined in the festivities for the first time since 1936, one could not help remembering all those tedious debates of the 1960s and 1970s concerning their membership.

Juan Antonio Samaranch, president of the International Olympic Committee, also remembered those luckless men and women who had been deprived by their Communist masters of attending these Games. 'We send a message from Los Angeles today to those of you who cannot join us,' he said. Those thousands of frustrated athletes missed a memorable afternoon which finished, not with the customary disciplined march out of the stadium, but with the competing nations holding hands and dancing as they usually do at the end of the Games. Let us hope this spirit of comradeship does not wither under the intense pressure of competition during the next two weeks.

---

2 AUGUST 1984

COOPER'S GOLDEN DREAM FULFILLED FOR BRITAIN

Colin Gibson in Los Angeles

In the shadow of the canyons of the Anaheim Hills in San Bernadino County, Malcolm Cooper struck gold for Britain last night. After five hours in the blazing sun at Prado Park, Cooper, thirty-six, from Hayling Island, fulfilled a lifetime ambition of winning an Olympic title. With it he equalled the world record set in Moscow in 1980 by Viktor Vlasov of 1,173 points, on a marvellous day for the British shooters on which Alister Allan, forty, took the bronze with 1,162 points. Runner-up was Danny Nipkov, of Switzerland, with 1,163 points.

Cooper began his quest for an Olympic gold in 1968 – the year in which Bob Braithwaite won Britain's last Olympic gold shooting medal in the Olympic trap event – but he had to wait sixteen years before achieving his target. He attended the Games in Munich and Montreal but said: 'I was probably too young in 1972. Of course, we did not go in 1980 but today I feel that the wait has all been worthwhile.' He began shooting seriously in 1962 but had always wanted to take up the sport since he was eleven. At that time, though, he received little encouragement. 'In fact, at the Royal Hospital School, Holbrook, I was always pestering my instructor to let me have a go on the range. Eventually he gave in, but when he brought back the target I had not hit it with a single shot.' It was a different story yesterday as he fulfilled his billing as the pre-competition favourite. He added: 'I always thought that if I reached my peak, especially in a technical sense, then I had the ability to win. But in the standing discipline I was caught out by a change of wind direction and it took me five or six shots to find the target again. Fortunately I kept calm,' he said.

---

6 AUGUST 1984

BRITAIN'S FIRST ROWING GOLD FOR THIRTY-SIX YEARS

Donald Saunders in Los Angeles

Britain's rowers earned their first Olympic gold medal for thirty-six years, at Lake Casitas in Southern California yesterday, with the coxed four finishing half a length ahead of the United States, who led New Zealand by a similar distance. Not since the double scullers and coxless pairs took home golds from Henley, in the 1948 Games, had a British crew finished first in the Olympics.

For Martin Cross, twenty-seven, from Hampton in Middlesex, it was truly a moment to savour, because he was a member of the coxless four who had to be satisfied with a bronze in the Soviet Union four years ago.

Cross, Steven Redgrave – the stroke – Richard Budgett, Andrew Holmes and Andrew Ellison, the cox, earned their success with a courageous finish that carried them past the Americans in the final stages.

From the start it had been a battle between the British and Americans, with the Italians and New Zealanders striving for third place. As the early morning mist began to lift to reveal the steeply rising Ojai Mountains, the Americans jumped into a lead of half a length. Setting a brisk pace, they were still in front as the race reached halfway on the 2,000-metre course. With five hundred metres to go, the Americans' lead had been shortened only slightly. Then, some three hundred metres out, Redgrave and his colleagues increased their stroke rate and edged in front. Urged on by the crowd's anxious chanting of 'U.S.A., U.S.A.', the Americans tried desperately to get back on terms over the final hundred metres. The British crew, calling on their last reserves of strength and courage, simply refused to allow the gap to be closed.

So fifteen minutes later, the Union Flag was being hoisted to the top of the flagpole and Britain's national anthem – a rare sound in California this past week – was echoing across the water. For the British quintet – a teacher, doctor, builder, landscape gardener and radiologist – and Mike Spracklen, their coach, the hard work of the past few months had been handsomely rewarded. No doubt, as he stood there watching the flag rise, Redgrave, in particular, heaved a sigh of relief. Having won the Diamond Sculls at Henley last year, he had planned to enter the singles here. Instead, he correctly realised what a good crew the coxed four could become and decided he would try to stroke them to Britain's first success in this event since 1912.

---

6 AUGUST 1984
McFARLANE AND REID EXCEL IN DEFEAT
Ken Mays in Los Angeles

Mike McFarlane, twenty-three, from North London, and Clapham's Donovan Reid came out of the sprinting shadow of Allan Wells to give Britain their best representation in an Olympic 100 metres final since 1948 when they finished fifth and seventh respectively in Los Angeles on Saturday. The two Londoners had battled their way through three rounds to join the powerful Americans, Carl Lewis, Sam Graddy and Ron Brown, as Wells surrendered his title by finishing last in the semi-final in 10.71 seconds. McFarlane produced a personal best of 10.27 seconds as Lewis swept to the title in 9.99 seconds, the first part of what he hopes will be four golds, while Reid, twenty, ran a magnificent 10.33 seconds. Graddy, the silver medallist, recorded 10.19 seconds, but it was Ben Johnson, of Canada, who split the expected clean sweep by the Americans as he finished in third place in 10.22 seconds.

It was a major disappointment that Wells, who had looked good in the opening two rounds on Friday, could not muster his old last-half burst, but said McFarlane: 'Don't write him off, he will be back, he is that type of athlete.' McFarlane, who tied with Wells for the Commonwealth title two years ago, went on: 'Wells will not lie down, and I refuse to call myself Britain's number one sprinter until the end of the season.'

The Briton had the misfortune of running against Lewis in all four rounds of the competition and as the outstanding American brought off the biggest winning margin in Olympic history, McFarlane said: 'He is an amazing man.' He went on: 'I learnt how to be cool in a hot situation with ninety thousand people all cheering for one man. I had hoped to make the semi-final, and to get into the final was unbelievable. It was a nervous situation and that drained a lot of energy out of me, but it was nice to have my training partner, Donovan, on the starting line.' Reid said: 'It is hard to describe the feeling of running in the final, but it is an experience that I would not have missed.'

––––––––––

8 AUGUST 1984

HOW SANDERSON BURIED MOSCOW MISERIES

Ken Mays in Los Angeles

Tessa Sanderson, the girl who walked out of the Lenin Stadium in Moscow in tears four years ago after a miserable failure to qualify for the finals of the Olympic javelin, wiped away those memories on Monday when she won the gold medal in the Los Angeles Coliseum. Miss Sanderson, twenty-eight, the Commonwealth record holder, threw 228 feet two inches (69.56 metres) in the first round, and then had to wait and hope that neither Tiina Lillak, the world champion from Finland, nor Fatima Whitbread, her British team-mate, who is the world silver medallist, would surpass it.

But with Lillak suffering a stress facture of the right foot and Whitbread not fully recovered from the after-effects of a stomach operation a few days before she arrived here, it never happened. It meant that for the first time in British athletics history, a javelin gold medal had been won at an Olympic Games and, just for good measure, the bronze. The Finn, who took only two throws, squeezed between for the silver at 226 feet four inches (sixty-nine metres), well below her world gold medal performance of 232 feet five inches (70.86 metres).

'I knew this was my last chance at an Olympics,' said Miss Sanderson, 'so I hit it well and it came off. After that I was experienced enough to realise the event does not end until the last throw.' The athlete born in Kingston, Jamaica, added: 'It was a fantastic final. We had three girls in the final [Sharon Gibson was the third]. That has never happened before and there was an amazing team spirit. I prayed for Fatima to do well when Lillak came up, but not hard enough for her to beat me.'

The gold medallist finished by saying: 'I knew after Moscow that I would come back because I was prepared to fight back. I have not been lucky in regard to injuries since then, but now I hope that even though I failed there, it is all dead and buried.' But it proved to the rest of the world that Britain is still a power in javelin throwing even though it had been left to Miss Whitbread to carry the flag, so to speak, over the last couple of seasons.

---

8 AUGUST 1984

COE SUNK BY CRUZ MISSILE
Ken Mays in Los Angeles

The kings are dead, long live the king. That was the message at the Olympic Games on Monday when Joachim Cruz, twenty, from Brazil, won the 800 metres gold, in one minute forty-three seconds, under the blazing Los Angeles sun. Cruz's victory ended Britain's five-year stranglehold on middle-distance running. Sebastian Coe and Steve Ovett blazed the trail, but the young Brazilian firmly put them in their places. Coe, despite his world record (one minute 41.73 seconds) at the distance, has never won a major 800-metres title. Again he was destined to take the silver, while Ovett finished off the night in hospital, recovering from bronchial trouble. Though Coe tried to match Cruz around the final bend and along the straight, the Brazilian came in for gold in the world's third-fastest time. Coe is the only man to have run faster.

When Ovett, who had been so fortunate to qualify the previous day, collapsed in the tunnel leading from the track it was Coe who called for medical assistance. Ovett spent his second night in a local hospital last night and, according to Dr Stephen Simmons, who has been conducting heart and lung tests on him, 'wants very much to run in the 1,500 metres'. However, Dr David Archibald, Britain's athletics team doctor, said that this was 'extremely unlikely'.

'We are too old for this game,' Coe had told Ovett after the finish, but before the 1,500 metres world record-holder collapsed with breathing difficulties and was taken from the stadium on a stretcher. 'I felt I had been mugged by a teenager,' Coe said. 'I'm not too disappointed, but we are getting a bit too old to play with fire like that. I'm still looking forward to the 1,500 metres because the conditions don't worry me. I came out here early to get used to them, and where I have been training it is even hotter than Los Angeles.' Coe was always in the hunt for medals and, though he made no impression on Cruz, he held off Earl Jones, who before this race had been the fastest runner in the world at this distance this year.

———

8 AUGUST 1984

LEWIS ALMOST GAVE UP CHASING OWENS'S RECORD

Ken Mays

Carl Lewis, the giant American who is hoping to emulate the late Jesse Owens by winning four gold medals at an Olympics, would have been prepared to surrender that aim in the long jump on Monday in Los Angeles. Lewis, who had won the 100 metres title on Saturday and will now attempt the 200 metres as well as the 4 × 100 metres relay, carried off the event at twenty-eight feet and quarter of an inch (8.54 metres), a lead of a foot over Gary Honey, the Australian silver medallist, with Giovanni Evangelisti, of Italy, in third place.

But it was achieved with Lewis's first and only jump, and if any of the competitors, who included fellow American Larry Myricks, the last man to have beaten Lewis, had bettered it, that would have been it. 'I was a little sore after the leap and if someone had jumped further than that I would not have come back,' said Lewis. 'I realised I was taking chances of destroying my aim of four gold medals, but that is the way I felt. But I felt confident about what I had done. Myricks is a very experienced and fierce competitor and capable of doing anything, and I'm pleased that the second part is over successfully.'

It was in 1936 in the Berlin Olympics that Owens collected his gold tally to make him the most outstanding American athlete of all time and Lewis intends at least to share part of that title. At the World Championships in Helsinki last year, Lewis, who claims to have lived, eaten and slept athletics since he was seven, won the gold medals for the 100 metres, long jump and the 4 × 100 metres relay.

---

11 AUGUST 1984

THOMPSON LETS RECORD SLIP IN STROLL TO GOLD

Ken Mays in Los Angeles

Daley Thompson proved without doubt that he is the greatest all-round athlete the world has seen when he won the Olympic gold medal in the decathlon for the second time in Los Angeles on Thursday. Thompson amassed a total of 8,797 points that left his greatest rival, Jurgen Hingsen, the West German and world record-holder, one hundred and twenty-three points adrift at the end of the ten-event competition.

But Thompson mystified his supporters by running such a slapdash 1,500 metres to finish off two days' of hard work that he missed taking the world record by a fraction. In what appeared to be total disregard of what he achieved in nine previous disciplines, Thompson ran like a jogger on a training spin to record four minutes thirty-five seconds in sixth place, a time that cost him the record by one point and one-tenth of a second. With a personal best of four minutes 20.1 seconds, Thompson had only to show interest in the record to have broken it for the fourth time, yet he ambled nonchalantly round the track and then had the audacity to look at the clock in disbelief when he found he had not cracked it. At a press conference afterwards in front of possibly the biggest gathering to see an athlete except that commanded by Carl Lewis, Thompson denied that he had come to America to set a record, and said that the gold medal was his sole target. 'I believe that I can take the world record anytime, but what I have won here has been worth the hours of seclusion and all the training I have put in. Getting the record would have been an extra, but it was not important. Hingsen is a great competitor. He scored the highest points ever by a loser, so I don't think he did too badly.'

Thompson, who had broken the world's best for a first-day score with 4,633 points, appeared to be in trouble on the start of the second day when he was beaten in the 110 metres hurdles by Hingsen and then dropped even further into trouble with a poor discus competition. At one time his lead of more than one hundred and sixty points had dropped to a mere thirty-four, but then Thompson responded by grabbing back more than one hundred points from a brilliant pole-vaulting competition that almost certainly tipped the scales permanently in his favour. 'I had thrown the discus so badly I was disgusted with myself, but the pole vault really sorted it all out,' said Thompson.

The Germans also had Siggi Wentz and Guido Kratschmer in the competition, no mean opponents in normal competition, but they proved not to be in Thompson's class. They had the good sense to congratulate Thompson before the 1,500 metres on his success, but even they were surprised that he could amble round and fail to break the record. Thompson said that his only thought in the 1,500 metres was that 'the sooner I got it over the sooner I could do the lap of honour', and as usual he did the lap with a Union Flag draped over him. The eighty-four thousand crowd responded to a tremendous performance from an athlete who has spent so much of his time living just outside Los Angeles.

---

12 AUGUST 1984

SLY SLIPS PAST BUDD-DECKER CONFUSION

Peter Hildreth in Los Angeles

If Aesop ever wrote another fable he could hardly pick a more compelling subject than Zola Budd, the waif-like runner from Stellenbosch, South Africa, by way of Guildford, Surrey, who joined the British team and underwent a vivid Olympic baptism of chance and misadventure in the 3,000 metres final. Not even the concerted thrust of publicity and contrivance which accompanied her arrival in England five months ago could have devised a more sensational sequence of happenings than crossed her path in this, her first full international track appearance.

Racing bravely but with little real hope of matching the overwhelming expectation heaped upon her, Zola was innocently involved in a two-way tangle with world champion Mary Decker, the punters' favourite and darling of the American crowd. As Decker crashed out of the race, Budd ran in to finish seventh. Then, amid general uproar the 18-year-old British citizen of recent history was disqualified, only to be re-instated almost within the hour when video replays of the incident had been studied by the track referee. In the general confusion it was almost overlooked that Britain's Wendy Sly had run on to take the silver medal behind Romania's Maricica Puica, an achievement almost certainly beyond the inexperienced Budd.

The unhappy Decker, who only a week ago broke Budd's world 2,000 metres record, and now reliving the Olympic disappointments of 1976 and 1980 when injury and boycott slammed the door on her dreams, was hurried to hospital for an X-ray which revealed a tear to the gluteus muscle of her left hip. Back in the interview room, Decker said: 'I don't think there is any question Zola Budd was in the wrong. I do hold her responsible for what happened. She cut in front of me and it was a matter of pushing her or falling. When I went down, I felt something in my left hip. I tried to get up but I couldn't.' At this point she broke down in tears and her fiancé Richard Slaney, the British discus thrower, who had carried her from the arena, bore her once again from the scene and she was driven away by Rolls-Royce before the news of Zola's reinstatement had reached the stadium.

In the frequent replays of the incident filmed from various angles it was possible to establish that Budd was in fact not culpable. She was in the lead after just over three laps when Decker, running close to her, twice tapped Zola's foot from behind. A short distance further on there was another, firmer contact for which the American girl was also responsible. This time Budd lurched, stumbled and, in recovering her balance, did a side-step over which Decker tripped, falling sideways on the kerb and rolling over on to the infield. Budd was lucky to stay on her feet and finish the course, but her strength ran out as Puica and Sly, who had both narrowly escaped the collision, raced on to claim the major medals. Puica's time was eight minutes 35.96 seconds, while Sly ran eight minutes 39.47 seconds and Budd eight minutes 48.80 seconds.

Although Budd's personal best of eight minutes 37.50 seconds suggests that a medal was within her compass, this was her twenty-third race of the year, counting a dozen in South Africa before her arrival in the synthetic world of sponsored sport wished upon her by a national newspaper. The cumulative strain of life in the headlines coupled with an over-lengthy season became too great a burden for her fragile frame and bare feet to carry. Mrs Sly said: 'I wasn't involved in the incident between Zola and Mary but it was very distracting. I had to concentrate hard to take advantage of the medal chance that was suddenly presented to me. I'm sorry for Zola, she's had a helluva time in the last few months, but so have I. I've had a succession of injuries and was just glad to make it here. I'm really happy to have won the silver.'

When layer upon layer of inhibitions are stripped away in the ordeal of Olympic competition, something of the person beneath the trained performer is revealed. In the case of Daley Thompson there is a brash propensity for juvenile solecism. Zola Budd is not yet a gold medallist, but she loses gracefully. In the tunnel under the stadium she went up to Mary Decker to say she was sorry about what happened. Decker said: 'Don't bother.' So Zola became the first British athlete since Chris Brasher in 1956 to be re-instated after disqualification in an Olympic final.

----

13 AUGUST 1984

BRITAIN RULE WITH COE AND CRAM ONE-TWO

Ken Mays in Los Angeles

Sebastian Coe and Steve Cram proved that Britain still rules as far as the metric mile is concerned when they swept up the gold and silver medals as the Olympic Games neared its close with the 1,500 metres before a ninety-two thousand crowd in Los Angeles on Saturday. Coe, who had been almost written off earlier in the year, ran a superbly controlled and designed race from start to finish to become the first man in the history of the event to retain the title, with a winning time of three minutes 32.53 seconds.

As he walked from the track, looking much more at ease than when he won the title in Moscow four years ago, his father and coach, Peter, was the first to greet him. 'No corrections, perfect,' said Coe senior, after months of planning the gold. It was a truly magnificent achievement for Coe timed his position perfectly throughout and then kicked at two hundred metres when Cram first threatened to challenge his supremacy.

Then for good measure when the World, European and Commonwealth champion had another attempt to get back in the final straight, Coe added his second change of gear to show that he was very far from being finished despite all the disasters of the past two years.

But the race also contained a poignant moment for Britain when Steve Ovett, the world record-holder and Coe's big rival, dropped out from exhaustion shortly after the bell and had to receive medical attention at the side of the track. Coe was unaware that the man who had caused him anguish in Moscow was in real trouble at that moment, because his main problem was the pace of the fair-headed Cram, who eventually finished in three minutes 33.40 seconds, almost a second in front of Jose Abascal, of Spain. Ovett had gone against medical advice to run after his breakdown in the 800 metres and was taken away on a stretcher from the track this time. 'As any athlete would, I felt sorry for Steve because it was a brave attempt by him after what had happened earlier,' said Coe. 'I just hope that he finds out very soon what the problem is and that he will be back as soon as possible.' After treatment at the medical centre to which he had taken earlier in the week Ovett said he was returning to England to have a thorough examination before he makes any commitments on his future activities.

Months ago Coe had also been involved in controversy when he had been beaten in the A.A.A. Championship 1,500 metres by the young pretender, Peter Elliott, on the day the team was finalised. It had been considered by some that his selection was unfair to the Rotherham athlete, but he proved those who had faith in him were right. But even Coe had his doubts. 'I was concerned at that moment because I thought I had blown my chances of defending the title even though I had been selected for the 800 metres,' he admitted. As to Saturday's race he was surprised that Steve Scott, the American hopeful, had decided to do the front running so early on, moving into the lead at five hundred metres and leading until Abascal took over at one thousand metres. Scott, who had thrown out the challenge throughout his European tour that Coe and Cram were only racing in their backyards and would not do so well in America, was made to eat his words as he finished seven seconds down in tenth place.

Coe hinted he would not be defending the title for the second time in South Korea in four years when he would be thirty-one, and his last major competition would be the European Championships, the event at which he was selected in 1982 but returned home without running after a surprise defeat in the 800 metres. 'My ambitions to win a major 800 metres despite the world record are now a thing of the past,' he said. Coe added that his victory was more satisfying than Moscow because of the long battle he has had with injury problems. He was just proud to have made the team, let alone win a gold medal in the 1,500 metres and silver in the 800 metres.

---

13 AUGUST 1984

LEWIS MAKES SOME HISTORY
Ken Mays in Los Angeles

Carl Lewis succeeded in establishing himself as the greatest athlete in American track and field history when he completed his schedule of four gold medals and shared in the only world record of the Los Angeles Olympics on Saturday. Lewis, who had earlier won the 100 and 200 metres as well as the long jump, finished off his magnificent achievement by anchoring the 4 × 100 metres relay team to the gold and world record of 37.83 seconds.

So Lewis had emulated the feat of Jesse Owens at the Berlin Olympics in 1936 of winning four titles, but the similarity will end there for Lewis is likely to be the most sought-after athlete in the history of the sport with about £7,600,000 to be earned. Yet the tall, slim Lewis, who had run with Sam Graddy, Ron Brown and world 100-metres record-holder Calvin Smith, is not the most popular of athletes in America. 'If I can make fifty dollars or fifty thousand dollars it does not make any difference. I have four golds and nobody can take that away from me. I have the same feeling for Jesse Owens: he is still the legend, I'm just a person,' he said. Lewis, who was timed at under nine seconds on his anchor leg, went on: 'I am very exhausted and my left hamstring is tired, but I am not injured in any way.'

---

14 AUGUST 1984

LEADING ARTICLE
GOOD TIME HAD BY ALL?

A British characteristic which foreigners sometimes find endearing is our enthusiasm for pursuits at which we do not particularly excel. This is true amateurism. Though in the absence of East European competition Britain may have won more medals than usual at the recently ended Olympics, our modest tally was below that of New Zealand or South Korea. Somehow even that old companion in gracious losing, Italy, outstripped us. Yet it would seem from the feverish television and press coverage of recent weeks that our men and women were achieving something very remarkable in Los Angeles. Of course very few of them did – Sebastian Coe, the mischievous Daley Thompson – and their names will no doubt be forever etched on the national consciousness.

Writ most large of course will be the name of Zola Budd. To some this may seem odd for Zola came seventh in her final. Truly the British love a failure, as a certain tabloid newspaper has not been slow to grasp. The Budd-Decker affair will be spoken of for many generations. Only a few days ago most of us had not heard of Mary Decker, though regrettably we knew somewhat more of Zola Budd. Now the whole country, possibly the whole world, asks the same question. Was Mary tripped or did she fall? It would be idle to suppose that with the passing of time the question will be less hotly debated. On the contrary. It will be remembered as the outstanding event of the Los Angeles Olympics, possibly of 1984, when Zola and Mary are tripping along amicably in the Elysian fields.

9
SEOUL 1988

LEADING ARTICLE
O TEMPORA!

Plato said that of the three groups involved with the Olympic Games, those who competed, those who watched, and those who went to buy and sell, the noblest were those who merely watched. We who will be forced to spectate from afar can bask in Plato's approval and reflect that the other two lots have nearly always come in for some measure of disapproval. Indeed, there is much nonsense being talked at the moment about the decline of the Olympic ideal. Those who sorrowfully contrast the razzmatazz of the Seoul opening ceremony and its one hundred parachutists with the chaste amateurism of the Greek games and its olive wreath prizes are indulging in so much misplaced *laudatio temporis acti*. The enormous sums earned in sponsorship by Mr Carl Lewis, who won four medals at the last Games, are nothing – relatively – to the cash benefits that were available to successful Greek athletes. In Athens, a supposedly democratic state, Olympic victors were fed out of the public purse for the rest of their lives. The announcement by Mr Sebastian Coe that he hopes to become a Conservative M.P. pales beside the performance of Cylon, who was so emboldened by his victories in the *stadion* and *diaulos* in 640 B.C. that he attempted a *coup d'état*. The idealistic view of athletics held by the modern founder of the Games, Baron de Coubertin, is in reality a Victorian aberration.

Nor is power politics a new feature. Nations have long been aware of the enormous commercial benefits of the Games. The quarrel between

North and South Korea over who should play host has an echo in the war between Elis and Pisata, over exactly the same thing, in 668 B.C. Only in one respect are the modern games worse than the ancient ones. Next week three million dollars' worth of equipment will be used to test the athletes for three thousand seven hundred banned drug substances. For the Greeks, obsessed as they were with glory, power and money, this kind of physical self-abuse would have been unthinkable. Indeed, the two months before the Games was a period of abstinence of all kinds. In this respect we can legitimately appeal to an historic Olympian ideal. For the rest, we can merely hope that our memories of Seoul will be of aspiration and achievement, rather than of wrangling and rancour.

---

20 SEPTEMBER 1988

INSPIRATION THAT KEPT MOORHOUSE ON MEDAL TRAIL
Michael Calvin

An Olympic gold medal fits snugly into the palm of a hand and, because it is only coated in the precious metal, is much lighter than expected. But, in the words of Adrian Moorhouse: 'The moment you hold it for the first time, that's it, you realise it's yours and think of what it means to people close to you, the people who matter.'

So yesterday, as he suffered from a headache triggered by the release of tension, Britain's latest Olympic breaststroke champion carefully folded a fraying piece of paper and placed it into his blue velvet medal case. It is a telegram, from Geoff Carter, his former Sunday school teacher in Bingley, containing the message: 'There will be a next time.' It was delivered during the Los Angeles Games where Moorhouse failed to win a medal and decided on a short-lived retirement. Now, after surviving the trauma of losing a world title in 1986 on a technicality, he is a winner. He promised himself that last night he would sleep with the gold medal around his neck.

That put into perspective the annual income of around £60,000 he is already thought to earn from swimming. Commercial exploitation of one's talent comes later; there is no reward greater than the gradual realisation that a lifetime's ambition has been fulfilled. Moorhouse, twenty-four, thought of his family in the stands, of the countless mornings when he has forced himself to rise before the sun to train. He thought of Peter Ackroyd, the man who taught him to swim. Mr Ackroyd, now a teacher in Hong Kong, was also in the Olympic pool. He had won a five-day trip to Seoul in a competition which demanded an answer to the question: 'Why should you go to the Olympics?' His answer was simple, but decisive. 'I want to see Adrian win,' he wrote. His wish was granted by one hundredth of a second, a fraction of an inch.

Though he had hardly slept for two nights before the final Moorhouse was calm in the warm-up area. Even when he trailed Volkov by 1.2 seconds at the turn he refused to panic. A champion's instinct takes over in such situations. Despite his limited vision, Moorhouse fixed his attention on 'this body, this mass of water'. It wore a yellow Soviet swim cap. Volkov was expected to tire but, as the Briton admitted: 'After seventy-five metres I thought to myself, "He's not dying. Maybe the Olympics mean something to him, too".' But, with five metres to go, he suspected he had won. It was only at the finish, when he turned to learn his fate on the electronic scoreboard at the other end of the pool, that he realised Hungary's Guttler had run him so close. 'At first, the shock of winning really hit my heart,' he said. 'But, then, I cringed for the Hungarian. I know what it's like to get so close, and yet so far. I almost felt guilty.'

---

23 SEPTEMBER 1988

COOPER MEDAL DOUBLE BOOST
Leslie Howcroft

Malcolm Cooper's achievement of Olympic gold for the second time is the most welcome news this publicity neglected sport has had for years. He put rifle shooting firmly on the map in Los Angeles and with the other world records and titles which followed, people were almost forced to pay attention.

Both Cooper and Alister Allan were determined from 1984 onwards to be on the Seoul winner's rostrum and no detail was spared in their all-out training. Equipment is, of course, paramount. Cooper used a Walther M.M.K. free rifle weighing six-and-a-half pounds with his own stock, hence the annoyance when it was damaged in Seoul, but Cooper, though in deadly rivalry with the Russians, has always been friendly with them and their armourer helped him effect repairs. Allan's rifle, a veritable

Rolls-Royce among weapons, slightly heavier, was hand-made in Switzerland and there are only twelve like it in the world. Ammunition, too, is crucial and Cooper, who always checks and rechecks, was not altogether satisfied with his the night before so he changed it. Ironically, under the old Olympic shooting rules, Allan, who had produced ten points better than his personal best, would have had the gold. His real forte is prone shooting; this gave Cooper the edge in the final which is shot from the standing position, Cooper's strongest style.

---

25 SEPTEMBER 1988

BIG BEN'S TIME WARP
BRONZE PUTS CHRISTIE UP AMONG THE ELITE

Peter Hildreth

Great sprinting acquired a new and dazzling criterion yesterday as Canada's Ben Johnson laid his mighty grasp on the Olympic 100-metres gold medal. With a fantastic world record of 9.79 seconds, the brawny Johnson cast down the defending champion Carl Lewis, putting a clear metre and a half between himself and the American's well-advertised ambition to become the first man to win sprinting's most coveted title twice. Lewis himself raced as never before, setting an American record of 9.92. And Britain's Linford Christie surpassed himself, taking the bronze medal with a United Kingdom and European record of 9.97. Lunging desperately for the line, Christie's final stride stretched a full three metres (nine feet ten inches).

Both Johnson and Lewis eclipsed the Olympic record of 9.95 held by another American, Jim Hines, since 1968. That was achieved with the benefit of reduced atmospheric pressure at high altitude in Mexico City. All the sprinters had yesterday was a legal following wind of 1.1 metres per second. It was warm; a perfect setting for the big race. The final had all the elements of last year's world championship in Rome. Except for Christie, the medals found the same destinations.

The fastest qualifiers were drawn, according to the rules, in the middle lanes. Christie was in lane four between Lewis and Smith. Johnson in lane six stood waiting for the starter's command with savage determination in his eyes, his lips moving like a witch doctor mumbling an incantation. To some he seemed in need of occult inspiration. Before the final Johnson did not look a likely winner. An hour and a half earlier he won his semi-final in 10.03 after Lewis had won his in 9.97. The American looked every stride superior. But so it was in Rome and Johnson knew how to turn it around in the final.

He still knew here in Seoul. The immense lift of arms and shoulders, the thrust of thighs like turbines, the strength synonymous with speed were all in evidence. But this time the race was not won on the blocks. Johnson's reaction time here was 0.132 to 0.136 by Lewis and 0.138 for Christie. In Rome it was all over by the first stride with Johnson reacting in 0.129, Lewis in 0.196. In this final Johnson imposed his will in the pick-up phase. The first fifty metres was the essential measure of the champion. There was no catching him after that. As much as Lewis applied his elegant and stylish genius, it was powerless against the pounding force of Johnson's impetus. Conceding three inches in height to the six foot two inch Lewis, the Canadian packed the greater thrust.

Lewis looked across four times to see where he stood, stepping out of his lane once in the process. This impeded nobody but Lewis who must have swayed to leave his lane even marginally. Johnson was sure where he stood, raising his arm in conquest at the line. Lewis said: 'I did my best, that's all I can do. I have three other events to think about. That's where my focus is now.' The press waited three hours for Johnson's interview while he went to doping control. No, he wasn't surprised at the record. He meant to give it his best.

To put this extraordinary event in an historical perspective it is necessary to classify it among the most superlative footraces of any kind on record. Apart from wind-assisted races, this was the first time four people have broken ten seconds with automatic timing in the same race. Johnson now stands out beyond question as the fastest human of all time over 100 metres. For Lewis there is the slight consolation of being the man who came closest to an Olympic 100-metres title double. For Johnson there remains a further dimension of sprinting prowess to be explored. He has yet to prove himself, as Lewis has done at Olympic level and may do again here, over 200 metres. But that is for another day. Yesterday was Johnson's day, or 9.79 seconds of it, anyway.

———

25 SEPTEMBER 1988
OARSMEN ON COURSE FOR DOUBLE
Chris Moore

The man from Marlow Bottom and the boy who was too lazy to play rugby were standing on top of the world in Seoul yesterday as they completed the first half of what could be a unique rowing double. Steve Redgrave, from the quaintly-named Buckinghamshire village, and Andrew Holmes, who chose rowing at Latymer Upper School, Hammersmith, to avoid the long bus ride to the playing fields, took their proud place on the rostrum as gold medal winners in the coxless pairs.

Britain's golden double act then dismissed suggestions that they are not exactly the best of friends. 'In fact, we have got on better than ever in these championships,' insisted Redgrave. 'It's always the same with the press. You get good sportsmen and they try to knock them down when they have produced the goods.' But their rowing future together still remains uncertain. 'We'll come away from here, go our separate ways and perhaps have a holiday. In a couple of months' time one of us will give the other a ring and say it's time to go out for a beer, and we will see what happens from there,' said Redgrave. Holmes and Redgrave, whose Olympic build-up has depended on grants and sponsorships, say their success should finally make people sit up and take notice of their achievements.

On a day at the Han River regatta course dominated by the muscular men and women from behind the Iron Curtain, Holmes and Redgrave led from the start, holding off a strong challenge from the Romanians, Dragos Neagu and Danut Dobre, to finish in six minutes 36.84 seconds. The British pair, who were due to race again in the coxed pairs final less than twenty-four hours later, could have been unsettled when the start of yesterday's race was delayed for thirty minutes when a stretcher broke on the Belgian boat. But Redgrave and Holmes refused to be disturbed by this temporary setback. 'We got out of the boat and sat in a car, determined to stay very calm,' said Holmes. The delay certainly had no effect on their concentration, with the British boat getting away to a perfect start. 'We had planned to lead immediately and, just as we expected, the Romanians came back,' said Redgrave. 'They almost drew level but we knew we had them. All we had to do was maintain that lead.'

Redgrave and Holmes, world champions last year, came to Seoul attempting to do the impossible – to win two gold medals. In the long history of Olympic rowing no rowers have ever won both the coxed and coxless pairs. How difficult would it be to achieve? 'Ask the crews who have raced in one final just what it takes,' said Redgrave with a wry smile. 'Racing in two finals on consecutive days is very difficult indeed. But that's what we came for: to win a double gold.'

26 SEPTEMBER 1988
FLO JO GLOWS IN THE SPOTLIGHT
Michael Calvin

When it mattered, with the world watching, Flo Jo glowed. She laughed, she cried, she posed and she pranced. She was the fastest woman on earth. Florence Griffith Joyner, the girl from the ghetto, had an Olympic gold medal around her neck and the hearts of the American nation in her pocket. No wonder her smile, set off by her red lip gloss, shone like a beacon. Yesterday was the day she could not contain the joy of knowing her talent is unmatched. 'I'll take care of the finances later,' she assured us, much to the delight of her newly-acquired business advisor. 'For now, sprinting is about excitement.'

A star to the tips of her four-inch fingernails, she knew she had provided one of the immortal images of these Games by laughing her way through the last thirty metres of the women's 100 metres final. It was the race of her life, no time to wear the outlandish racing costumes which make her look like an extra from a Flash Gordon film. She started well and, when she looked around her at the halfway mark, she could see no one. She was on her way to a time of 10.54 seconds, the second fastest in history. 'I knew I was winning the race,' she recalled. 'I was so relaxed, and looking forward to crossing the line. I was smiling because I was happy, I guess.' There is a natural grace about her long, high stride, which is reminiscent of the white horses of the Spanish Riding School in Vienna. But there is also an awesome power in her legs that is, in her words, 'the result of hard work, determination and dedication'.

Mrs Griffith Joyner, twenty-eight, began running at the age of seven, when she beat boys in races for underprivileged children staged by the Sugar Ray Robinson Foundation in Watts, the riot-torn Los Angeles ghetto. She reached the turning point of her career at last year's World Championships in Rome where she watched Ben Johnson before winning her silver medal in the 200 metres. 'I was so frustrated with my starts at that time I used to cry,' she said. 'Then I saw Ben set his world record. I looked at his start and said to myself, "That's what I've got to do".' Al Joyner, the triple jumper who became her coach after marrying her last October, videotaped the race. She watches it every day, usually when she listens to her motivational cassettes. Her physical effort mirrors Johnson's fitness regime. She does one thousand sit-ups a day, has a hamstring-extension machine in her kitchen, and endures a 90-minute weightlifting session each evening.

Like Johnson, she must live with those who suggest her improvements are aided artificially. Her answer is unequivocal: 'I don't think a person has to use drugs. There is no substitute for hard work.' Evelyn Ashford, who pipped East Germany's Heike Dreschler for the silver medal, hails her American team-mate as 'a phenomenon'. No one argued yesterday when she added: 'Only a man can run faster.' The difference is that *Playboy* have not been on the telephone to Johnson.

———

27 SEPTEMBER 1988

BEN JOHNSON IS STRIPPED OF HIS GOLD MEDAL
DRUG TEST FAILED BY WINNER OF FASTEST EVER 100 METRES
OLYMPIC CHAMPION FACES LIFE BAN

Charles Laurence and Colin Gibson in Seoul and Brian Oliver

Ben Johnson, the fastest man on earth, was stripped of his Olympic gold medal in Seoul early today after being found guilty of using drugs to win last Saturday's 100 metres race. Johnson, twenty-six, from Toronto, shattered the world record in winning the Olympic title, watched by millions of television viewers across the world. The medal was officially withdrawn from Johnson on the unanimous recommendation of the International Olympic Committee's chief executive board. A spokesman for the I.O.C. said the board had considered a suggestion that the anabolic steroid, stanozolol, had been administered by a third party, but had rejected this because it did not fit the 'drug profile'. A decision whether to upgrade the silver and bronze medal holders has not been confirmed, but the I.O.C. spokesman said this was likely.

Senor Juan Antonio Samaranch, president of the I.O.C., said: 'This is a blow for the Olympic Games and the Olympic Movement, but shows that the I.O.C. was right in the firm stance that it has adopted to keep sport clean.' In one of the most astonishing chapters in Olympic history Johnson, also the world 100 metres champion, now faces a life ban and international disgrace. Reports last night suggested that the Jamaican-born athlete who ran the 100 metres in 9.79 seconds to win Saturday's race, had already left South Korea.

His business advisers, however, say Johnson will be appealing on the grounds 'that his urine sample was mishandled by officials'. His manager, Mr Larry Heidebrecht, said early today in Seoul that the news of Johnson's drug test was a 'shattering disappointment' and that the athlete had 'absolutely never taken drugs'. He said Johnson was the most tested athlete in recent history and no traces of drug taking had ever been found. 'I can only say at this moment it is a tragedy, a mistake or sabotage.' Mr Heidebrecht claimed he was investigating 'peculiar things' that may have led to the drug test report. 'Ben is certainly not guilty of anything. He has absolutely never taken any drugs of any kind. He has kept to the same training and he has proved in numerous meetings that he can break records without using drugs or any other form of unauthorised training.'

Mr Roger Jackson, the Canadian Olympic Association president, said: 'We met until 2.30 in the morning reviewing all the evidence that was before us. The reports were consistent with the evidence we have been given. They suggest that an anabolic steroid had been used.' Mr Paul Duprey, the president of the Canadian Athletic Board, was called to the I.O.C.'s hotel in the centre of Seoul for urgent talks late last night. Mr Lyle McCosky, Canada's assistant deputy minister of sport, also attended the meeting. The incident is a great embarrassment to the Canadians who led the fight against drugs in international sport. Mr McCosky said Canada had strong views about drugs in sport and had 'tried to bring about a level playing field and common strategy throughout the sport world'. He added: 'Our policy is if any athlete is confirmed positive on drug use, then the Canadian Government would withdraw all financial support for the rest of his life. The whole thing would be painful for Canada.'

Now that Johnson has been disqualified, he will automatically be banned for life by the International Amateur Athletic Federation and forfeit the world record he set in Seoul. But his previous world mark of

9.83 seconds, set at the World Championships in Rome, is expected to remain in the record book as the Canadian's dope test there proved negative. It is believed that Johnson's gold medal will go to the runner-up, Carl Lewis, the American who held the Olympic title until Saturday. Britain's Linford Christie would move up to the silver. The American Calvin Smith, who came fourth, would get the bronze.

---

29 SEPTEMBER 1988
LEWIS ACCEPTS DEFEAT WITH ADMIRABLE GRACE
Michael Calvin

Joe DeLoach was consumed by a strange sense of guilt when he prevented Carl Lewis from winning his second set of four Olympic gold medals. Lewis knew his fate in a single, despairing glance three metres from the finish of the 200 metres final. DeLoach, his friend and training partner for the last two years, was fractionally ahead. They watched together a replay of the race, won in an Olympic record time of 19.75 seconds, on the stadium's electronic scoreboard. When it was over Lewis turned to the champion and said: 'Congratulations. It's over.'

DeLoach confessed: 'I really hated that I was the one who came between Carl and his dream. He is the best runner in history. He has helped me so much. Before we met I could run fast, but I didn't understand racing. He has such a feel for it.' It was natural that DeLoach, who failed to reach the American Collegiate 200 metres final earlier this year, was struck suddenly by the implications of his achievement.

Lewis appeared destined to repeat his Los Angeles clean sweep in the sprints, long jump and relay. Tom Tellez, who coaches both Lewis and DeLoach, believes Lewis suffered only his second 200-metres defeat in thirty months because of the physical demands of the long jump. Yet Lewis was not looking for excuses. 'I'm happy with what I've got and I'm proud of what Joe has achieved,' he insisted. Though in cold print that may appear trite, Lewis was genuine. He admits he has been obliged to examine his motives by the global controversy stirred by Ben Johnson's disgrace.

In Los Angeles he was perceived as an arrogant, one-dimensional character. In Seoul he has matured, winning friends and influencing people by his grace under pressure. He senses a greater commitment to rid sport of drug abuse and used his platform to argue: 'As a society we promote winning too much. Coaches, managers and some athletes want it all. But an athlete is not a machine. All he can be is his best.'

---

3 OCTOBER 1988
GAMES MARK LAST ACT FOR MOST OF BRITISH SQUAD
Chris Moore

The sixteen men in Britain's magnificent hockey squad, who crowned eight years of rehearsals with a dazzling performance in the final act, will not play together again. By beating West Germany 3–1 in Saturday's Olympic final at Songnam Stadium, Britain not only won their first hockey gold for sixty-eight years but also qualified automatically for the next Olympics. That means the squad will not be re-formed for at least three years, the individual home countries taking over international commitments. By then all but a few of the gold medal winners will have retired. Already several have announced they will depart from the international scene, with others under domestic and business pressure to join them.

Ian Taylor, Paul Barber and Kulbir Bhaura, all well into their thirties, have played their last games at top level. Richard Dodds, a doctor who takes up a new post in Chichester shortly, will also depart. Reserve goalkeeper Veryan Pappin is thirty and Richard Leman is twenty-nine. For them the pressure of combining relentless training with earning a living is a continuing strain. Even for younger players like Jon Potter, twenty-four, and Imran Sherwani, twenty-six, there are big decisions to be made. Potter is in the early stages of a marketing career and Sherwani, who marries later this month, is a newsagent whose working day starts long before most people are awake. 'It was hard enough to go through the training regime when we were striving to win an Olympic title,' said one player wryly. 'Now we have our gold medals personal motivation will be even tougher.'

Britain's performance in the final, against the nation who beat them by the only goal in the 1984 semi-final, did not always provide the most attractive hockey. But it was precise, clinically efficient and tactically perfect. Starting with careful build-ups, Britain struck in the twentieth minute when Sean Kerly and Steve Batchelor set up a scoring chance which was finished off superbly by Sherwani. With West Germany struggling to contain the hard-working British inside forwards, Leman and Robert Clift, Kerly added the second – his eighth in seven games in Seoul – from a forty-sixth-minute short-corner. A long ball from Barber set up Batchelor who rounded two defenders before laying on the third goal for Sherwani. With only eighteen minutes left even a reply from Dopp was not enough to put Britain in jeopardy.

––––––––

4 OCTOBER 1988

I.O.C.'S STRENGTH TURNS SCANDAL INTO SUCCESS

Michael Calvin

George Orwell, who regarded international sport as a substitute for war, would have approved of the perverse logic which suggests the Seoul Games were a triumph. In his classic book *1984* he introduced the concept of Newspeak slogans, which insisted: 'War is Peace, Freedom is Slavery, Ignorance is Strength'. In 1988, south of the 38th parallel, scandal was success.

Nothing is gained by ignoring that, for many, the credibility of the twenty-fourth Olympiad ended at 3.30 a.m. on Tuesday, 27 September, when Ben Johnson reached into his holdall and handed over the gold medal awarded to the world's fastest man. But, by the very act of exposing sport's greatest weakness to the world, the I.O.C. strengthened immeasurably their hand. After years of prevarication they applied moral leadership when it mattered most. Of course, there were disturbing side-effects. Instead of being saluted without reservation, great champions like Florence Griffith-Joyner and Jackie Joyner-Kersee were subjected to a whispering campaign implying they, too, had had artificial help.

Since the air of mistrust which polluted these Olympics can only be cleared by concerted international action, it is significant that Soviet and American officials have promised a joint approach on drug abuse. Their declaration was an acknowledgement that, by 1992, when the Olympic Flame is rekindled and borne to Barcelona, the movement must have come to terms with the problem. The pleas of honest athletes, it seems, are finally being heeded. The strength of their argument for life bans for anyone involved in the perpetuation of the drug culture cannot be resisted. Such champions as Sebastian Coe and Ed Moses should be encouraged to assist someone like Dr Arnold Beckett, of the Chelsea College, in setting up an I.O.C. drug-testing squad, with powers to investigate anyone, anytime, anywhere.

There are happier flashbacks: to the well-rehearsed dignity of Carl Lewis and the utterly genuine delight of Britain's hockey players. But, most of all, one remembers smiling faces and the sense of awe which radiated from Korean children. The world came, gas masks packed, expecting the Games to be staged behind barbed wire. They have not been perfect but, then, neither is life.

10

BARCELONA 1992

21 JULY 1992

REWARD FOR DEDICATION AS ATHLETES AWAIT THEIR FINEST HOUR

The Princess Royal, I.O.C. member and former Olympian, takes issue with critics who argue that only potential medal-winners should be allowed to compete at the Games and salutes the self-sacrifice of Britain's best

This weekend the 1992 Summer Olympic Games start in Barcelona, and if you are not already aware of that fact, you soon will be. The media in all its forms will make sure we see and read an enormous number of results, stories and opinions. Some reporting will be good but, if the Winter Games are anything to go by, some of it will be negative. There are as many viewpoints as people but, in this instance, my sympathies lie with the competitors. Our athletes qualify to go to the Olympic Games to a standard set by the International Olympic Committee, the relevant international sports federation or their own national Olympic committee. The qualifications achieve two things: to limit the numbers and to ensure a level standard of competition.

In each individual sport every athlete knows what he or she has to achieve and many will not manage to reach those levels. Those who do know they have worked hard and sacrificed much to reach their goal of competing at an Olympic Games. Once every four years is not often in a sporting career and that chance may come only once. Many will recognise that they have no chance of winning a medal but, as the number of 'personal best' results indicate, most will return knowing they could not have done better. Some will fail to achieve their own or their expected goals, which will be difficult enough to live with by their own high standards, never mind the added pressure of criticism from elsewhere. That criticism is often unaware of or uninterested in relevant information.

But, whatever you think about an individual sports performance, or indeed the Olympic Games, I cannot believe many people would agree with the post-Albertville opinions or comments on British athletes' performances which queried the point of sending athletes to compete in a discipline when they had no hope of winning a medal. Critics also said it was a waste of money. Whose money? The British Olympic Association raise the funds from sponsors and the public, and I do not believe those supporters would think much of any competition where only 'winners' were allowed to appear. One thing the Olympic Games have not tried to do is to limit the competition only to those athletes who are capable of winning. That would hardly be a festival of sports for the world's young, and not so young, sportsmen and women from the greatest number of countries. Taking part may not be important to the media timetables but it is seriously important to an awful lot of potential and hopefully persistent Olympic competitors – and they are the people who matter most at the Games. Without their ambitions, hopes, efforts and talent there would be no point in the I.O.C., the television coverage, the sponsorship and all the other hangers-on.

Some of those athletes will experiment with artificial means of improving their natural talent or lengthening their sporting careers, but many will reject that path for what it is – cheating, a threat to their physical health and a risk to their credibility and future careers if they are caught out. I believe the I.O.C.'s Medication Central Programme, led by Prince Alexandre of Merode, has set an example in its efforts to achieve consistency in testing, but the Olympic Movement have let themselves down through lack of consistency in punishing the guilty. However, the I.O.C. need support from the international sports federations and national Olympic committees. The athletes need to understand and accept that they belittle only themselves by 'cheating', whatever form that may take. The random testing programme that the B.O.A., many national Olympic committees and national federations run on a regular basis will help everyone avoid making real fools of themselves – athletes, trainers, coaches and administrators. Those athletes who do abide by the rules deserve the support of the authorities, and by that I mean the application of sanctions and laws should be upheld by the relevant bodies. Then, maybe, the athletes would have more faith in the ideal of 'clean' sport.

However, the Olympic Games are not only about your sport and performance. They are also about a unique mixture of people of all ages and nationalities. A chance to be part of that mixture is still an important part of the Olympic experience for many competitors. How much you make use of that opportunity is a very individual decision, but a central 'village' can create the good atmosphere at the Games which contributes to their success from the competitors' point of view. So, when the Barcelona Games hit your screens and newspapers, you will be seeing real people who are not play-acting, though the press coverage will not be on the minds of the competitors when they step into their respective arenas. The athletes will be concentrating on what they have been training for over the past months and years, and out there they will be on their own. Selection for and competing at the Olympic Games is still a unique commitment for any individual, and I wish them all fair competition and fair reporting – especially those who are British and carry the goodwill of thousands of supporters with them.

---

24 JULY 1992

EMOTIONAL RETURN TO OLYMPIC FOLD FOR SOUTH AFRICA
Michael Calvin

Enos Mafokate shed a surreptitious tear. Edmund Hellenberg said a silent prayer for the townships. Tshakila Nzimande savoured the fresh air he is denied in the gold mine. Three men, black South Africans, captured at the moment of sporting history they shared at precisely 10.21 yesterday morning. They turned their eyes right, over a half-filled ornamental pool, to see their Olympic flag being raised in the athletes' village. Thirty-two years of isolation were at an end.

The scene, given suitable gravity by the security helicopter which hovered overhead, was obviously emotional. For, standing to attention alongside the South African squad were the Jamaican team. There were four whites representing the Caribbean island which had led vehement opposition to sporting contact with South Africa during the years of apartheid. There were a minority of twelve black faces among their ninety-seven South African neighbours.

Mafokate, Hellenberg and Nzimande, coach, manager and athlete, had typical tales to tell. They were laced with an innocence that belied the scarcely-concealed inter-racial bickering that marked the team's arrival in Barcelona. They carried far greater weight than the self-conscious philosophising of the village mayor, who spoke of the occasion being 'the final convergence of all human beings'. Mafokate's words were the most emotional. 'I'm shaking,' he said. 'When I first looked down at my feet on Spanish soil, I couldn't open my mouth for two hours. I'm still choked. When I saw that flag go up I was so happy. I just wish you could open my chest and see what I'm feeling. Just look at us. The same uniform, the same team. We have made it. Left and right. Black and white. Together. Things like this have never happened to us before. It must be good for our children.'

Nzimande, twenty, might have been hiding behind designer sunglasses, but he was still prepared to wear his heart on his green and gold sleeve. His only other Olympic experience was acquired through a videotape of the Seoul Games. The 200-metre sprinter, whose cold, picked up in Britain, has been eased by the Mediterranean warmth, lives in Bloemfontein, the heartland of Afrikanerdom. Like many coloured runners, he works at a local gold mine, the President State Fund. It is hard, unrelenting work in dirty, noisy surroundings. But he quickly became accustomed to a strange celebrity status. Workmates gather around him at lunchtimes, when he trained alone. And when Barcelona began to loom on the horizon, idle curiosity was replaced by admiration. 'This gives the people I have left behind something to aim for. They can see me here, and believe anything is possible. It's something to tell the children about,' said Nzimande. 'I lost faith several times in the past year. I didn't think we would come. There were so many problems, but, two months ago, I began to believe again.'

As he spoke, Sam Ramsamy, the former London-based anti-apartheid campaigner who is head of the South African Olympic delegation, was being presented with Kobi, the ubiquitous mascot of these Games. The gesture, somehow, seemed a little out of place. It belittled an occasion which, even if reality can still be masked by symbolism in the minefield of African politics, was uplifting. 'The most important thing is we are here,' said Ramsamy. 'Medals will be a bonus. This will be a tremendous help in reducing tension in South Africa. It was right that we should be made to wait until this moment, when we have a truly non-racial team. The sight of black and white together will radiate throughout Africa ...'

Ramsamy, besieged by a posse of photographers, played his traditional role of spokesman for what is, to all intents and purposes, a new member of the Olympic family. 'This is the first time a non-racial team from South

Africa has ever taken part in the Olympics,' he said. 'It's of tremendous importance to us, and the emotion is too great to express.' But he, above all, appreciates that sport does not exist in a vacuum. It may even speed the end of the township violence at home, which put the trip in doubt. 'It's going to play a tremendous role,' he said. 'We had to do this because we feel the non-racialism that we are imbuing in our sportsmen and women is going to penetrate to all aspects of society.'

———

30 JULY 1992

BOARDMAN ON RIGHT TRACKS TO STRIKE GOLD
Colin Gibson

It took little more than four minutes in the Val d'Hebron velodrome in Barcelona yesterday for Chris Boardman to win Britain's first gold medal of these Games. After setting two world best times in the heats of the 4,000 metres pursuit, Boardman simply humbled the world champion, Jens Lehmann of Germany, in an outstanding display. From the moment the final day of cycling began, Boardman again appeared invincible.

The confidence that had surged through the young carpenter since Lotus Sports unveiled the 'dream machine' bike to Boardman, twenty-three, from Hoylake on the Wirral, stayed with him throughout the nerve-racking evening. His dream came true in a blur of technological genius and cycling determination when Boardman demolished the challenges of everyone who was ushered on to the Val d'Hebron track to face him. Lehmann, from eastern Germany, had been unrivalled in the world until Boardman's recent advances. The German and his engineers had watched and wondered what Boardman might be capable of on board his carbon-fibre, aerodynamically-shaped machine. They have filmed and photographed the bike since its first public race at a track in Leicester a month ago, but they had dismissed its capabilities rather too lightly. The British team continued to make subtle changes to fine-tune the Lotus Sport machine. The technicians, like racing car test driver Rudi Thomann, worked tirelessly. Last night the hours of energy and countless thousands of pounds were rewarded, and now Lotus can proudly add the name of Boardman and the Barcelona Olympics to the roll of honour in their Norfolk factory.

While Lehmann had been forced to break new ground with his fastest time in the semi-final when challenged by London-born Gary Anderson, representing New Zealand, Boardman had a much more comfortable success against Australian Mark Kingsland. This, Boardman appeared to have decided, was no time for heroics. The most important target in his sights was not a world record but the gold medal that has eluded British cyclists since the Antwerp Games of the 1920 Olympics. He took no chances. He cruised through the semi-final, conserving energy for what he expected to be the closest of finals. In the end it turned out to be the most spectacular of successes. No world champion can have been humbled so comprehensively.

From the moment the gate opened Boardman ate into the distance between himself and his talented German rival. With every passing lap the thunder of the approaching Boardman must have grown louder and louder for the anxious Lehmann. After two thousand metres victory was already assured; by three thousand metres Boardman had closed to within fifty metres of the world champion and then, with less than two laps to go, the British champion pulled out and slipped effortlessly by the German. His timing was perfect because his moment of glory came within feet of his wife Sally Anne who had, on the spur of the moment, flown out to share what she always felt would be the greatest day of her husband's life.

----

2 AUGUST 1992

CHRISTIE TAKES OLYMPIC CROWN
OLD MAN OF THE TRACK LEAVES RIVALS GASPING

Peter Hildreth

Linford Christie gloriously lived up to the promise of his finest season when he won the Olympic 100 metres final in Barcelona last night. With his eyes staring from their sockets in savage effort, he powered across the line in 9.96 seconds to become, at thirty-two, the oldest man to win the biggest prize in sprinting. In overcast and humid conditions, with the floodlights glinting through the gloom, Christie had one of his better starts and was never headed, claiming his title by a margin of almost a metre from the American-based Namibian Frankie Fredericks (10.02), whom Ron Roddan, the Londoner's coach, told me would be the chief adversary over both 100 and 200 metres. The American challenge, once thought unbeatable, was limited to a bronze medal for Dennis Mitchell (10.04) as Leroy Burrell (10.10), runner-up to Carl Lewis in the World Championships, faltered badly to finish fifth behind Canada's Bruny Surin (10.09).

'I showed that not only Americans can win,' said Christie. 'I ran for my life and was never relaxed. I had no doubts that I would win. It's always been my ambition to be number one in the world. It's taken a long time, it's been a slow process – and I'm clean. The Olympics is the pinnacle of every athlete's career. At thirty-two they said I was too old, but I did it. I have been going to championships since 1986, and it is great to hear *God Save The Queen*. I had to do this for everyone – for the morale of the team.'

There was a false start, debited to Burrell, who twitched and set Christie moving too. On their marks for the second time Mitchell raised his arm complaining of noise. Christie, a model of concentration, insisted the hold-ups had not worried him. 'All I had to do was focus. Nothing was going to distract me from what I came out here to do. From sixty metres I knew I had won it because no one finishes as fast as me. I was easing up when I crossed the line because I knew I had it sewn up.'

Emerging from doping control two hours after the final, Christie said: 'I can't afford to celebrate otherwise my other races, the 200 metres and the relay, will suffer. It's a shame Carl wasn't there, it would have been an even better race with him.' A final without the commanding presences of Lewis or Ben Johnson never seemed likely to live up to the epic scenario of a contest for the title 'fastest man on earth'. It was not the greatest race, but Christie was unquestionably the greatest on the night.

---

2 AUGUST 1992

DREAMBOAT COMES IN FOR REDGRAVE AND PINSENT

Geoffrey Page

The dream came true for Steve Redgrave when he and Matthew Pinsent overwhelmed the opposition in the coxless pair final at Banyoles to take the gold medal with the outstanding performance of the day. It brought Redgrave a remarkable third consecutive Olympic gold rowing medal, the first time this has been achieved by a British oarsman. It had been Redgrave's target and principal source of motivation this year, and he had to overcome some setbacks earlier in the season when he had been suffering from colitis. The pair looked the likely winners from their first heats, but anything can happen to upset form in Olympic finals. However, the Leander pair, the reigning world champions, made no mistakes and were in magnificent form.

Germany, the Lucerne winners, led initially but Britain had taken the lead by the 250-metre mark and were a length up after five hundred metres. They were now in full control, rowing at a powerful thirty-four, with most of the opposition striking a pip or two higher. Britain were a quarter-of-a-length clear at halfway, with less than three lengths separating the other five pairs. Pinsent raised the rate to thirty-five after fifteen hundred metres and to thirty-eight at seventeen hundred and fifty metres and the opposition could not match the pace. Redgrave and Pinsent crossed the line at forty-two well clear of the Germans, who took the silver medal by a narrow margin from the Slovenians, last year's world silver medallists, who had twice beaten the British pair earlier in the season when Redgrave was not fully fit.

Redgrave's collection of international medals is now extensive. Apart from his Olympic wins in the 1984 coxed fours, and the coxless pairs with Andy Holmes in 1988 and yesterday's win, he also took a bronze medal in the coxed pairs in Seoul. He has won three world titles, two in coxless pairs and one in coxed, on the latter occasion at the expense of the Abbagnale brothers from Italy.

Pinsent, who learnt his rowing at Eton, won a world junior gold in coxless pairs in 1988, and a senior coxed four bronze in 1989. He was again a bronze medallist in the pair with Redgrave in 1990 before winning the world title last year. He has twice rowed for Oxford but dropped out of the last academic year to concentrate on the Olympics. He is the Oxford president for next year's Boat Race and is now the first O.U.B.C. president to be a world and Olympic champion while holding office.

———

3 AUGUST 1992

SEARLE BROTHERS SURGE TO FAMOUS VICTORY AS ITALIANS WEAKEN

Geoffrey Page

An outstanding performance by Jonathan and Gregory Searle brought Britain a second gold medal in the most dramatic finish of a superlative day's racing in yesterday's finals at Banyoles. After Steve Redgrave and Matthew Pinsent's overwhelming victory in the coxless pairs on Saturday, the coxed pair's race could hardly have been more different. The young British pair were facing the Italians, Carmine and Guiseppe Abbagnale, seven-times world champions and seeking, like Redgrave, a third successive Olympic title.

The Italians were clear of the field at five hundred metres, with Britain in fourth place, and had stretched their lead to two lengths by the 1,500-metre mark, where the Searles were still only third. It began to look as though the real battle was going to be between Romania and Britain for the silver medal until Greg Searle went into overdrive; he was striking forty at sixteen hundred metres and Britain were beginning to close the gap. At seventeen hundred and fifty metres, it was clear that the Italians were beginning to feel the pressure. Britain were past the Romanians and, in the final row-in, the Italians suddenly wilted. Striking forty-three, the Searles caught Italy with half a dozen strokes to go and the gold was theirs. It was a spectacular and famous victory, one of the most dramatic in Olympic rowing history. The Italians have been beaten only twice in the world championships since winning in 1981, one of these defeats coming from Andy Holmes and Steve Redgrave, who took the title in 1986.

The Searle brothers – ten years younger than the Italians – have been in this class of boat only since April and their finishing pace in their heat and semi-final astonished the crowd. Greg, at twenty, three years younger than his brother, said: 'Everything was going black. I didn't know what was going on. It was lucky that, being brothers, we switched into the same auto pilot.' 'Greg was brilliant,' said his brother. 'He kept us in touch with them all the time.' Garry Herbert, their cox, said: 'I wanted them to be prepared to die for this, and they nearly did.'

6 AUGUST 1992

GOLDEN GUNNELL DESTROYS FIELD TO BRING HOME HURDLES TITLE

Colin Gibson

Sally Gunnell, a farmer's daughter from Chigwell in Essex, became only the second British woman to win an Olympic track title. Gunnell, second at the World Championships in Tokyo last year, produced a 400-metres hurdles performance last night in Barcelona that brimmed with courage, commitment and determination. Her reward was to become the first woman since Ann Packer won the 800 metres at the Tokyo Games of 1964 to hold a track gold medal, and the Montjuic Stadium rose to acclaim her achievement.

Her victory, in 53.23 seconds, guaranteed her place in British sporting history. It was a moment to savour for Gunnell, twenty-six last week, who had suffered the disappointment of having the world title snatched from her by the Unified Team's Tatyana Ledovskaya in Japan. But there was never a danger that the Russian, or the highly fancied Sandra Farmer-Patrick, of the United States, would ruin her night.

The tension gripping the woman from the Unified Team was obvious – she was responsible for a false start – and she never really found her rhythm. From the moment Gunnell went over the penultimate hurdle in the lead there seemed no chance that she would be caught. 'When I went over that hurdle I thought that I must not waste the lead that I had established.' Not only did she not squander the advantage but she actually increased the distance between herself and her rivals after the final hurdle. Farmer-Patrick searched for the acceleration that might have caught the Commonwealth champion, but by then Gunnell already had the finish line and the Olympic gold fixed in her sights.

Farmer-Patrick, who held on to claim the silver ahead of her compatriot, Janeene Vickers, admitted that there was little she could do once Gunnell had passed her on the home straight. 'Sally was a bit of a surprise when she came up alongside and a lot of my concentration evaporated,' said the American. 'She made the least amount of mistakes and deserved to win.'

Gunnell, whose winning time was only six-hundredths of a second outside the Olympic record set by Debbie Flintoff-King in Seoul four years before, always felt confident that she could take the gold for Britain. 'I always thought that I could do it,' she said, 'I had the experience of winning the silver medal in the World Championships in Tokyo last year and so I knew what to expect in this race. The disappointment of not winning in Toyko made me a little bit more determined to win here in Barcelona. I was delighted that the race went well in a technical sense. I wanted to make sure that I did not fall down on that aspect of the race. I just gave it everything that I could but I have to say that there is not much of the race that I remember. It is just beginning to sink in.' Wrapped in a British flag and clutching a Teddy bear, Gunnell – who becomes only the fifth British woman in the history of Olympic track and field to win a gold medal after Packer, Mary Rand, Mary Peters and Tessa Sanderson – headed out on a lap of honour to the accompaniment of a standing ovation from the crowd which was heavily laced with support from home.

---

7 AUGUST 1992

EMOTIONS RUN HIGH AS LEWIS INCHES TO VICTORY

Michael Calvin

Three centimetres. Just over an inch. By such margins are legends embellished and losers embittered. Just ask Carl Lewis and Mike Powell. Lewis won his seventh Olympic title last night with his opening long jump of 8.67 metres. He produced the Stars and Stripes with a flourish, acted as cheerleader for the crowd and savoured the moment. As the champion milked the applause, Powell walked, shoulders drooping, to a bench which offered no sanctuary. He turned away from television cameras and buried his face in his hands.

His prayers had not been answered. The instant the electronic scoreboard recorded his last leap as 8.64 metres he imploded. Lewis swamped him in a telegenic embrace, but his taut body barely responded. 'When I hit the sand I heard the noise of the crowd and I knew it was going to be close,' he said. 'I looked back at the board, but I just couldn't tell. Carl was meant to win.' Lewis traditionally refines his emotions and thinks before revealing his deepest feelings. But guaranteed tangible reward for a season scarred by his failure to qualify for the Olympic sprints, he was suitably animated. The only gold medal that has meant more – his first, for winning the 100 metres at Los Angeles in 1984 – went into his father's coffin when he was buried in 1987. 'This was my most difficult gold to win,' he stressed. 'The challenge was so intense.'

Lewis has reduced his run from fifty-five to forty-nine metres to ensure he is accelerating when he hits the take-off board. The long jump is a technically precise event, yet it also defines an athlete's character. The stadium, bathed in bright evening sunshine, was packed to its sixty-one thousand capacity. For all he was aware of that mass of humanity, Lewis could have been in the middle of the Kalahari Desert. His routine was constant. Even apparently spontaneous gestures were regimented. On every attempt he licked his lips, exhaled in short, sharp bursts and composed himself by focusing on the runway. His first jump was an object lesson in the avoidance of distraction. As he prepared himself, Powell gambolled on to the track to embrace Kevin Young, who had just broken the world 400-metres hurdles record. The crowd were exultant, yet Lewis, lost in his own search for excellence, spoke urgently to himself. The first jump, normally a statement of intent, proved decisive.

There was no visible sense of satisfaction. Powell, dressed in a tracksuit that gave him the appearance of a psychedelic zebra, reacted with studied indifference. Yet his introduction to the finals was to be equally instructive. His left hand, trailing in the sand, reduced his distance to 7.95 metres, a metre short of his world record. He rarely seemed at ease with himself. Recent back and hamstring injuries affected his preparations, and the burden of attempting to become the first man to defeat Lewis in an Olympic long jump competition was etched on his expressive face. 'I was bewildered,' he admitted. 'There I was at the Olympic Games and I wasn't excited. I told myself, "Get it together", but I couldn't.' The solitary consolation was that Lewis, too, was not at his peak. He was visibly angry after two successive no-jumps in the middle of his programme and rarely threatened to exceed his initial effort.

The climax was the theatre the world had anticipated. Spectators all around the vast concrete bowl of the stadium clapped rhythmically. It was the sound of ultimate opportunity. Powell squatted down at the end of the runway like a Muslim at prayer. He clapped his hands, exhaled and, arms flailing, sprinted towards his destiny. 'I was praying quite a bit out there, believe me,' he said. 'It's been a really difficult year for me and I was asking God to enable me to compete to the best of my ability. That opportunity was all I could have asked for. It was within reach, but my body just felt flat. I felt great in the warm-up, but I just didn't have that pop.'

Lewis had been sitting alone, isolated by his impotence. He thought back to the World Championships where he, too, had failed to make the most of his last chance. 'It was all out of my hands,' he reasoned. 'We've all had experience of being in that situation. I just had to sit and wait, knowing Mike could pull it off.' He tried, but failed. Carl Lewis was, once more, an Olympic champion. By three centimetres. Just over an inch.

---

10 AUGUST 1992

CATALONIAN FIESTA IS TREASURE TROVE OF SPANISH GOLD

Michael Calvin

A sea of people flooded down the mountainside, past the fairytale palace and the floodlit waterfall, and into Placa Espanya, a Barcelona landmark. There was no more appropriate place on Saturday night to celebrate Spain's Olympics. Elderly men mirrored the wonder of grandchildren who clung to them in the crowds. Everyone, irrespective of age, class or sex, wanted to bathe in the reflected glory of thirteen gold medals.

Barcelona was locked in a delirious traffic jam, which parted to reveal a taxi. On its roof was a member of Spain's triumphant football team, waving his gold medal. No Roman emperor had a more adoring audience. Spain, who had won only four golds since the modern Olympics began in 1896, and never more than one in any previous Olympiad, had exceeded its wildest expectations. The self-congratulatory mood cut across all social barriers.

The city seethed on Saturday night. Fermin Cacho's epic victory in the 1,500 metres was that of a man emboldened by an entire nation. He was propelled to the line by prayer. King Juan Carlos and the Queen embraced Cacho before rushing to the Nou Camp Stadium where they oversaw a last-minute Spanish winner of Wagnerian intensity in the football tournament. Even though the water polo squad had to settle for silver when they lost 9–8 to Italy in over-time yesterday, the achievements of the Spanish squad have surpassed all expectations.

Before the Games, national Olympic committee president Carlos Ferrer said: 'We are moderately optimistic because we are only a minor sporting power. We are seeking to triple the four medals [1–1–2] we won at Seoul.' The Spanish Government invested more than £100 million in the preparations of elite competitors, and state-controlled firms such as cigarette company Fortuna, offered a range of financial incentives. Banks provided a range of pensions, payable in a lump sum on the fiftieth birthday of any instant Olympic hero. A bronze medal was worth £250,000, a silver £400,000 and a gold £500,000. The Barcelona authorities, who spent £7 billion on facilities, fostered an invaluable sense of civic pride. A seven-second delay on TV transmission gave scope to edit out political demonstrations, and the Spanish royal family received more air time than Magic Johnson. As a result, they were Spain's, rather than Catalonia's, Olympics.

Zola Budd was outclassed in her 3,000 metres heat. But she was unrecognisable from the tortured, self-defensive waif whose only previous Olympic experience, in Los Angeles in 1984, ended in vilification by the crowd. She was representing something far bigger than herself. For when her South African team-mate Elana Meyer won a silver medal in the 10,000 metres, she united, however briefly, a nation that once institutionalised division.

Gail Devers, of the United States, overcame disease to become 100 metres champion. She fell when the hurdles gold was within reach. Her reward was to be subjected to unsubstantiated allegations of drug use by Gwen Torrence, her team-mate. Torrence, who apologised for her comments immediately after winning the 200 metres, had succumbed to the underlying frustration of modern athletics. Drugs pollute the bodies of the guilty and infect the minds of the innocent. It does not do to be too parochial in the Olympics, however admirable the performances of Steve Redgrave, Sally Gunnell, Linford Christie, Chris Boardman and the Searle brothers. One would like to think the most significant British victory was the moral lead offered by denying Jason Livingston, Andrew Davies and Andrew Saxton the right to sample the Olympic experience. China's emergence aroused inevitable suspicion.

The fragmentation of the Soviet Union was put into stark context by the misnamed Unified Team, who, today, cease to exist. Their accustomed place at the head of the medals table was deceptive. Top names, like the gymnast Vitaliy Shcherbo, who won six gold medals in Barcelona, are fearful of retribution in their homelands. The 'Dream Team', the multi-millionaires of American basketball who were the dominant personalities of the Games, did not merely move the Olympic goalposts. They chopped them up and used the splinters as tooth picks. Juan Antonio Samaranch, the I.O.C. president, was possibly star-struck when he 'received' Magic Johnson, who responded to the solemnity of the occasion by wearing Bermuda shorts. Their team bus was protected by a helicopter, eight motorcycle outriders, three police cars and two armoured vans with guards toting pump-action shotguns peering out of open doors. The crowds reacted like teenyboppers. Even in the Placa Espanya, at the height of Spanish celebrations, the Americans' gold medal was cheered. The world was suddenly a smaller, much smaller, place. The Olympic Games do matter, after all.

CHAPTER 11
ATLANTA 1996

16 JULY 1996

FROM HICK TO SLICK IT'S THE REAL THING AS CITY COMES OF AGE

Iain Macleod in Atlanta

The Games of the twenty-sixth Olympiad approach and this southern city, so desperate to live up to its boast of being 'the world's next great city', finally stands on the threshold of completing its 163-year transformation from modest cotton town and transportation hub to international metropolis. Torched by General Sherman in 1864 during the American Civil War, the city's treasury was left with $1.64 million when rebuilding began and it is ironic now that the symbolic moment that will usher Atlanta towards the fulfilment of its dream also has blazing connotations. The lighting of the Olympic Flame on Friday evening will be Atlanta's coming of age, and the party will last for sixteen days.

The conversion of the city from hick to slick has been remarkable. When Atlanta, in 1990, won the right to stage the centennial Games, the city, which one local described as 'just a bus stop on the way to Florida', had little to commend it. To some extent that is still true, though occasionally there are moments which are purely southern. There is no industry here other than hype and commerce, the epitome of the city, at least until now, particularly as it is also Coca-Cola city; you cannot escape the images of the Games' longest-serving sponsor.

Amid the gaudiness of Coca-Cola city, there is another side that the Atlanta committee for the Olympic Games do not want visitors to see; it is said that as part of the reinventing of the Olympic city, the undesirables who blemished the commercial skyline were offered a one-way ticket to nowhere. This is a city governed by blacks but dominated by whites; it is the city of Martin Luther King and the Ku Klux Klan; it is the city which has spawned so many dreams in recent years, whether they be of racial harmony or Olympic glory. And, frankly, my dear, they do give a damn.

Criticism of the city has known no bounds and while Atlanta may not be entirely aware of what it has taken on, there is a deep-rooted yearning for the twenty-sixth edition of this extraordinary event which Billy Payne, the man whose vision brought the Games to Atlanta has called 'the greatest peacetime event in the history of the world', to be nothing more, nothing less. Anita de Frantz, one of the U.S. members of the International Olympic Committee, and one of their more gifted talents, says that whatever problems are perceived in the build-up to a Games, 'when they begin they have a momentum of their own'. She should know, given her involvement with the 1984 Games in Los Angeles which led to the Games' metamorphosis from penury to a multi-billion dollar entity.

The gremlins, though, are starting to appear. The I.O.C., publicly, always defend the organising committee even when relations are at their lowest ebb; privately, it is different and already many of the Olympic family complain that for all the willingness of the volunteers, some appear ill-trained for their assignments. Accreditation, which takes place close to Hartsfield international airport, is already creaking; waiting time has been up to four hours, and each day the tension increases as the volume of foreign visitors intensifies. There are fears that transportation, the perennial Olympic problem, could paralyse the city when the Games begin; taxi drivers have hiked up charges despite frequently being totally unaware of where their destination lies; meanwhile, undistinguished restaurants will, for the duration of the Games, add a twenty per cent service charge.

---

22 JULY 1996

ALI'S NIGHTMARE AND KING'S DREAM VIVID AT GREAT AWAKENING

Paul Hayward

The last time Muhammad Ali had been on an Olympic podium a gold medal dangled from his neck as he embarked on the most illustrious career in sporting history. Thirty-six years later he stood alone, like a fading emperor wheeled out in front of his people, trying to control a violently shaking left arm and light the Olympic Flame that would declare the Atlanta Games open. In the control room of the opening ceremony staff, Don Mischer, the creator of a show that was watched by forty-seven per cent of American television viewers, was saying through his headset: 'Get ready to help him. Help Ali light it.' The hands that had destroyed so many men would not now lift a torch to a wick that would rise on a wire one hundred and seventy feet to ignite the Olympic Flame. Those hands, the Ali hands, so close to letting go.

Ali had appeared unexpectedly on a stage overlooking the Olympic Stadium in white trousers and official torch-bearer's T-shirt. The Flame had been carried for eighty-four days across fifteen thousand miles of America and had been passed via boxer Evander Holyfield and Janet Evans, a young Californian swimmer, to Ali, trapped inside a body that no longer works. The Olympics – the whole of sport – trembled on the edge of a terrible pathos as Ali planted his shaking left hand on the torch and the flame crept perilously close to scorching his right arm. They waited for the clatter of metal on stage. They waited for the medics to rush out. Neither happened. He clutched the torch long enough and straight enough to send the wick skywards, and before those eighty-three thousand dazzled souls could look down again Ali was being helped into a black Transit van at the back of the stadium and taken back to his hotel. Another victory, another foe overcome.

The problem is, what should we think of this brutal exposure of Ali's injuries? Was he being used? Was he cheated for the thousandth time in his ruined life? One common view about Ali is that he lived more than most of us could in fifty lifetimes, and so is in no need of our sympathy or remorse. In the end, that theory doesn't work. Ali has severe brain damage because he boxed too much, and he boxed too much because so many people stole his money. He is a father and grandfather, and his family have to see him that way without the luxury of detachment that the rest of us voyeurs can enjoy.

The symbolic importance of Ali's appearance, though, was unquestionable. For the American South these Olympics have taken on a cathartic quality. They are seen as an opportunity to escape forever the legacy of segregation and racism which was challenged by Atlanta's most famous son, the Reverend Martin Luther King Junior, who lost his life in the struggle. For the local columnist, Dave Kindred, the opening ceremony brought together 'the world King spoke of on a day a generation ago'.

'THE GAMES WILL GO ON' PLEDGE IOC

Colin Gibson sees shadow of 1972 disaster darken the city of Atlanta

François Carrard, the International Olympic Committee's director general, was insistent. 'The Games will go on,' he said yesterday morning in downtown Atlanta. 'The Games will go on.' The question now is for how long and where? Moments after the bomb exploded in Centennial Park, the I.O.C. and the Atlanta Committee for the Olympic Games (A.C.O.G.) began trying to rebuild confidence in the Games. It is a challenge that the I.O.C. have faced before. In Munich twenty-four years ago the Olympic Movement had their biggest crisis. Israeli athletes had been massacred by Palestinian terrorists. In Munich, just as in Atlanta, the Games continued in sombre and subdued mood. The I.O.C. felt that they could not be held hostage to terrorism and that to cancel the Games would have been the final surrender.

After Munich the then I.O.C. president, Avery Brundage, insisted: 'We have only the strength of a great ideal. I am sure that the public would agree we cannot allow a handful of terrorists to destroy this nucleus of international co-operation and goodwill.' Yesterday in Atlanta those words were echoed by Billy Payne, the president of A.C.O.G. He argued: 'We must continue in the spirit of the Olympic Movement. The Olympic family mandate that we must continue even though we feel discouraged or dismayed by these events. We must link arms and march together to protect the Olympic Movement who are one of the bright hopes for the future. We cannot be deviated from that aim.'

But just as after Munich, the I.O.C. now recognise there must be a price to pay if the Olympics are going to continue in their present form. Unlike Munich, Atlanta was on the highest security alert. More than forty thousand members of the armed forces and national guard had been brought into the city. Every street corner was manned by Army or Air Force guards, every building was surrounded by massive police security. After the explosion on TWA flight 800, security in Atlanta had been raised to the highest in the United States since the Gulf War. It was a city ringed in steel but it still proved vulnerable. It was an expensive ring. The costs of security in Atlanta are estimated at $300 million, and with the Defence Department budget alone being suggested at $50 million, increased measures are certain to push that bill higher. 'No one can ever guarantee that every public place at an Olympic Games is entirely safe,' said Payne. If that is the case, are the Games really worth the price in terms of money and human life?

———

REDGRAVE'S MASTER STROKE

Brough Scott on the high cost of Olympic gold on Lake Lanier

They did it. They truly did it. But don't let anyone suggest that it was anything but agony. Up on the wooded shores of Lake Lanier, Redgrave and Pinsent took on the titanic task of moving our attention away from the worries of bomb-hit Atlanta to haul themselves once again to gold. They led the coxless pairs all the way. Two seconds up on New Zealand at five hundred metres, 2.8 over France at one thousand, 2.4 over the Australian pair at fifteen hundred, who had reduced that to 0.93 seconds when Redgrave and Pinsent crossed the line after six minutes and 20.09 seconds of what could be their last row.

Afterwards you could see the toll it had taken. Matthew Pinsent had the energy to punch the air, those strangely British red cheeks blooming with the effort. But behind him in the boat, Steven Redgrave, the mighty Redgrave, was utterly spent. He lolled to his side, trying to get breath and strength from somewhere. It was a history-making performance. The first rower to take gold at four consecutive Olympics: Los Angeles, Seoul, Barcelona and now Atlanta. Soon he was to tell us of the cost. Once he and his partner had oxygen enough to get themselves upright, they paddled slowly across to the far side of the lake, where the interviewer was waiting. 'If anyone,' gasped Redgrave, 'sees me go near a boat again, they have permission to shoot me. I never want to get into another boat in my life.' Pinsent was later to say something similar, and if it is indeed the end of their astonishing unbeaten sequence, we must treasure the memory of two athletes of the strongest steel.

Only a tiny fraction of us have had much to do with a rowing skiff. Indeed if almost any two of us tried to get in Redgrave and Pinsent's bamboo-like craft, we would capsize it in an instant. But we know perfection when we see it, mind and body, arms and legs and oars, and skimming water. Redgrave and Pinsent represented an absolute. You have to hang on to them while you can. Pinsent has, of course, become much more than the gangly lieutenant he was in Barcelona. He is a terrific and articulate sportsman in his own right. But he is the first to give the bow to Redgrave; to an athlete who in so many senses has become a man apart.

Redgrave can soon return to the smiling splendour which adorned his features as he carried the Union Jack like a mainsail out in front of him through the Olympic Stadium. Within a few days the agony of yesterday's efforts and the exhausted thoughts at his interviews may prompt a rethink. But the memory will remain not just of him in full power afloat, but of a phrase he dropped as the tension mounted on Thursday. Someone asked him why he was being uncharacteristically short with his answers. He took the question; he was not rough with it, but his reply was a million miles from an apology. 'You've got to realise it's been a long time now. This is what we've worked and trained for. This is serious. We've got to begin to tighten the focusing.' He looked round our assorted company. Just a gaggle of hacks in a marquee in upstate Georgia. Just another set of microphones begging for words on which to feed. He could say them, but could we comprehend? 'It's like this,' he said. 'The mind has got to tighten in. I'm going somewhere else now. I'm not really with you any more.' Yes, he would have to go there for this one final time. To another country, where only the great champions can breathe. To a mountain-top where the inspiration lies, to bring back the strength which we watchers will never forget.

---

31 JULY 1996

LEWIS'S LEAP ANSWERS THE CALL OF HISTORY

Michael Calvin in Atlanta

Carl Lewis has lost the arrogance of invulnerability. He has endured adversity, responded to ridicule and self-doubt. Age has given him grace, grey hairs and the glory of a record ninth gold medal. When he won the Atlanta long jump early yesterday, and joined Al Oerter as the only track and field athlete to win four consecutive Olympic titles, he was feted as much for his fallibility as his unique ability. 'A lot of people thought I didn't have it any more, that I couldn't win,' he acknowledged, without rancour. 'They laughed behind my back, saying, "Heh, heh, he won't make it!" There were so many years when I was invincible. But this year I had to do blue collar work. I had to jump like a dog before I got my confidence back. That's what makes this the most special medal. It took the most pain.'

His longest leap, 8.50 metres (twenty-seven feet ten and three-quarter inches), was the shortest of his four winning distances dating back to 1984, when he announced himself as Jesse Owens's heir by dominating the Los Angeles Games. It was all so easy then. Too easy. His natural nonchalance bred resentment. He knew his own mind, and spoke it, with monotonous regularity. His achievements were booed. His talent was begrudged. But in Atlanta, 'twelve years, sixteen hairstyles and miles and miles of training' later, he was redeemed. The eighty-three thousand crowd savoured his struggle, acclaimed his success with unprecedented warmth. The dilettante had revealed himself as a fighter.

He had missed last year's World Championship with a hamstring injury that signalled the inevitable deterioration of his 35-year-old body. He secured selection for the U.S. team by a single inch, and reached the Olympic final with his last qualifying jump. Then, with his third leap in the final, he answered the call of history. Instinct took over. The moment Lewis landed, he leapt up, as if the sandpit was filled with scalding water. He immediately glanced over his shoulder at the measuring board. He knew the magnitude of what he had done.

World champion Ivan Pedrosa, making a premature return from surgery, failed to make the final three jumps. World record-holder Mike Powell sustained a groin injury and writhed in agony as his dream died. That left Joe Greene, the third string American who had seen Jamaican James Beckford supplant him in second place in the final round. Lewis lounged backwards, leaning on his hands, with his face a mask of apparent indifference. Greene sprinted, threw himself forward. He, too, glanced over his shoulder, only to find an official flourishing a red flag. Carl Lewis had equalled Paavo Nurmi's record of nine Olympic titles.

It was only later, however, when Oerter emerged to laughingly suggest 'this man is too old to do such things', that he could begin to put the accomplishment into perspective. 'I've always been honoured to touch people's lives,' Lewis reflected. 'But, I tell you, today they reciprocated. Millions of them stood up and gave something back to me. I think about Jesse Owens on days like today. I've read a lot about Paavo Nurmi lately, and we have a lot of similarities. People call me a legend, but I still see the same person in the mirror. I've taken a lot of abuse over the years. I've taken a lot of heat but, at the same time, a lot of joy from what I have done. I've never wavered from what I believe in. It has always been full speed ahead. I don't think track and field wants another Carl Lewis. They may want the athlete, but they don't want the whole package.'

————

31 JULY 1996

JOHNSON GLISTERS ON GOLDEN TRAIL
Paul Hayward

Michael Johnson is athlete number 2370 at these Games, but he really ought to be contestant number one. His gold lamé shoes have already carried him to the 400 metres title and tonight he will set off across a glittering landscape of flashbulbs in pursuit of a unique men's 400-200 metres Olympic double. With Johnson in the 400 metres there is a race A and a race B. Roger Black, of Britain, can reasonably claim to have won gold in race B while Johnson streaked away with the real title in that curious Gumpish way of his. 'I won't say what I said to myself when he came past me,' said Iwan Thomas, of Newham and Essex Beagles, who finished fifth. 'I knew he was coming, though. I felt his presence.'

The flashbulb count is a good way to register an athlete's popularity. When Johnson set off in the 400-metres final on Monday night a great rolling wave of fairy lights twinkled across the packed stands of Atlanta's Olympic Stadium. Johnson has taken from Carl Lewis the role of America's foremost track and field athlete and at last is receiving the recognition his magnificent talents deserve. No longer is he known purely as Eddie Murphy's double.

Watching Johnson assert his dominance is a privilege which even Black seemed to acknowledge. Those kind of opportunities come once every generation, as the American public are now realising. In the first heat of the 400 metres he overtook the runner on his outside long before he had rounded the first bend. Turning towards the straight you would think he was running past traffic bollards, not the best of the rest of the world. For pub trivia questions, remember that Sugath Thilakaratne, of Sri Lanka, actually managed to beat Johnson in one of the heats when the champion slowed almost to a walk after scorching the opposition on the bend. You half expected him to get a picnic hamper out.

It's a measure of Johnson's stature that his victory over Black and Davis Kamoga, of Uganda, was tinged, for some, with disappointment. For a runner who is unbeaten in major races over 400 metres since 1989 it amounts to something of a failure to break only the Olympic record. 'A lot of people were talking about the world record but I'm not disappointed at all,' said Johnson, 'I'll have other opportunities to win a world record. Everybody said at the start of this race, "Hey, you're blowing 'em away. You're playing with them. It looks so easy". But nobody was going to say, "Hey Mike, here's the gold medal".'

Johnson, whose running style is close to the great Jesse Owens's, is not a flamboyant character. Lewis ungraciously suggested he is short on 'charisma' and therefore the wrong heir to his title of America's leading athlete. Johnson has had to endure this calumny for four years so it was inevitable that Lewis should partially upstage him on the same night by winning his fourth consecutive Olympic long jump. 'That's great,' said Johnson when asked what he thought of Lewis's victory. The long silence that followed revealed more about his feelings. 'I've never said he needs to pass the torch to me. I said I think he should step down from trying to be the premier athlete of track and field. I'm not in competition with Carl. I'm just trying to win as many gold medals as I can and put my name up there with the great athletes. Carl Lewis is one of those.'

The one extravagance in Johnson's make-up are those gold running spikes, which he bought for these Olympics and are a gaudy reminder to his opponents of how far he is ahead. 'I just chose that colour because I felt good about my chances for gold,' he said. 'I guess it worked.' The T-shirt bore the warning 'Danger Zone'. And that, in athletics terms, is what he is. 'It's just the mindset I'm in,' he said, before retiring for the equivalent of a quick nap between events. 'The 200 is a completely different race and I've got to get into it. The guys are already talking about what they're going to do to me and saying I'm vulnerable because I've run the 400.' He paused for a moment, lowered his voice and said: 'That's a big mistake.'

A BLUE BLUR, THEN A SWOOSH AS JOHNSON STRIDES INTO HISTORY

Michael Calvin

Pandemonium. The public address announcer screams: 'It's hard to describe the magnitude of what we just saw.' To mark an historic Olympic occasion he plays a New Age punk rock song in honour of Michael Johnson. *You're Unbelievable.* The message contained in the repetitive three-chord chorus captures the moment. Johnson has, in 19.32 seconds, contemptuously defied conventional athletic thinking. He is the first man to add the Olympic 200 metres title to the 400 metres gold medal. He has matched speed and endurance, and produced the type of world-record performance that occurs once in a generation.

Turn the clock back ninety minutes. Johnson has won his semi-final with absurd ease, recording a time of 20.27 seconds. He opts to take a bus back to the warm-up area rather than submit himself to introspective study by his peers. 'Why sit there under the stands, staring at each other?' asks his coach, Clyde Hart. He first met Johnson as a gangly youth, and retained faith in him when he finished third in the 200 metres at the Texas High School Championships. 'Michael had the qualities I was looking for,' he explains. 'He was a good student. He came from a good family. He was a youngster I was never going to have problems with. That's the key with him. He'll work hard for you. People doubted him, but I knew he possessed something different. That leg speed. That was something he had when the doctor smacked him on the bottom and he said hello to the world.'

Coach and athlete work for forty-five minutes while others stew in the juices of an Olympic final. Hart stresses how disturbed he had been by Johnson's speed around the bend as he prepared for the semi-final. Even other athletes, absorbed in their own preparatory rituals, stood to watch. 'Slow down,' he orders, and halves Johnson's traditional warm-up routine. He does one practice start, followed by two laps of the track. Hart then institutes reaction drills 'to key up his fast-twitch muscle fibres'. Johnson allows himself thirty minutes to return to the Olympic Stadium. Hart reminds him: 'Everyone is a suspect. Go for them all.' Johnson is healthily nervous and walks with his head bowed, concerned to the point of paranoia about stubbing his toe. He is impassive as he waits on the blocks. He is telling himself: 'This is the one I want.' Frankie Fredericks sucks his lower lip, like an insecure schoolboy. Ato Boldon, in a black zip-up sweatsuit and wraparound shades, exudes aggression.

One final exhalation, to control the tension, and Johnson gets to his marks. His block for his left foot is two feet behind the starting line. His right foot fits into one precisely forty-two and a half inches from the line. He reacts well to the gun, leaving his blocks in 0.161 seconds, but stumbles momentarily. He knows he has disobeyed his coach and tried to get upright too quickly. 'That cost me hundredths of a second,' he admits. 'I was afraid of how fast I could run. I wanted to make history.' By his fourth stride, he was on schedule. 'I've never known such pressure in my entire life,' he is to reflect, much later. 'It's been with me for six months. Every newspaper, every magazine I picked up talked of this double. Every telephone call seemed to be about it. People reminded me of it as I walked down the street.'

But no one runs bends better than Johnson. He has short legs, from his knee to his ankle, for a man of his height, six foot one. Bio-mechanists believe his speed of stride, which allows him to skim the track, makes him the most efficient sprinter in the world. His feet touch the ground for eight-hundredths of a second, one hundredth of a second less than the best 100-metres sprinters. That advantage, allied to the strength of an intriguingly well-ordered mind, is unbeatable. Oblivious to the clamour of the crowd, Johnson consciously relaxes and, by eighty metres, has the gold medal won. All that has to be decided is the margin of a legendary victory. 'Coming off the curve, into the straight, I felt I was running faster than ever before,' he says afterwards. 'You can always tell at that point. I knew I had a shot at the record. I was in control.'

Boldon, the brash new kid on the block, is about to discover the facts of life. 'I noticed a blue blur and a swoosh. As he went by I thought, "There goes first".' Fredericks is overhauled within two strides, but beats off a brief Boldon rally to claim the silver. 'It will take a perfect race to beat Michael. I don't really know what to say. I doubt if we can get close to that.' That propels the eighty-three thousand spectators off their seats. Johnson, who according to official statistics had covered the first hundred metres in 10.12 seconds, completes the second half of the race in 9.20. Hart, in the stands, has hand-timed the splits as 9.85 for the first hundred and 9.47 for the second. No matter. Johnson is still running in excess of 25 m.p.h. He experiences a twinge of cramp in his right hamstring three strides, or five metres, from the line. Bizarrely, given the magnitude of the moment, he begins to think ahead to his duties in the 4 × 400-metre relay team (in fact he later withdrew with the hamstring strain). As he crosses the line instinct tells him he has run 19.5 seconds, what Hunt calls 'the magic number'. But as he begins to decelerate Johnson glances over his shoulder and sees his time, highlighted in yellow lights on a rectangular scoreboard. 19.32. You're unbelievable.

---

6 AUGUST 1996

BARBED BOUQUET FOR ATLANTA AS I.O.C. PRESIDENT MAKES HIS EXIT

Rampant commercialism of past fortnight will not be repeated, says Iain Macleod

The normally cheery farewell wave from Juan Antonio Samaranch, the president of the International Olympic Committee, seemed to contain a veiled thumbs down for Atlanta as the twenty-sixth Olympiad ended here on Sunday night. Amid the customary pomp and ceremony, Samaranch unusually refused to give an unqualified endorsement that these Games were the greatest. 'Most exceptional,' was as far as he would go. In I.O.C.-speak that can be considered a rebuke to Billy Payne, president of the Atlanta Committee for the Olympic Games, all the more so as the ceremony was shown live around the world, and Samaranch had earlier stated that 'commercialism must not run the Games'. Samaranch added: 'We need commercialisation, but this must be controlled by the organising committee or the I.O.C. Without commercialisation it's impossible to organise the Games.'

The private entrepreneurial exercise that cluttered the streets and became one of major derogatory images from Atlanta will not be allowed to happen again. The relationship between the I.O.C. and the A.C.O.G. has been somewhat fractious during the seventeen days that were characterised in the first week by seemingly never-ending transportation problems and systems failures and the bomb in Centennial Park, and in the second, by a magnificent track and field meeting that helped to salvage some of Atlanta's reputation. But the fact remains that for all the wonderful moments in the sporting arenas, the Games will be remembered for much more than that, even if Michael Johnson's monumental world 200 metres record of 19.32 seconds was probably the defining moment.

The argument that any Games should be judged by the quality of its sporting achievements is to misunderstand the awesome responsibility that is bestowed on a host city in the modern era. The Games have become far too big, too much of a logistical nightmare, to be left to well-meaning amateurs. And that, effectively, is how many I.O.C. members viewed A.C.O.G. and their hierarchy. Neither did A.C.O.G.'s relationship with the city council provide succour; one senior I.O.C. official, unhappy about the street vendors in that they undermined commercial potential, said 'the city did everything it could to sabotage the Games', as the privately-funded Olympics scrambled around desperately, right up to the opening ceremony, to meet a $1.7 billion budget.

The Atlanta committee did not always seem to understand the magnitude of what they had taken on. The I.O.C., clearly unhappy about the shoddy organisation, should take some blame; it is not as if the I.O.C. co-ordination commission, under the chairmanship of Canada's Richard Pound, were unaware of potential problems. Pound, during the first week when the debacle was at its worst, said that the I.O.C. had 'been banging the drum' about transportation for over two years – to little effect, as it transpired. Samaranch said on Sunday that a small working group related to the co-ordination commission could be set up so that they could visit Sydney more frequently. It is to be hoped the I.O.C. show greater awareness than they did with Atlanta. Samaranch is said at one stage to have asked an aide how the I.O.C. had come to choose Atlanta (over Athens). The reply came that 'they [A.C.O.G.] lied'.

William Berry Hartsfield, the former Atlanta mayor, is rumoured to have said that: 'If you're going to Heaven or Hell, you've got to change planes in Atlanta.' Many of those who have departed the city in the last couple of days have no doubts about which location they have left. The Centennial Games did not fulfil expectations; there was too much rhetoric and not enough substance for these to be the greatest Games.

12

SYDNEY 2000

10 SEPTEMBER 2000

THE GOLD STANDARD

Steve Redgrave, aiming for his fifth winner's medal, looks forward to the greatest sporting event in the world

I've stood on that rostrum with an Olympic gold medal round my neck four times now, and it's a strange experience. The focus you have is to win that medal. The medal is everything. I've thought long and hard about winning gold in Sydney, but I haven't thought about winning a fifth gold. I look at it as securing a medal I've spent four years working damn hard to obtain. I don't see it in historical terms at all.

I remember Matthew [Pinsent] trying to explain what winning Olympic gold felt like. He ended up comparing the experience to watching a firework. Matthew said, if you tried to describe a firework to someone who had never seen one before and you referred to the force of it, the power of it, the colours, you could never do it justice. That is similar to what winning gold is like. It's a number of different sensations and experiences coming together, hopefully at the right time, culminating in a massive sense of achievement. Strangely, receiving the medal itself is not as big a thrill as you would imagine. Knowing what you've done on that particular day is all that you need. The award ceremony is special and emotional, but that's more to do with the timing of it, the release of pressure, and the reduction of all the stress than its significance as an event.

The Olympics themselves are really special. There are so many people there, there's something for everyone. There will be some whose highlight is just getting to Sydney. That's their pinnacle no matter how they perform. Some of the swimmers will do their one event almost straight after the opening ceremony. They will race in their heat and if they don't get through that's it, that's the Games over for them.

I think that, to be an Olympic sport, the Olympics have to be the biggest thing in that sport. That should be the criterion. You shouldn't sacrifice everything to the commercialism of showbusiness. Sport is about genuine, meaningful competition. That's why people watch it. When I was growing up, the two main sporting events worldwide which stuck in my mind were the Olympics and World Cup and the Games were way ahead of the football in terms of status and importance. I remember, as a kid, watching the swimmer Mark Spitz on television. Spitz remains one of my Olympic heroes to this day, and I can still recall him winning his seven gold medals and a headline in one of the papers – 'Spitz gets six' – charting his progress en route to his final haul.

Another great Olympian, for me, was the 400 metres hurdler Ed Moses. I met Moses at a Games once and I was completely dumbstruck. I just didn't know what to say to the guy and felt bloody stupid. But the Games can do that to you no matter who you are or what you've done. There are only a few people on this planet who have never heard of the Olympics. They are simply the biggest sporting event there is.

———

16 SEPTEMBER 2000

AUSTRALIA PUTS HEART AND SOUL INTO GAMES

Peter Foster and Barbie Dutter in Sydney

The four-hour spectacular Olympic opening ceremony in Sydney yesterday was an unqualified success, embodying the life and soul of the host nation. From the moment one hundred and twenty stockmen burst into the arena on horseback to a soundtrack of thundering hooves the show pulsed with breezy informality. The riders, ordinary horsemen and women from rural Australia, set the tone for what was to follow – cheeky, quickfire and informal. How many nations would have dared to include a sequence of one hundred dancing lawnmowers in their opening ceremony? They were driven in formation by men in garish shirts and lime-green sunhats – a witty tribute to suburban Australia.

Even the more choreographed sequences, such as the 'Deep Sea Dreaming', which sought to dramatise Australia's relationship with the sea, brimmed with a sense of organised chaos. Acrobats suspended by cables twirled and somersaulted high above the arena as beneath them pantomime fish swam through a sea of billowing blue silk. A ponderous eel with thirty pairs of shuffling feet followed a barracuda, while all about shoals of minnows – young children with fish-like tails – ran about the arena. There were no pretty patterns or obviously symmetrical formations; it seemed as if David Atkins, the artistic director, had told his little fish simply to go out and run their socks off. They did not disappoint him.

After the extraordinarily self-possessed performance of 13-year-old Nikki Webster, who played the crowd like a singer twice her age, the star of the show was undoubtedly the Tin Symphony. Primitive contraptions that, according to the official programme, were intended to convey the 'energy, humour and ingenuity that powered the settlement of the bush', clanked around the arena like a scene from the Mad Max films. By the time the parade of athletes, led by Greece, entered the arena the crowd of one hundred and ten thousand packed into Stadium Australia was in a state of near-frenzy. A special reception was reserved for the North and South Koreans, who marched together for the first time. As a symbol of the growing understanding between the two sides the pan-Korean flag was carried jointly by two athletes, one from each side of the divide. As they entered the stadium the spectators rose to their feet in a spontaneous burst of approval. Only the Australian team, who, in keeping with the relaxed atmosphere, threw hundreds of rubber kangaroos into the crowd, received a bigger cheer. Even the orchestra's string and brass sections joined in, waving their bows and trombone slides in appreciation of the home team.

With the more than eleven thousand athletes in place, the time came to light the Olympic Flame. Olivia Newton-John sang her duet before judges and athletes swore an oath of allegiance to a fair and drug-free Games. Juan Antonio Samaranch, the I.O.C. president, paid a 'special tribute' to the Aboriginal people, who have used these Games to highlight some of the wrongs committed in the past, before he declared the Games of the twenty-seventh Olympiad officially open. The only remaining question was who would light the Olympic cauldron, a subject of intense speculation in Australia over the last few months. The great cricketer Don Bradman had been mentioned, as had the wheelchair-bound Betty Cuthbert, the golden girl of Australian athletics who won eight Olympic medals between 1948 and 1964 but now suffers from multiple sclerosis. In the event the choice was Cathy Freeman, the Aboriginal 400-metre runner who won silver in Atlanta last time and is the darling of Australia's sport-obsessed public. Many believe that she is destined to become the face of the Sydney Games. In a skin-tight white suit Freeman stood, the torch held aloft, at the foot of a spectacular waterfall that had burst down the north end of the stadium. She applied the flame but for an agonising minute it seemed as if the flaming bowl would fail to make its ascent to the summit of the stadium wall, where it will burn for the next sixteen days. A nervous titter broke out around the crowd as the flaming crucible juddered to a halt, threatening humiliation in front of a worldwide audience of more than three billion people. Then it was free, gliding serenely skywards to the relief of everyone, not least Ric Birch, the director of ceremonies. 'There was a little hiccup,' he said afterwards, 'and everything had been going so well until then. But then all's well that ends well.'

---

18 SEPTEMBER 2000
QUEALLY HITS TOP GEAR
Andrew Baker

Before he had time to come to terms with winning one Olympic medal, Jason Queally won another. After a near-sleepless night spent glancing at the gold medal from the one-kilometre time-trial, which dangled from the door knob in his room, the quiet Lancastrian emerged on to the Dunc Gray Velodrome track with his two team-mates in pursuit of another in the Olympic sprint. Queally, Craig MacLean and Chris Hoy came within a bike's length of another gold, but were defeated by the French trio. So Queally now wears two shiny tokens of the sporting world's esteem on blue ribbons around his neck, and still cannot quite understand what has happened to him.

Queally has fought in the past, against poverty and apathy and appalling injury, and the ease of his victory on Saturday night came as a surprise, a relief and a richly earned reward. 'Normally, it hurts so badly,' he recalled last night with both gold and silver medals dangling on his chest. 'I've finished races and been in such agony afterwards that I've had to send fellow riders up to collect my medals. But not this time.' What Queally found, in one minute 1.609 seconds of first wobbling, then swooping speed around the Velodrome, was a level of performance that he has often achieved in practice but never been able to produce when the occasion demanded it. His start was slowish, and his progress around the track often strayed from the black line of perfection towards the red of untidiness, but his power and speed through the final five hundred metres were unmatched by the three riders who had a chance to defeat him. Each threatened, but fell away, and the gold was Queally's.

———

19 SEPTEMBER 2000
THORPE STANDS TALL AS A NATION IS SILENCED
Paul Hayward, Chief Sports Writer

They called it a race to stop the nation but it turned out to be the event that stopped Ian Thorpe. The news from Sydney is that the 17-year-old swimmer with size seventeen feet is fallible after all. Not that he was diminished one drop by a defeat which threatens to send the Olympic hyperbole industry into liquidation. The expectation was that the most dazzling talent to emerge at these Games would swim through undefeated to become the twenty-first century's Mark Spitz. That romantic plot developed a kink when he was beaten by Pieter van den Hoogenband, of Holland, in the 200 metres freestyle final in a world record-equalling time. Australians had begun the day queueing to buy the new Ian Thorpe commemorative stamp. Then they rushed home to see the wonder boy get well and truly licked.

Normally one might fear for such a callow performer exposed to such giddy expectation in front of a near-hysterical home crowd. The sound that greeted him before his third gold medal attempt was more of a scream than a cheer: pop-star-at-the-airport stuff, which confirmed Thorpe's symbolic status as Australia's hero son. When the long Dutch fingers of Van den Hoogenband touched gold ahead of him, the noise in the 17,000-seat aquatic centre collapsed as if someone had yanked the nation's electric plug from the wall. Yet Thorpe is no less inspirational than twenty-four hours before, when he was clutching two gold medals and threatening to become only the third Australian to win a third of those cherished medals at a single Games. He may yet do it, in the 4 × 200 relay or the medley, if the Australians shuffle their team.

'I was pretty happy with how I raced tonight. Happy with the result,' Thorpe said. 'I know I gave it my best shot and came out with the best result I could have on the night. This is the Olympic Games and I'm privileged to be swimming here. It's an opportunity that so few people get to have. A great athlete beat me.' Maybe. Van den Hoogenband comes from the same Dutch stable as Inge de Bruijn, winner of the 100 metres butterfly on Sunday. Jacco Verhaeren, personal coach to both, must be some kind of sage. For the orange of Holland read newly smelted iron.

Incredibly, Van den Hoogenband's own world record survived from the previous night. The tips of his fingers touched the sensor at the same moment in the semi-finals: one minute 45.35 seconds. 'I thought the world record would only last for two minutes. Now it's survived two days,' he said. Ha, ha, very funny, the Australians must have thought. It was Thorpe's record that the Dutchman cruelly passed. Was he downhearted? Was he hell. The sensation of collecting a first Olympic gold at seventeen came back to him ('standing there, feeling numb, not knowing what to do, feeling time slow down; you just want everybody to be able to experience that'). No, an excitable audience had not burdened him with inflated hopes. 'I think I was just maybe a bit flat from the first day of the competition. I don't really like the Olympic programme, but not many people get to change it. I'm not going to win every race. I'm not going to break every world record. It doesn't always happen like the dream that everybody wants to plan. You don't always get it your own way.'

---

23 SEPTEMBER 2000
FIVE IN A ROW FOR REDGRAVE
Sue Mott

Steve Redgrave hauled himself into Olympic legend today, powering Britain to a gold medal and himself to the fulfilment of a 20-year quest. The quiet achiever has done it. Five gold medals in five Olympics. A monumental intent backed on the day by a monumental performance from Redgrave and the three men who shared the vision.

As the British coxless four, seeded fourth by an Olympic committee, but the rampant favourites in the hearts of the rowing fraternity, crossed the finish line, the sell-out crowd at the Sydney International Regatta Centre filled the crystal blue air with celebration, admiration and respect.

The Union Jack and bedlam were everywhere. The crew had triumphed in a united adventure beyond the grasp of most mortals and now they were free of the nag of posterity. Not to mention totally and utterly knackered.

When the psychological joy kicked in, Matthew Pinsent, now a triple Olympic gold medallist, climbed over Tim Foster and fell into the arms of a laughing and crying Redgrave then leapt off the boat. James Cracknell waved and whooped. Foster fell forwards punching the air. For Redgrave, crossing that magical line was the moment a colossus became a legend. They won by 0.38 of a second, which looked like a lick of paint over the fast finishing Italians, with Australia, yelled on by thousands, crossing the line third. As the triumphant four took a lap of honour around the course, a former gravel pit in Penrith became a crucible of British glory. They stayed on the water for ages, lapping up the transcendental relief, taking the cheering acclaim of the crowd who had just witnessed human endurance at its peak. In those last moments when the blue-bowed British boat was under final assault, it was survival of the fittest.

Cracknell and Foster, in the days when they were the new boys, spoke of the awe Redgrave and Pinsent inspired in foreign opposition. They remembered Romanians gazing up at them on the victory rostrum, wildly happy to come second. It was thought, wishfully, that the ageing process and illness would deprive Redgrave of the energy to pursue his fistful of gold. A 38-year-old diabetic is not necessarily sporting god material. He has fundamentally disproved that line of thought. Age was never going to wither his intent. The strength his body has surrendered in the onslaught of time was more than made up for by a determination that could launch a space shuttle let alone a 45-foot rowing boat. Sped along by the complementary passions of his companions, they were simply unbeatable.

Walking to the start and settling themselves into the boat had been the worst moments. Foster's girlfriend was in tears of dread anticipation. Redgrave was primed to hear the voices of his children clamouring for his success as his little daughter, Natalie, had done to spur him on in Atlanta. Redgrave and Pinsent knew they could ask Olympic victory of themselves. Cracknell and Foster were being asked to explore the extent of their own nerve and delivery for the first time. They had won World Championships together, but this was the ultimate test. The measure of their ecstasy was expressed by its opposite in the brimming eyes and shocked exhaustion of Greg Searle and Ed Coode who came fourth in the men's pairs. They, like the four, had fully expected to win. 'But that's the nature of sport,' said Coode, tears of devastation in his eyes. It was that nature that Redgrave, for five successive Olympics, has tamed by the power of his will. No man or woman, in any walk of life, has deserved the dais more. He must be pretty pleased no one shot him in Atlanta after all.

---

25 SEPTEMBER 2000
LEWIS TURNS HER GRIT INTO GOLD
Paul Hayward, Chief Sports Writer

Denise Lewis once said: 'The instinct to survive when things are bleak is innate in me.' She was raised by a single mother and would travel for an hour and a half on cold winter nights from her home in Wolverhampton to train at Birmingham's Alexander Stadium. That instinct drove her through the pain barrier in Sydney yesterday and all the way to an Olympic gold.

Three golds in a single weekend, and five for the British team in all. Not since Melbourne in 1956 has *God Save The Queen* had to be rolled out for a sixth time at the Games. Lewis's gold in the heptathlon was the first for a British track and field athlete since Sally Gunnell and Linford Christie in 1992. The new Mary Peters, the female Daley Thompson: and all with an Achilles tendon injury that almost wrecked her coronation with a single event to go. She limped through a door into another life and the world of hyper-celebrity will now drag her in. She possesses the holy trinity of talent, intelligence and looks. Terry O'Neill, the fashion photographer, once said that she reminded him of a young Naomi Campbell (though without the temper). Most elite athletes do one thing brilliantly. Lewis has to do seven things exceptionally well. 'I don't think my life will be hugely different. I'll still be me.' Still visible, amid the snowstorm of contract offers that will blow her way today.

As her body threatened to disintegrate within touching distance of financial Utopia, the barriers seemed never ending. First the 100 metres hurdles, then the high jump, shot put, 200 metres, long jump, javelin and 800 metres, her least favourite event. After the long jump she was barely able to walk. 'It completely locked my foot,' she said. 'I had the scare going into the javelin. My physios tried everything. You don't come this far only to give up in the penultimate event.' They strapped her up and sent her back out. And in truth a strong show in the javelin won her the gold. The spear sailed 50.19 metres and took her to the head of the field. Stop watches and calculators were grabbed. She finished seventh in her 800 metres heat but it was enough.

The stadium had almost emptied by the time they hung the medal round her neck. 'It's a disgrace. You don't do a medal ceremony with only two people in the stadium,' her coach Charles van Commenee said. 'They wouldn't do that with the 100 metres.' But no audience was needed for the magnitude of her achievement to strike home. She jigged on the podium and waved to a throng of British admirers flourishing Union flags. With the help of an earpiece she spoke to her idol, Peters, who won her pentathlon gold in Munich in 1972, a week before Lewis was born.

The cold rain might have taken her back to all those lonely training nights in Birmingham, when school work was still waiting for her when she got home. It took eleven years to get here and two minutes 16.83 seconds of sheer survival in a lung busting race for Peters to finally hand on the torch. Only her high jump on the opening day had let her down. As a child she sang in a choir and learned tap-dancing and ballet. She admits to having a penchant for theatricality on sport's great stage. With Lewis there could never have been a straightforward finale to forty-eight hours of unceasing effort. She needed to be no more than 4.29 seconds behind Natalya Sazanovich, of Belarus, and a maximum of ten seconds behind Yelena Prokhorova (Russia) in the 800 metres to seize gold. At the start she shook her injured left foot and fiddled with her hair and the number on her shorts. Moistness formed in her eyes. It was easy to imagine a mid-race breakdown and a tearful wailing at the gods.

Tenderly, with her head erect and her stride choppy, she forced herself round the damp track and stayed close enough to the two eastern Europeans to hang on. The mathematicians in the crowd leapt up. Eunice Barber, the world champion, had already pulled out in bits. All evening, heptathletes staggered across the finishing line in disarray. Lewis always said it would be thus, like an American dance marathon where the last one standing wins. 'Survival of the fittest,' she said. 'It's easy when you're in great shape and riding the crest of the wave. It's when you've got injury problems that it becomes so hard.'

Growing up with a single parent taught her, she says, that 'you don't get everything you want on the day that you want it'. Her patience and fortitude saw her through. Something else she said when the Olympic dream was still a thousand training sessions and a few more injuries away:

'At the end of my career I'm going to be standing in the arena after my last competition thinking, "Did I give it my best shot? Am I satisfied?" If those questions can't be answered in the right way I'll be left with a very big void for the rest of my life.' The gold is hers, the void filled.

———

26 SEPTEMBER 2000

FREEMAN'S SPRINT INTO HISTORY RELEASES POLITICAL TENSIONS

Paul Hayward, Chief Sports Writer

Two hundred years of Australian history have been loaded on to Cathy Freeman at these Games and the weight of them finally knocked her down at the end of a paralysingly intense 400 metres. Shock and bewilderment pushed her over, and so there she sat, gulping for air and encased by the sound of 112,524 erupting souls. Australia's racial politics are a matter for Australians, but all of us here have been transfixed by accounts of Freeman's Aboriginal family history. The country's one hundredth Olympic gold was a first for an individual indigenous athlete. It bore many of the qualities of France's victory with a multi-ethnic side in the 1998 World Cup. It has prompted a whole nation to wonder out loud whether race can be turned into another discredited 'ism', swept away by the unifying power of sport.

'Sport is this great arena for drama; it's a reflection of life,' she advanced nobly while being pressed repeatedly to say something profound. 'Sometimes favourites don't win. My Olympic dream came true when I crossed that line.' There will be many grander feats than Freeman's victory over Lorraine Graham as well as Katharine Merry and Donna Fraser from Britain. But many of us doubt whether we will ever be so moved again by a single sporting act. 'I was part of a very special race this evening and I'm very privileged to have run with Cathy in an Olympic final,' Merry said. Such was the political significance of Freeman's searing run that Michael Johnson's subsequent victory in the men's 400 metres was reduced to a loose page of the night's plot flapping in the breeze.

'Ten days ago you lit the cauldron. Tonight you set the stadium alight again,' said the M.C. at Freeman's press conference. He ought to have been a headline writer. For the race of a thousand flashbulbs, the object of all this photographic attention appeared in a skin-like one-piece complete with hood, as if trying to seal the athlete inside and keep Australia's expectations out. She had no chance. The noise that rattled the Olympic Stadium as Freeman set off must have shaken the blood in her head. 'I was pretty nervous, but there was a voice in my mind saying, "Just do what you know",' she said. And what she did was come bursting off the final bend in third place into a canyon of sound. 'There will be a lot of changes with all the corporate and business stuff, but the main change in me is that I've weathered the pressure and come through with a gold medal. To ease the pressure, I tried to absorb every experience so I could use them to help teach my children.'

The journey took 49.11 seconds, a seasonal best, and at the end it was finally possible to see what Freeman has been carrying since Sydney was chosen as the host of these Games. She had to stop running for it to show. She sank to the ground, looking as if she was about to throw up. 'It was just relief and I was totally overwhelmed because I could feel the crowd all around and all over me. I just felt everyone's happiness and joy. I just had to sit down and make myself feel normal and get comfortable.'

According to a book by Adrian McGregor called *Cathy Freeman: A Journey Just Begun*, Freeman's grandmother, Alice 'Mero' Sibley, was taken to a penal settlement for 'troublesome Aborigines' after being stolen off the streets at the age of eight. Her whole past is shot through with institutionalised prejudice, with the missing and the damned. This is nothing new. In 1960 Cassius Clay travelled to Rome from a country where blacks were living under apartheid across large swathes of the South. Jesse Owens sprinted past Hitler and the psychopaths of the Third Reich. The Olympics have a way of entangling themselves with politics. Australia's search for 'reconciliation' between settler and Aboriginal is a much more subtle and complex problem than those faced by Muhammad Ali or Owens; but on the day of Freeman's final, the ethnic question seemed to come alive again as the weight of the responsibility she was carrying began to build.

More than ten million Australians watched on television. There were tears and long silences as those lucky enough to have tickets tried to take it all in. Again, the mood in the stadium was reminiscent of Paris two years ago, when the team of many colours beat Brazil, and France seemed to become a less divided place. It was probably an illusion, just as it is to believe that Freeman's triumph will eradicate ancient tensions in Australia. But if sport is about escapism and fantasy then yesterday it certainly worked. 'Top Work Cathy', read a banner in the crowd. And maybe it really was as simple as that. Certainly, Freeman sounds happiest being an athlete rather than a moving symbol in spikes. 'Running definitely comes more naturally to me than doing the creative stuff. At the opening ceremony I was really concerned about falling into the water when I walked across the cauldron. Running is like breathing to me. The Olympic gold is more personal to me than the Olympic Flame. My family are a constant reminder of my Aboriginal heritage. It just gave me a really big thrill to see them happy. I know they'll settle down again when this euphoria is gone and I'm just a normal family member. I'm going to go back to them now, where I feel loved and safe and secure.'

---

26 SEPTEMBER 2000
GOLDEN NICHE FOR EDWARDS
Tom Knight

Jonathan Edwards played his part in the greatest single night of athletic action in Sydney by crowning his career with an Olympic gold medal in the triple jump. He may have had only a support role in the drama surrounding Cathy Freeman's glorious triumph in the 400 metres, but Edwards was savouring every moment inside Stadium Australia. In front of a record crowd of 112,524, the Briton earned his own place in history by soaring out to 17.71 metres on his third-round jump. The distance was short of his five-year-old world record, but it was his best of the season and good enough to win him the title he missed so despairingly four years ago in Atlanta. His team-mate Larry Achike might have joined him on the podium, but was shunted into fifth place by a final-round jump of 17.47 metres by Yoel Garcia, which earned the Cuban the silver medal. It was fitting that the 34-year-old Edwards, whose performances in the last five years had done so much to bolster the wavering fortunes of the sport in this country, should win the gold, Britain's sixth at these Games. The British team have already matched their country's best post-War tally, at the 1956 Olympics in Melbourne, and one more gold medal will leave them the most successful since the 1924 Games in Paris.

Since breaking the world record twice in his World Championships victory in Gothenburg in 1995, Edwards has always won medals at major championships without achieving the same level of success. After his run of twenty-two successive wins came to an end with his silver medal in

Atlanta, he won the 1998 European title, took silver at the 1997 worlds in Athens and bronze at last year's World Championships in Seville. He said: 'I've become used to carrying the expectation of the nation. Every year since I won the 1995 world title, I've been seen as our main hope for a medal. I haven't had that much success since then, so it's great to finally win something again. We were a bit of a sideshow tonight, there's no doubt about that, but I was prepared for the commotion I might have to walk into. I was overwhelmed at the end. I was on the point of crying a number of times and I had to choke back the tears. I couldn't believe I was in this stadium, at the Games and that I was the Olympic champion. It was almost too much. This was a hard competition. Gothenburg was about world records, big jumps and feeling great, but this was a battle. I had to work really hard. I was nervous for days beforehand. I thought if I was going to win an Olympic title, it would be in Atlanta. To come here, at thirty-four, and win the gold medal has been fabulous.'

For Edwards, who has become a millionaire through his triple jumping, victory meant he had at last achieved the goal he set himself after his disappointment in Atlanta. But it came at a price. A devout Christian, Edwards's struggle to regain the form which brought him so much success has seen him constantly question his motives and commitment to the sport. At the start of the year he proclaimed himself the greatest triple jumper of all time only to have his Olympic preparations collapse after poor performances. His lack of confidence sent him looking for inspiration by training in Israel with his best friend on the circuit, Rogel Nachum, who was the first to congratulate him after last night's win.

---

30 SEPTEMBER 2000
AINSLIE GAINS REVENGE AFTER GOLDEN DUEL
Tim Jeffery

The winds were modest, but yesterday was a mighty and magnificent day for British sailing: four medals won, two of them gold for Shirley Robertson and Ben Ainslie. Robertson, thirty-two, became the first British woman to steer an Olympic gold medal-winning boat with her victory in the Europe class. The only other female gold medallist was Dorothy Wright, in a crew of four who won in 1920. The only occasions when more than two golds have been won were in 1908 and 1900, while 1956, the last time the Games were in Australia, was the only regatta in the modern era in which Britain had previously won more than two medals of any colour. Finn class sailor Iain Percy guaranteed himself a silver, and Ian Walker and Mark Covell in the Star a bronze. All this on top of Ian Barker and Simon Hiscocks's silver in the 49er, secured last Monday.

Ainslie reversed the outcome of the 1996 Games to wrest the Laser gold medal from Robert Scheidt in a thrilling confrontation. For four years, Ainslie has dwelt on how the Brazilian finessed him across the start line in the deciding race. Scheidt could afford a false start then, Ainslie could not. Older, certainly wiser but no less steely, Ainslie faced the same all-too-awful possibility of coming up one short as Scheidt moved into a nine-point lead with one race to go. 'I'd trade two silvers for one gold,' admitted Ainslie afterwards. 'Every day of my life for the last three years has revolved around winning this gold medal.'

Advised by coach John Derbyshire, Ainslie decided that trying to beat Scheidt by ten places in the final race was too risky. It would be better to 'try to sail Robert down the fleet'. With sailors allowed to ditch their two worst results from eleven races, Ainslie calculated that if he prevented Scheidt from finishing twentieth or better, he would win. Extreme measures? Possibly, but not an unknown strategy when only two competitors can win the big prize, and not the first time it has been used to secure a medal. As two of the quickest men in the 43-boat fleet, giving Scheidt the freedom to sail his own race carried a high risk for Ainslie. Strait-jacketing the Brazilian and removing his options was the safest strategy.

And so another furious pre-start battle followed, the pair twisting and turning, Ainslie seeking control and Scheidt endeavouring to escape. Scheidt, with three world championships to Ainslie's two, and four years his senior at twenty-seven, had helped the Briton with advice in the build-up to the 1996 Games. Since then, their battles have been full of vim and respect in equal measure. The balance of power has inexorably moved Ainslie's way. He pricked Scheidt's invincibility with world titles in 1998 and 1999 before the Brazilian bounced back ominously in 2000.

Ainslie induced Scheidt to collide with him just before the gun, causing the Brazilian to take a 720-degree penalty turn. Ahead, and with both their fates in his grip, Ainslie clamped his boat in front of Scheidt's, tacking every time he did. There must have been thirty tacks, perhaps more, and their synchronicity was so perfect it looked as though the two boats were attempting to perform in unison. The eye contact was intense as Ainslie sailed the opening upwind leg looking backwards as much as forward. Scheidt committed a second foul at the windward mark. As Ainslie blocked him out, Scheidt gybed around and came up underneath the Briton with right of way. Scheidt's head was pressed into Ainslie's sail as they collided, but he had altered course so suddenly the Briton had no opportunity to keep clear.

Still, the outcome was far from settled. In the last two legs, Scheidt recovered to twenty-second place. If he had made it to twenty-first, he would have tied with Ainslie and won gold with four race wins to two. Ashore, both men protested. 'I think he did a good job,' said Scheidt, his praise a shade grudging. 'The only problem was that some rules were broken.' Ainslie believed that, too, but was sure the only person at fault was Scheidt. Five hours after finishing the race, Scheidt was disqualified by the race jury and Ainslie confirmed the winner.

By contrast, Robertson's progress to the top of the podium was serene, though there was a moment in her final race when the gold slipped briefly from her grasp, as Dutch rival Margriet Matthysse moved to the lead and the Scot dropped two places. But Robertson's new-found cool resilience saw her recover to third, and twelve years without either a world title or Olympic medal came to a glorious end.

---

2 OCTOBER 2000

BRITAIN'S GOLDEN AGE
Paul Hayward, Chief Sports Writer

Best Olympic performance for eighty years. First heavyweight boxing gold since 1920. Perfect symmetry to end the Sydney Olympics. Team GB are now beating up other countries instead of themselves. There were two last golds for Britain before the F-111 jets blasted through the night sky and turned Sydney into bacchanalia. Stephanie Cook and Kate Allenby took gold and bronze in the women's modern pentathlon while an injured Audley Harrison jabbed his way to victory in the super-heavyweight division in the ring. The three had breakfast together in the Athletes' Village. 'Audley was on the big fry-up. We were on the muesli and bananas,' Cook said. Harrison's valediction to amateur fighting included a rap poem and a quote from a seventeenth-century French dramatist. Things are definitely looking up.

There are eleven gold medallists to honour when the British flight touches down tomorrow and twenty-eight jewellery-winners in all. In Atlanta four years ago, Britain were buried deeper than Scarlett O'Hara. At thirty-sixth in the medal table, they were below Ethiopia, Algeria, North Korea and Nigeria. Now they have risen to a perky tenth; not world-threatening, but a miraculous improvement on 1996. 'We've proved that Britain is great again. We've produced the goods,' said Harrison, who fought with a swollen hand to win his country's first boxing gold medal since Chris Finnegan in 1968. 'To have two Brits on the podium is spectacular. What a way to finish,' raved Cook. There was euphoria and incredulity in the British camp. It seemed like a bad time to point out that Britain won thirty medals fewer than Australia, a country with less than half the population, or that Holland, Italy, France and Germany all won more golds. It was not the point. Britain's Olympic revival has been one of the major themes of these Games and ought to be felt across every boxing gym and kayak club.

Steve Redgrave, who held the team in Atlanta afloat, carried the flag into the Olympic Stadium last night like some redoubtable British officer who had survived a terrible onslaught and emerged at the head of a revitalised troupe. Eleven golds is the minimum Britain should expect, given their sporting history and economic clout. This ought to be only the start. Five golds in three days produced a rousing finish; there were three in two days in the yachting and then a double in two of the most gruelling sports yesterday. Australian zeal is now officially an infectious condition. Body language alone suggested that many of Britain's three hundred and twenty-one athletes drew strength from the force field which sustained these Games, and which turned the sky over Sydney last night into a radiant constellation of loudly exploding colour.

A final scout round the erupting city yesterday could produce nobody who thinks there has been a better sporting carnival. Some who remember *la dolce vita* in Rome in 1960 are prepared to enter a token debate. But it never lasts long. Australia is above all a positive country, a sport-devouring land capable of breaking every Olympic attendance and ticketing record (6.7 million tickets sold, nine billion hits on the official website). On day eight, 400,345 squeezed into the Olympic Park with barely a cross word or a transport snarl-up. No worries. This was the slogan of the Games. Every night in that vast Olympic Park, an announcer asked the multitudes pouring on to the excellent train network to applaud the forty-seven thousand volunteers who managed to stay cheery through two weeks of leg-ache and smile-fatigue.

They were clapped and cheered every time, and no wonder. A statistician worked out yesterday that they gave five million hours of their lives.

Uniquely, in modern sport, the Olympics find room to celebrate frailty as much as strength. These Games were a factory for tragicomedies: the Australian walker who was disqualified two hundred metres short of a gold medal, wailing: 'No, no, not me.' Yes, you. Upset of the fortnight was Alexandre Karelin's first wrestling defeat in thirteen years. The greatest choke was Spain in the men's football final, the finest race Haile Gebrselassie winning the 10,000 metres by the width of his teeth.

On to the roster of grade-A global recognition go Ian Thorpe, Inge de Bruijn and Pieter van den Hoogenband from the pool, and Marion Jones, Denise Lewis and Cathy Freeman from track and field. We will remember Freeman not running but sitting down, knocked to the track by history's juggernaut at the end of a 400-metre race which, however irrational this sounds, seemed to alter the trajectory of Australian history. Defeats for the two greatest middle-distance runners of modern times left a void that no number of lucrative Wednesday night Grand Prix victories can fill. Wilson Kipketer (800 metres) and Hicham El Guerrouj (1,500 metres) were tactically off target. So, in truth, were the impresarios of track and field, who crammed too many stellar events into the first three days and so failed to sustain the dramatic tension.

But for three days in mid-Olympics there was the danger of ending up like Freeman, bowled over by melodrama and the unceasing buffeting of big events. Redgrave's fifth gold medal rolled into Denise Lewis's heptathlon victory and thence to Freeman and the emotional crescendo of the Games. For Britain, Atlanta was one long autopsy. This time the Team GB good-news bulletins hummed until the end. Athletes and officials raced off into a long night of celebration, for once not feeling the need to dodge disgruntled British fans. The legacy left by Redgrave, Pinsent, Lewis, Edwards, Ainslie, Harrison and the rest was that Britain were not excluded from the wild festivities of last night. The light from the fireworks detonating over Darling Harbour shone on British achievements as much as anything we saw in the fortnight. The Sydney Games were so good that they made the forty or so drugs busts seem like welcome news. In another place they might have been taken as further evidence of the corruption of the Olympic spirit. Here, they seemed to express an intolerance of cheating, a willingness to stop pretending at last that all is clean and well. A star burst is what it was, and it put eleven British athletes in the Olympic firmament.

13

ATHENS 2004

14 AUGUST 2004

GREECE'S VICTORY TURNS PYRRHIC

Paul Hayward in Athens

Two young Greeks claim to have fallen off a motorcycle here on Thursday night. Nothing unusual in that, given the way Athenians hurtle through their streets. But this routine road 'accident' in the southern suburb of Glyfada did more than tip two riders off a bike. It upended the whole historical fantasy of the Olympics coming home two and a half thousand years after men raced round in chariots. On the eve of last night's opening ceremony, the twenty-eighth Games were rocked so violently that another couple of chunks of rock might have fallen off the Parthenon. Suddenly the starlit cavorting inside the main Olympic Stadium elicited not only admiration but an equal measure of pity. The Games were turning from gold to rubble before a rocket had gone up, before a universal human theme had been explored. Greece's national victory in beating a thousand construction deadlines was turning pyrrhic in front of billions of pairs of eyes.

These were no ordinary nightriders buzzing through the dusty labyrinth of the city. On board – so the story goes – were the two most famous names in Greek athletics, who were supposedly racing through the night to take a drugs test they had missed, Rio Ferdinand-style, when officials turned up at the Olympic Village expecting to take urine samples from the two dashing local heroes. Kostas Kenteris, the Olympic 200-metres champion, and his training partner and fellow air force officer, Ekaterini Thanou, who chased home Marion Jones in the women's 100 metres final in Sydney, were nowhere to be seen when the testers called. The visiting officials were told by members of the Greek delegation that Kenteris and Thanou had gone home to 'pick up a few personal possessions', having arrived in Athens that afternoon from their American training base in Chicago. A few hours later, Kenteris was in hospital, reportedly in a neck brace, with 'a cut to the head, bruising to the nape of the neck, bruises to both knees and scratches to the right leg', while Thanou was being diagnosed with 'abdominal bruising, bruising of the right hip and bruising to the abductor muscles in her right leg'. That's a lot of bruising to precious limbs, but it's not half as bad as the damage to the tissue of these Games.

Yesterday morning, as the Olympic torch was winding its way down from the Acropolis to the main stadium for the most symbolic part of the opening ceremony, Kenteris and Thanou were summoned before a three-man International Olympic Committee disciplinary hearing set up, on the orders of the I.O.C. president Jacques Rogge, to determine 'the exact reason why the tests were missed'. It added poignancy to this much larger re-run of the Ferdinand affair to learn that Kenteris was being tipped to light the Olympic Flame. Neither athlete made it to the disciplinary hearing. Shortly before 2 p.m., Christos Artinopoulos, the hospital's chief administrator, issued a statement: 'The two athletes must remain in hospital for at least forty-eight hours.' With no one to place in the dock, the I.O.C. suspended the inquiry until Monday, by which time the Games will be in full swing and Kenteris – if one rumour is to believed – will have announced his retirement.

The Olympics love a conspiracy theory. They adore a high-speed rumour and a shock announcement. And Kenteris has been the subject of more dark mutterings than most. A graduate in physical education and sports science, this 31-year-old three-time Greek Athlete of the Year rarely runs outside his own country and trains away from prying eyes. His talent for peaking in major championships has aroused the curiosity of the track and field community. He has loaded an impressive cargo of muscle on to a slender frame. Though his recognition rating outside athletics is low, two years ago he became the first sprinter to hold the Olympic, world and European titles. In Sydney, where he shaded Britain's Darren Campbell, he was Greece's first male gold medallist since 1912. So you can see why the Greek track and field campaign was built around him. Thanou, who also emerged from the Olympiakos athletic club, is almost equally popular. Four times she has worn the crown of Greek

Female Athlete of the Year. There was a degree of symbolism in the two jumping on the same motorbike and riding into a major scandal.

The plot darkens still further when you discover that it was Christos Tzekos, their coach, who lent them his two-wheel chariot for the wardrobe dash back to their homes. Nowhere in the elite coaching manual does it advise star athletes to ride pillion through busy streets at night, a week before they take to the track. Of course, there are plenty here in Athens who doubt whether the pair ever fired the ignition on Tzekos's bike. Having missed the tests, they were already guilty of a doping offence, and so a pretty spectacular explanation was going to be needed to get them off the I.O.C.'s hook, which has expanded since the Canadian Dick Pound took charge of the World Anti-Doping Agency (W.A.D.A.) and Rogge succeeded Juan Antonio Samaranch as the president of the I.O.C. In one corner, Olympic experts theorise that the new culture of intolerance in relation to performance-enhancing drugs gave rise to a bold but risky raid on the Greek camp. If Kenteris and Thanou had been there and had tested positive, the cost to Greek self-esteem would have been outweighed by the credit the I.O.C. would have drawn for conducting such an audacious bust. Some say the Americans were in revolt at the number of tests their athletes were being subjected to – and that powerful figures inside the U.S. team demanded that the spotlight be turned equally on the Greeks.

It should be pointed out that neither Kenteris nor Thanou has ever tested positive for drugs. But it's hard to see how the I.O.C.'s disciplinary committee can accept such a convoluted explanation for their failure to submit to the tests within the two-hour period specified by W.A.D.A. One of the key questions is: were the athletes contacted directly by the testers, or did they rely on team officials to pass on the notification? Either way, it appears significant that the testers chose to descend just hours after the pair had touched down from Chicago.

---

17 AUGUST 2004

DETERMINED THORPE PROVES HE IS STILL THE BIGGEST FISH OF ALL

Sue Mott in Athens

This was the night the Olympic Aquatic Centre turned into a piranha pool. There were such deadly intentions in that churning blue water, you almost expected it to turn red. And when the thrashing was over, from the suddenly still water one man emerged, ripped off his yellow cap, clenched a fist in the air and roared his delight. Ian Thorpe, of Australia, the mighty Thorpedo, is still the greatest of them all. After a phenomenal body of hype and speculation, another phenomenal body, that of black-suited Thorpe himself, emerged the victor of a race that was billed the most potentially compelling of the entire Athens Games.

On paper it was the men's 200 metres freestyle final. In the water it was an emotional war between the 2000 Olympic champion, Pieter van den Hoogenband, of Holland, the wave-making teenager from the United States, Michael Phelps, and the sultan of swim himself, Thorpe. Now we know. Australia's hero swam to victory and an Olympic record of one minute 44.71 seconds. Van den Hoogenband, with one solid block of orange-clad Dutch supporters going wild in the stands, finished 0.52 seconds behind him. Phelps was a phlegmatic third. He beat his best time by half a second but not the two best sprint freestylers in the world. 'I'm pretty pleased with that,' he admitted.

He is right to be. The two men in front of him are swimming machines of quite spectacular order and they both had something to lose. The Olympic title in the case of the Dutchman, not to mention a grudge that the race had been condensed by the American/Antipodean media as a straight Thorpe versus Phelps dish, with no orange dressing. He proved them wrong. It was the Dutchman who responded most dramatically to the start gun, blazing into the lead at a world-record pace. But Thorpe, mysteriously bulleting through the water despite that deceptively languid stroke, stayed with him. Phelps had already been left behind by the first turn. As his coach had promised: 'This was the best against the best at their best.' That's hardly a float on a lily pad.

But for Thorpe, once monarch of all he surveyed through his goggles, the stakes were highest. He was the world record holder. He was the winner of three golds and two silvers in Sydney. He is the superstar who symbolises Australia's almost mystical attachment to the water. A chlorine king in robes of skin-tight black Lycra. There were fears, maybe in his own 21-year-old head, that he was starting to lose hunger and momentum. Not so. He surged into a lead midway down the third lap and never lost the advantage again. The partisan cheers of an internationally patchwork crowd rang round the open air stadium, bathed in Athenian sunset. It was close but not close enough to deprive Thorpe of his victory and these Games a moment of genuine sporting theatre.

As he clutched Van den Hoogenband in a post-race embrace of relief and congratulation afterwards, he said to the Dutchman who beat him four years ago: 'Now we're even. It will be an even tougher race in Beijing.' It will be if Phelps matures to join them. The ludicrous projections that he might win eight gold medals at these Olympics, surpassing the record of Mark Spitz, may have vaulted him on to the cover of *Time* magazine but, unfortunately for him, not to the forefront of the 200 metres freestyle when it mattered. He's a lad. He still likes chocolate pancakes for breakfast and drives a Cadillac augmented with toys. The mental and physical toll of the clash of the pool titans was more than he could endure at this stage in his development. Then he lost to Britain's Stephen Parry in the 200 metres butterfly semi-final, which says it all.

---

20 AUGUST 2004

SILVER LINING AS BRITISH PAIR'S FIGHTBACK FALLS SHORT

Paul Hayward, Chief Sports Writer

British badminton's HQ at Milton Keynes was said to be overrun and 'overwhelmed' by excitement and media interest yesterday. It was a red-letter day in Buckinghamshire but a Red Flag afternoon in Athens, as a Chinese pair conquered Nathan Robertson and Gail Emms at the end of an epic struggle for gold in the final of the mixed doubles. Milton Keynes requires quite a prod to rouse it from its slumbers. Normally it reserves its bunting for changes to the roundabout system or the building of a new numbered street. 'As the magic hour approached in Athens this afternoon, a media circus overwhelmed us,' declared the website of the Badminton Association of England. The trouble is, Robertson and Emms were overcome as well in a contest that should draw many converts to this intense, acrobatic and raucous sport. The two darting, dashing Britons finished up with silver medals after going down 15–1, 12–15, 15–12 in a contest that will have opened many eyes to the joys of the shuttlecock shuffle. With typical British understatement, Andy Wood, their coach called it 'an extremely significant' day for the sport, even though it was Jun Zhang (the man) and Ling Gao (the woman) who occupied the top of the medal podium.

'Badminton's coming home!' Robertson and Emms might have announced had they been able to capitalise on an 11–8 lead in the third 'game'

– badminton's equivalent of a tennis set. Though the sport traces its origins to the fifth century B.C., its modern foundations were laid by the British Army in India in the Victorian age. When the Duke of Beaufort introduced the game to royal society at his country estate – Badminton House in Gloucestershire – the resoundingly English name was applied. Knowing this, we are entitled to wonder why Robertson and Emms were the first British players to reach an Olympic final. 'I think we've had a fantastic tournament. We were seeded fourth, so really the best we could hope for was bronze. To get silver was amazing,' declared Emms after mopping up copious tears. 'In the final we did everything we could, but it just didn't come off today.'

The Goudi Olympic Hall rocks with flags, chants and generally exuberant spectators. You walk in expecting to find all the atmosphere of a library and bounce out with ringing ears. British and Chinese ardour clashed head on. It was the Proms against a Beijing rally. Great fun it was, too, until Zhang and Gao ambushed the British couple and annexed the first game 15–1. These painfully one-sided opening exchanges had the Union Flag brigade squirming in their seats. As Zhang smashed the shuttlecock at Emms again and again he borrowed the sound effects of Bruce Lee, punching home his points with a terrible yelp. It was badminton as martial art. 'I've never seen anyone come out so fast,' Emms agreed. 'He was smashing so hard in that first game, and I just wasn't ready. Fair play to them. They were confident and just blew us off the court. When that happens, you just have to accept it. Then get on with it.' Robertson's attitude was: 'Forget that and move on. And that's exactly what we did. They caught us with speed in the first game.'

The counter-surge was impressive, and soon the British duo were levelling the match at one game apiece. In the deciding session they recovered from 3–0 down to lead 7–3 and then 11–8 before the Chinese regained their hold to win seven of the next eight points. 'I must say the British team played excellently today,' said Zhang with more grace than he showed on court (gamesmanship is a major component of this deceptively belligerent sport). 'We got so close, and when we came off my first emotion was to be absolutely gutted. I felt sick,' Emms said. 'It was so close and it could have gone either way. But now I've got an Olympic medal round my neck and my name has gone down in history so that can't be bad. This is more than I expected.' 'We came here today to give the performance of our lives and our reward for it was the silver medal,' Robertson continued. 'We've been the best-prepared team I've ever been involved with. I don't think we lost control of the match. The last few points to win an Olympic gold are going to be hard ones, and the Chinese have had more experience of that situation. It was our first time in the final and they were a bit more positive at the decisive stage.'

There was something faintly Henman-esque about their defeat: the slow start, the valiant response and the missed opportunity right at the end. The enthusing about the silver medal was also a little overdone (not that Henman ever exaggerates the merits of his quarter- and semi-final appearances at Wimbledon). The chance was there and then surrendered. You see this a lot in sport. People who have to fight their way back from such a calamitous start rarely have the emotional reserves then to push on through to glory. 'This has given me an appetite for more,' Emms promised. 'We want to go out and win some more things.' No prizes for noticing that Britain are performing best in the middle-class or middle-England sports: sailing, rowing, equestrianism, archery and now badminton. England's rugby team win the World Cup. England's footballers seem doomed to go out in quarter-finals. It is a talking point, anyway. Milton Keynes was doubtless subdued last night. The day started with this battle cry from Lars Sologub, Britain's performance director: 'We will do everything we can to "go for gold", as it says on the seams of our Ben Sherman suits.' But the Red Flag flew over Buckinghamshire.

---

20 AUGUST 2004

GOLDEN BLONDES SET STANDARD FOR BRITAIN

Andrew Baker in Glyfada

The sticker on their car reads 'Legally Blonde' but Shirley Robertson, Sarah Ayton and Sarah Webb are now legally, triumphantly and incontrovertibly gold. The trio yesterday afternoon won Britain's first gold medal of the Athens Games when they secured top spot in the Yngling class at the Olympic regatta in Glyfada. Robertson, who also won gold in the Europe class in Sydney, became the first woman in history to win Olympic competitions in two different classes of boat. 'I'm completely thrilled,' she said. 'We have all worked so hard together, and it is very sweet to be sharing this moment with the two Sarahs.'

Jubilant members of the British sailing squad danced on the dockside as Robertson steered her boat back into the port, before treating the victorious crew to the traditional ducking. With British sailors handily placed to collect more gold at the weekend, they may not be the only ones to take a dip in the harbour. The Yngling crew can now afford to sit out the final race of the series, having scored so consistently over the past week that their closest rivals, Denmark, cannot now beat their total. Yesterday's race developed into a tactical battle between the two crews, with Robertson knowing that she needed to finish no more than three places behind her rivals to secure the gold. The Danes were fifth, the British eighth. Job done.

That was a brief culmination to years of effort. The strain has been not just physical and mental, but financial too. The Norwegian-designed Yngling – the name means 'youngster' – is an expensive boat, and Robertson and her crew had to rely on the generosity of friends to fund the purchase of their craft. 'Our boat is owned by thirty-six people, who each put in £1,000,' Robertson explained. 'Without everyone's belief that we could nail it, we wouldn't be in this position. I'm just overwhelmed that we have put it all together and made it happen.'

The three blondes intend to enjoy their unexpected time off. 'We're going to get our hair done,' Robertson said. 'The last thing any of us wants to do right now is get back in that boat.' Shades of Redgrave, there. Any chance of going for a third medal in Beijing, Shirley? 'It's always a possibility,' she said. 'But I think my husband would quite like his wife back.'

---

21 AUGUST 2004

QUICKSILVER HOY STRIKES GOLD TO SHOW HE IS THE REAL McCOY
Jim White

The Saltire is fluttering with an extra flourish: the Scots are in the ascendant. After Shirley Robertson skippered the Yngling crew to victory in the sailing, Chris Hoy repeated Jason Queally's performance of four years ago and yesterday won the first available gold medal on the Olympic cycle track. Those who were privileged enough to be there for the men's kilometre time-trial will all agree they witnessed one of the finest sporting performances by a Briton in a generation. With an effort of quite astonishing control, nerve and grit apparently carved from the foot of

Edinburgh Castle, Hoy was obliged to beat times nobody could have predicted. Here is how tough a race the Scot won: the Australian rider Shane Kelly surpassed the Olympic record set by Queally in Sydney and didn't even make it on to the medal rostrum.

'I was in complete shock when I'd finished my ride,' Hoy said after setting a record of one minute 00.711 seconds, burning round the track at an average over 37 m.p.h. 'I looked up at the scoreboard, saw the time and couldn't believe it. To be honest, I still don't believe it.' High above the vertiginously banked wooden track at the new Olympic velodrome, some British supporters had hung a banner which read: 'Chris Hoy is the real McCoy.' Among the over-hyped reputations of modern sportsmen this was no idle boast. Before his ride Hoy was faced with quite simply the most demanding responsibility in Olympic cycling history. Because of his world ranking position, he was drawn to go last of the seventeen riders to venture out on the Athens track. He had watched his British team-mate Craig MacClean briefly hold the lead, before the drama was ratcheted up almost beyond the bearable. In turn, the old Olympic record was smashed by the three riders who preceeded Hoy. Sitting there at the start line, as the queue diminished and his turn slowly came, he knew, to say the least, that he was up against it.

'It was pretty horrible, to be honest,' Hoy said of those nerve-shredding moments as he watched first Kelly, then the German Stefan Nimke, then the French giant Arnaud Tournant go faster than anybody had gone before at the Olympics. But if he was feeling edgy, he didn't show it. As Tournant's time of one minute 00.896 seconds registered on the scoreboard, to yelps of disbelief from the French team, the man from the right side of the Edinburgh tracks merely applied more grip-friendly chalk to his hands. After months in the gym, Hoy has a sprinter's physique: thighs the size of small buses, calves apparently hewn from steel and a backside voluminous enough to house a nuclear power plant. When he set off on his bike – specially tailored from some twelve thousand pieces of carbon – that physique pumped so aggressively, the ground appeared to shudder. What a start that power gave him; after the first trip round the 250-metre circuit he was already up on Tournant's time. In the stands, the large British contingent roared on every muscular thrust.

'The cheering was unbelievable,' Hoy said. 'I heard this huge roar after the first lap, so I knew I was up, and I thought I've got to keep up.' He did: burning ahead of Tournant at every time split, he broke past the finish line 0.12 of a second faster than the Frenchman; slightly less time than it took to blink in disbelief. When he looked up at the scoreboard he almost fell off his bike in astonishment. But he recovered sufficiently to grab a Union flag and take a slow, steady lap of honour, to bellows of amazement from supporters and rivals alike. 'I've watched the Olympics since I was a kid,' he said. 'I've dreamt of this moment. It's an experience you just can't put into words.'

––––––––––

23 AUGUST 2004
AINSLIE'S FRENCH FEUD CREATED A MONSTER
Andrew Baker

Ben Ainslie is not a demonstrative man. Self-effacing to the point of shyness, Britain's gold medallist in the Finn class sailing event believes in letting his sporting performances do the talking for him. His rivals have for years regarded him as a determined, if rather quiet, competitor. But over the past week they have found out what happens when Ainslie gets annoyed. A Frenchman named Guillaume Florent lit the touchpaper. He and Ainslie were in close company during the second race for the Finn fleet last Saturday. Words were exchanged but no incident took place that registered with Ainslie. So he was shocked to find himself the target of a protest from Florent, stunned to find himself disqualified from a race in which he had finished second. It was one man's word against another: the jury believed Florent.

That decision saddled Ainslie, the pre-event favourite, with a maximum score for that race of twenty-six points. Under the rules he could drop the score from his eventual total, but would then be forced to count his next worst score. In other words, one more poor race or misdemeanour and Ainslie would have no chance of a medal. Ainslie was, quite uncharacteristically, beside himself with fury. He kicked a fence. He stamped on his sunglasses. But his Team GB sailing squad colleagues rallied around. 'We told him to put it behind him,' Shirley Robertson recalled. 'We said, "If anyone can get it back, you can".' So the 27-year-old from Lymington set out to channel his anger at the Frenchman's conduct into his racing. The next morning he carved through the fleet from sixteenth place to win race three. He won race four from the front, and went on to dominate the rest of the week's racing. Long before Ainslie wrapped up the gold medal on Saturday, people were starting to point at Florent on the dockside between races. 'That's the one who wound up Ainslie,' they would mutter. 'Fat lot of good that did the rest of us.'

Ainslie won the silver medal in the Laser class in Atlanta, and followed up with gold in the same category in Sydney. His gold here elevates him into the pantheon of multiple Olympic medallists but, typically, he claims not to feel at home in such company. 'Good grief, no,' he said. 'People like Matthew Pinsent and Sir Steve Redgrave are my Herculean rivals. I'm miles away from them – I just try to focus on each challenge as it comes.' His colleagues disagree. Shirley Robertson, herself a double Olympic gold medallist, summed up their feelings. 'We all think Ben is superhuman,' she said.

---

23 AUGUST 2004

AS WE HEARD THE CHEERS, ALL OF US WERE CRYING

James Cracknell

Over the past thirty-six hours the most frequently asked question has been 'how does it feel?' The answer is proud. Proud of the guys I raced with, proud of my coach, proud that my sport could yet again produce such a dramatic event, but most of all proud that so many British supporters made the journey to cheer us on.

The forty-eight hours preceding the final were incredibly emotional as we prepared our bodies and minds for the challenge both would be facing on Saturday morning. Six minutes would determine whether four years of training had been worthwhile and, to me, only one result would have made the sacrifices seem like a wise investment. In spite of the injury-plagued season we have endured, there had never been any question of us lowering our expectations. Which is why the pressure from outside did not affect us; nobody could put more pressure on us than we had ourselves. What made the last couple of days so hard was that we knew we had to race at a new level if we were to have a chance of winning – very different to four years ago.

We left the hotel at 5.30 a.m. in the dark and in total silence. There was nothing more to say – each of us was ready for what we had to do. It was just light when we climbed into the boat for our pre-race training session.

As we paddled into the last five hundred metres we could hear shouts for Great Britain. Hundreds of Brits had got there at 6.30 to get the best seats so they could watch us race over the finish line. All of us were crying when we got off the water. Feeling that support made me realise how lucky I was to have a chance to race for gold again, and that people cared whether we won or lost was a huge inspiration.

All along I had visualised the race as being incredibly close. Canada, like us, like to dominate races, so there was never going to be any quarter given in the first part of the race. They have a strong middle section but, in my opinion, have always been suspect in the last five hundred metres. Every time I had thought of the race I envisaged us being level with two hundred and fifty metres to go: whoever was prepared to dig the deepest would come out on top.

The most relaxed I had felt in forty-eight hours was when we got in the boat for the final, at last we were in control of everything. No more hanging around – this was what I had trained four years for. I had no doubt that we would win and I was prepared to battle all the way down the course. Matt Pinsent and I hugged on the stage before getting in the boat, something we have never done in nearly ten years of rowing together – we knew this was going to be the toughest race of our careers. In a high-pressure race there is nobody I'd rather be in a boat with than Matt: he steps up his performance when it really matters. In Ed Coode we had someone who transfers that rhythm seamlessly down the boat. Steve Williams and I are both aggressive and committed to powering that rhythm along. I had no doubt that we would win, it would be incredibly hard but we would survive.

That belief never left me, even when Canada were nearly half a length up with five hundred metres to go. The sprint for the line was what sport is all about. We knew it could go either way: for the winners a surge of pure ecstasy that you only get from achieving a lifetime's ambition, and for the losers total devastation from knowing they were so close but would never come out on top. We came out on top and I've enjoyed every second of it since we crossed the line. The second most frequently asked question is 'has it sunk in yet?' The answer is yes. I'd raced that final a thousand times in my head and most of the time it ended like it did yesterday.

———

23 AUGUST 2004
RADCLIFFE LEFT FRAZZLED AND FORLORN
Paul Hayward

Whatever she mumbled to herself when she sat on that grass, with her Olympic dream thoroughly cooked, it looked like 'help me'. Now we know why they say long-distance running is the loneliest job in sport. Paula Radcliffe was a picture of desolation here yesterday when her gruesome journey down from the hills of Marathon ended in tears and exhaustion on the streets of Athens. In the beautiful stone tunnel of the Panathinaiko Stadium – the amphitheatre where the Olympics were reborn one hundred and eight years ago – super-fit women lay around in physical disarray. Dehydrated, dizzy and flooded with lactic acid, they flopped on to mobile hospital beds or simply collapsed on the track after crossing the line. Soon Radcliffe would join them, wrapped in a silver cape, accompanied by her family and husband, Gary Lough, after the most dispiriting night of her distinguished career. She said only that she was 'devastated'.

On the most savagely hot day of the Games so far, eighty-two women set off in 35-degree temperatures down the route taken by Pheidippides, the messenger who lost his life to fatigue after telling the people of Athens that the battle with the Persians had been won. Radcliffe travelled the last of those miles in an ambulance. Alan Storey, the technical director for British endurance running, described her as 'emotionally drained'. The great reception that hundreds of ecstatic supporters had planned for her went cold as Mizuki Noguchi, of Japan, hauled herself round the tight finishing track to become the Olympic champion in two hours twenty-six minutes twenty seconds.

After Britain's rowing triumph on the lakes on Saturday morning, Team GB's travelling clan were expecting to see Radcliffe confirm her position as the odds-on favourite and the fastest woman marathon runner of all time. She was the track and field team's only banker of these Games. But her journey ended more than four miles from the end of her scheduled journey of twenty-six miles and 385 yards. Moments after being relegated to fourth place by the Ethiopian, Elfenesh Alemu, at the 35-kilometre mark, Radcliffe stumbled to a halt, put her hands on her knees and leaked hot tears of sorrow. Glancing behind her to see how fast the rest of the field was approaching, she broke into a half-hearted jog but then stopped again after a few groggy steps. This time her despair was overwhelming. The contortions in her face spoke of a terrible realisation. At thirty, she may already be too old to add an Olympic gold to those she won at 10,000 metres in the European Championships and Commonwealth Games. This was not the happy weeping of the rower, Matthew Pinsent, from the day before. It was the grief that comes over athletes when they realise that thousands of hours of training and austerity have come to nought.

Liz Yelling, Radcliffe's fellow Great Britain marathon runner, who came in twenty-fifth, did manage to mutter a few words through the fog of her own exhaustion: 'I'm totally gutted for her. I know how hard she's worked – her dedication and the sacrifices,' Yelling said. 'The course was much harder than I thought. Maybe Paula just underestimated the course.' Britain's other representative, Tracey Morris, was twenty-ninth. Sixteen failed to finish.

Those sacrifices are now legendary – and they took Radcliffe to the point of apparent invincibility, though many good judges did doubt whether she could withstand the rigours of this especially brutal test. Since the crushing disappointment of her fourth-placed finish in the 10,000 metres in Sydney four years ago, Radcliffe's attention had been fixed with laser-precision on winning an Olympic gold. To prepare, she ran one hundred and forty miles a week in the thin air of the French Pyrenees, with twice-daily long-distance jogs and post-exercise massages lasting two hours. The last training stop was an undisclosed location in Spain, where the sun and humidity provided conditions similar to those in Athens. Before Pheidippides was dragged out of the history books and his famous run revived, Radcliffe had run three of the top four Marathon times of all time. Her world record of two hours fifteen minutes twenty-five seconds is three minutes twenty-two seconds faster than her closest rival's personal best. Before the start of yesterday's race, she wore an ice vest for thirty minutes to lower her 'core temperature'. Bobbing on her chest was the necklace with the five Olympic rings given to her by her mother.

But none of this was any good to her when the awful physical reality of the Athens Marathon began to strike the contestants. Down at the stadium, trolley beds and drips were being lined up in the tunnel. At the start some runners hid from the roasting sun under umbrellas. They set off past the BP garages and car showrooms for the biggest physical trial of their lives. Within fifteen minutes, Radcliffe's head was starting to bob. There was an extra desperation in the sucking of drinks as the field rumbled towards the ancient town. The sun was so pitiless that you could feel it burning the skin beneath your shirt. The women filed past the Tomb of the Athenian Warriors. Radcliffe's running style was never a pretty sight. With head jerking and eyes rolling in their sockets, she renders it almost impossible to judge how well she is going. 'Radcliffe on another rampage,' proclaimed one banner near the finishing line – which must have seemed far, far away. Not this time. Something inside her was about to break. At twenty-five kilometres Noguchi and Alemu abruptly opened up a 20-metre lead, which then stretched to eighty metres as the field began the latest in a succession of uphill slogs. Three-quarters of the way into the race Radcliffe toiled into second place, but then the Kenyan, Catherine Ndereba, who took the silver, attacked, and Radcliffe headed towards her resting place, on a suburban grassy bank.

There had been rumours that Radcliffe carried an injury into these Games – but there was no talk of an infirmity here last night. Rather: the tank of an athlete's energy is finite, and Radcliffe, in conditions that didn't suit her, reached the bottom of hers. To run through a furnace over an undulating course in pursuit of an Olympic medal is about as brave as you can be in sport. Maybe it was right in these circumstances that the winner should come from the land of the rising sun.

———

24 AUGUST 2004

STUNNING HOLMES SNATCHES GOLD
Jim White in Athens

The look on Kelly Holmes's face as she crossed the line at the end of the women's 800 metres was one of pure amazement. There she was, seizing Britain's first middle-distance gold medal in twenty years, since Sebastian Coe ruled Los Angeles, and she simply could not believe it. Arms out-stretched, she was momentarily goggle-eyed. Then grim reality seemed to strike her. She stopped, put her arms down and stared at the scoreboard. Even at the last, such had been the course of her career, she assumed this crowning moment was not to be, that someone else had done it, sneaked through in that crowded, elbow-jarring, chest-thrusting finish, meaning she was destined forever to be the runner-up.

'When I crossed the line, I could not believe it,' she said, glowing so much vibrancy, they could have lit Athens from her smile. 'I wanted it for so long, and I've dreamt about it so much, so I was shocked that it all worked out. I really needed the confirmation from the others to accept that I'd won.' When it came, when her name arrived in orange letters high above the Olympic Stadium, she jumped in the air, she gasped, she shrieked and then she embarked on the longest, most joyful lap of honour imaginable. There wasn't a television camera she didn't stop for, not a radio microphone she could resist, not a notebook she did not want to fill with her victory tale. This was her moment and Kelly Holmes was going to live it.

Holmes was up against Maria de Lurdes Mutola, who won the gold in Sydney and subsequently re-defined women's middle-distance running. The pair are firm friends. They share a coach, they share training schedules. The only Mozambique athlete to win an Olympic medal is the one against whom Holmes measures herself. Five months before the Games, Holmes moved away with the express purpose of defeating her friend. 'She knows my weaknesses,' said Mutola, who finished a desperately close fourth. 'Kelly Holmes really deserves her gold medal. Congratulations to her. She ran the best race when it counted.'

She did that. With her hair braided in zigzag corn rows, Holmes looked a slight figure as she waited at the blocks for her race to start. But those slight looks are deceptive. Holmes is a scrapper, a tough, determined competitor, driven by an unspoken desire to prove everyone wrong. Her reserves of competitiveness were schooled in a household in which she was the oldest of six and honed by nearly a decade in the Army. Over a long career which took in a bronze medal in the 800 metres in Sydney, she has become a canny tactician, with tungsten-grade mental strength, never phased by the task ahead.

From the gun, she does what she always does, settled into a position near the back of the eight runners, allowing others to set the pace, holding back, watching. At the bell, the veteran American Jearl Miles Clark led the field, and Holmes was still seventh, still biding her time. Then she gradually moved up the field, and on the bend at two hundred metres she was on Mutola's shoulder, waiting for the Mozambique runner's kick to come, knowing that it would. As the field rounded the last bend, she was fourth, but ready to strike. Mutola kicked, her face contorted with the effort, but the hamstring was not functioning fully. With the line in sight, Holmes moved smoothly to the front. Up till then, she said, everything had gone according to plan. But others had plans too. Notably the Romanian Yolanda Ceplak and the Moroccan with the featherweight step, Hasna Benhassi. Both seemed set to condemn Holmes to the position of gallant loser once more. Somehow, though, the British runner held them all off, even the muscular thrust of Mutola, fighting to the last for her title.

---

26 AUGUST 2004
DYNAMIC DUO SAVE THE DAY
Jim White

It was enough to make Matthew Pinsent blub again with pride. The golden oarsman was one of hundreds of British fans crammed into the sweaty confines of the Athens velodrome last night to watch Bradley Wiggins and Rob Hayles come third in the madison, the wild, 36-rider free-for-all, the penultimate event of the Olympic cycling programme. The pair scored twelve points, behind the Swiss Franco Marveli and Bruno Fisi with fifteen and the Australians, Graeme Brown and Stuart O'Grady, with twenty-two.

For Wiggins, adding the bronze to the gold and silver he had already trousered, there was history in becoming the first Briton in forty years to win a trio of medals at the Games. For Hayles there was consolation after coming fourth in the individual pursuit. And for both of them, there was a huge sense of relief, vindication after they had dramatically crashed on the last lap in the same event in Sydney while occupying the silver position and ended up with nothing. 'I never thought I would be pleased with a bronze medal,' said Hayles as he sat alongside the interpreters in the post-race press conference. 'But for myself and Brad we're really, really chuffed. And I don't know how that goes in French.'

Not that it was easy. About halfway through the 200-lap race, Hayles spun on a corner, clashed wheels with another bike and ended up splattered on the trackside. For a horrible moment, there was silence among the British supporters: it was Sydney all over again. Hayles thought much the same. 'When I went down I was thinking the British public must be thinking I'm a proper idiot,' he said. Wiggins, though, stepped into the breach and rode ferociously until his partner had recovered. Though, with typical modesty, he played down his role. 'Actually it happened at a time when the pace was pretty slow,' he said. 'As soon as I saw Brad go down, I joined in the pack and just kept going until he was ready to get back on his bike and join in again.'

For those new to the discipline, the surprise was that Wiggins could work out what on earth was going on. The madison is a race in which eighteen pairs of riders set off on a 50-kilometre spin, trying to accumulate points as they go in timed sprints, while also trying to outflank their opponents by lapping them. Riders belt round the track for nearly an hour, in huge convoys of bikes, working in pairs, one sitting out while the other sprints, tagging each other like wrestlers every ten laps or so. At any one time there are riders sprinting, resting or tagging. And since there are thirty-six of them out on the track, the velodrome resembles a particularly hyperactive ants' nest. It is a discipline which requires equipment from across the sporting range. Riders need the stamina of the Marathon runner, the thighs of a 200 metres sprinter and the mental calculator of the darts player. Plus a fly-half's ability to pick his way through carnage unfolding in front of him. At times, it is utterly confusing to watch. But then it bursts into sudden, viscerally exciting life. As it did when Hayles and Wiggins made an enormous surge through half the field with eight laps to go to make up the ground lost when they had crashed. As they belted after the teams ahead of them, zig-zagging through back markers at nearly 40 m.p.h., the entire velodrome rocked to the cheering. 'To come back after a crash like that was just great,' said Wiggins.

---

30 AUGUST 2004
ELEMENTARY, MY DEAR HOLMES, JUST ELEMENTARY
Sue Mott

Just before daybreak yesterday, the morning after the night before when she became an Olympic legend, Kelly Holmes sat on her balcony in Athens and talked to her mum on the phone. 'You're in the history books now, Kel,' said her mother from Tonbridge, with the noise of a party raging in the background. 'Aw, mum, shut up,' said Holmes, accurately reflecting her continuing wonder that the weight round her neck is no longer a thwarted dream but the solid reality of two Olympic gold medals. It was clear to anyone who spent time with her yesterday that the enormous fact of her role-reversal, from nearly-girl to really-girl, is having trouble penetrating her electrocuted brain.

'It's weird. It's bizarre. It's surreal,' she said, and several other things along those lines. She smiled and stuttered and kept repeating her belief all through these Olympics that something, anything, would go wrong as usual to deprive her of her life-long ambition. When it didn't, when she calmly, expertly and convincingly won the 1,500 metres to add to her whisker-wide victory in the 800 metres last Monday, she entered an alien realm. She is now joyous and agog simultaneously. This condition could clearly last until Christmas. 'When I lay down on all fours after the race I was so tired, worn out, happy and half-crying. Everything suddenly let down. I couldn't walk another step. I really needed one of those buggies to do the lap of honour,' she said, her little, light-boned face still wide-eyed in amazement. At the age of thirty-four, she had run a lifetime personal best, broken the national record and become the first British double gold medallist at the two middle distances since a War hero in 1920. 'If I had been told beforehand I'd have to run that fast, I wouldn't have turned up,' Holmes said that night, still in shock after her three-minute-57.90-second four laps. 'I really can't believe it's happened to me.'

Yet it did, and with such visible self-determination. She walked out for the 1,500 metres final with the javelins flying, the high jump raging, Union flags jigging and a full moon beaming, yet her concentration did not waver once. 'Guts and tunnel vision. That's what I had,' said the former Army sergeant with proper self-analysis. Coming off the final bend, following her plans to the tactical letter, she surged into the lead, carefully checking for the Moroccan Hasna Benhassi in her wing mirrors. No sign. All clear. This time she smiled through the line. A tumult of emotions then registered across her face of which the most readable was simply: 'Cor!' Indeed.

---

30 AUGUST 2004

THE UNDERDOGS HAVE THEIR DAY
AT LONG LAST

Jim White

When Mark Lewis-Francis crossed the line at the end of Saturday's 4 × 100-metres relay final, the initial reaction among many of those watching was that he was celebrating rather extravagantly for a runner-up. When the words 'Great Britain' were displayed on the stadium scoreboard as the winning team in 38.07 – just .01 of a second ahead of the United States – there was a momentary silence, a split second of mute disbelief, an assumption there had been some sort of computer error. Which was not surprising. Not since 1912 had gold hung round the necks of a British sprint team.

At almost every Olympics since, the British effort has ended with a dropped baton or disqualification. Even when the current team got it right, as they did in the World Championships last year, it was to finish second to the Americans, and then subsequently to be stripped of their reward after Dwain Chambers was exposed as a drug cheat. And here they were up against a U.S. team, three-quarters of whom had occupied the podium in the individual sprints, a team going for a world record. Here they were, none of them having made that final. Nobody expected this. Except the runners themselves. 'The crazy thing is, we knew we'd do it,' said Darren Campbell. 'It's hard to explain, but we knew it was ours.'

Yes, there was vindication in this race. Gardener, so graceful off the blocks on the opening leg, was thrilled to have overcome a double hernia operation in March which had threatened his participation in the Games. Devonish, so unheralded that he didn't even enter the individual events, simply stared at his medal and giggled. And, after he had just edged out the former Olympic champion Maurice Greene on the line, Lewis-Francis was bounding from interview to interview: 'I'm the Olympic champion, man. You gotta write positive things about me now.'

But injured pride was not the reason the Britons won. The devil was in the detail. The Americans just assumed speed would win out. When they emerged on to the track before the race, the nailed-on favourites went through the most cursory of warm-ups; Greene barely bothered to pace his run-up. Gardener, on the other hand, was obliged to walk past all the flag-waving hullabaloo of Holmes receiving her gold medal. He appeared not even to notice, and stared straight ahead at the track. 'It's called focus,' he said afterwards. The focus paid off. Once the race got underway, at the crucial change-over stations, where micro-seconds are there to be won, the Americans fumbled. The Britons moved like a well-oiled machine. 'I wouldn't say that,' said their coach, Steve Perks. 'I spotted some room for improvement. We'll be working on that.' You cannot imagine the Americans doing the same. A slightly embarrassed Greene admitted that he was not entirely sure how many times his team had got together before the run. 'Three. No two. Was it two? Yeah, two times. But you know, it's kinda difficult with all our individual commitments.' When Perks was asked how the British had prepared, he gave a lengthy break-down of training schedules and holding camps, practice runs and race planning.

Even misfortune has worked to British advantage. After Chambers's disgrace, all the times in which he had participated were stripped from the record. From being second best in the world, the team slipped to fifteenth, in danger of missing qualification for the Games. They had to race often over the past year to secure the necessary times. Practice paid off. 'We knew we couldn't beat them on flat-out speed,' said Campbell. 'The only way was baton skills. Every year we've worked harder and harder, every year we've got closer and closer. Finally, we got that little bit of luck. It proves God loves a trier.' The glory for the British team was they did not win by default. Unlike in the women's event, the Americans got round the track, baton in hand. The British proved themselves a better team. They worked so well that, on the final leg, Lewis-Francis found himself three paces ahead. By then, it didn't matter that Greene was closing on him like a Ferrari in the rear-view mirror. Immortality was theirs, by all of 0.01 of a second. The celebrations will last a little longer.

---

30 AUGUST 2004

MISSION ACCOMPLISHED AS TEAM GB BRING BACK THE MEDALS

Andrew Baker

Memo to staff manning the metal detectors at Gatwick Airport: you are in for a heavy afternoon. The Cyprus Airways flight from Athens at 3 p.m. carries the British Olympic team with medals from thirty events slung around their necks, and they will be mighty reluctant to take them off. The squad boarded their plane at Eleftherios Venizelos airport in Athens this morning with nine gold, nine silver and twelve bronze medals, two more in total than the team earned in Sydney. Simon Clegg, the *chef de mission* of the British team, had promised before the Games 'an end to the sorry summer of British sport', and yesterday he admitted his relief at seeing his prediction fulfilled. 'I'm proud of our athletes,' he said. 'In some respects we can say "mission accomplished".'

Sporting comparisons are odious — venues, equipment and opponents change, athletes age — but British achievements in Athens will inevitably be measured against the results from Sydney, generally reckoned to have been a very good Games for the national team. Britain won two fewer medals in Sydney, but more gold: eleven compared with nine here in

Athens. By the gold standard, British performance has slipped a little. But the higher overall total, and the fact that three of the golds were won in prestigious track events, compensate to some extent for the reduction in winners.

The final weekend of the Games was a triumphant conclusion to the festival for the British squad. On Saturday night Kelly Holmes added the 1,500-metres title to the 800-metres prize, while the men had a sensational win in the 4 × 100m relay. Yesterday 17-year-old Amir Khan won Britain's final medal, taking the silver in the lightweight boxing category. Holmes carried the Union flag at the head of the British team in last night's closing ceremony, and behind her most of her compatriots will have been reflecting on their performances with satisfaction. Even the exceptions — one cannot think of Paula Radcliffe without a pang of sympathy — will surely one day consider themselves fortunate to have competed in the home of the Games.

There were blots on the landscape, because no modern Olympics will ever be free from controversy. But doping scandals, disappearing Greek athletes and questionable judging will weigh lightly in the scales of posterity set against the host nation's achievements. Contrary to most predictions, the Athens Olympics quite simply worked. So did Team GB. Those elements of the squad expected to perform lived up to their hype. The sailors once again led the way with five medals while cycling and rowing again made strong contributions. A patchy performance in track and field was rescued by the brilliance of Holmes and the sprinters, and while the swimming squad will have been disappointed with just two bronze medals, they would consider themselves a work in progress. Four years hence, they must rise to the challenge again in Beijing.

14
BEIJING 2008

II AUGUST 2008

COOKE TIMES HER MOMENT TO PERFECTION
Brendan Gallagher in Juyongguan

The Union flag flew proudly over the Great Wall of China last night after Britain's Nicole Cooke conquered savage monsoon weather as well as the world's best cyclists to win the Olympic gold medal she has dreamt of and the victory Great Britain have planned for meticulously. Her stunning victory in the women's road race was Britain's first gold medal in the event and the first gold won by a Welsh competitor at the Olympics since Richard Meade in the three-day event in 1972. And it had a Welsh feel. Torrential rain swept off the surrounding mountains and the temperature plunged, but Cooke was in her element as she weaved under and over the Great Wall. It could have been Snowdonia in the middle of a winter storm with Caernarvon Castle in the background.

After a disappointing – by her own standards – fifth place in Athens four years ago, Cooke had no intention of squandering this chance and rode with native *hwyl* to bring the spoils home. All of Wales, and Britain, can be proud. Coming off the final bend under one of the wall's watch towers she was handily placed in fifth. But she then unleashed an unstoppable surge on the uphill sprint to roar past Sweden's Emma Johansson and Italian Tatiana Guderzo to claim Britain's first gold medal of these Games. As she crossed the line Cooke let out a shriek — mostly of joy but also a venting of past frustrations. 'We did it, it was perfect. It's a dream come true,' she said. 'I came over the line and there were so many emotions that were coming out all at once. I made so much noise because I guess that's just the person I am.

I want to thank all the people who've been there from the start. I've worked so hard, I'm so happy. I don't think it has sunk in yet. I still feel like the normal Nicole from before the race. But it's just so exciting.'

Cooke, who in previous years has ploughed a lonely furrow on GB duty, profited enormously from her selfless colleagues, Emma Pooley and Sharon Laws, both specialists in hilly terrain. They forced the pace relentlessly on the first circuit after the peloton had arrived at the hill circuit pretty much intact. Pooley, in particular, set a punishing pace to help draw the sting of rivals such as Holland's outstanding pre-race favourite Marianne Vos, who would have preferred an easier pace to conserve her sprint finish. After breaking clear with the four other riders eight kilometres from home Cooke approached that last, crucial, treacherous stretch. Every racing muscle in her body will have wanted to lean into the racing line, but her brain was working overtime and women's team manager Julian Winn was counselling caution on her earpiece. Cooke was on state-of-the-art, ultra-light tyres – a calculated risk in such weather – and had religiously avoided leaning the bike too far all afternoon. Now was not the time to start. And there were the other four riders to think about, all riding on the edge with thoughts of an Olympic gold medal swamping their minds. If one of them pushed too hard and fell, Cooke would perish as well. So she opted for the conservative line, though, as Winn later admitted, Cooke allowed slightly more of a gap than they had planned. No matter, out on the road Cooke was calm and confident – grace under pressure. She had looked around and taken stock and knew she had the beating of her opponents. This was her moment. Off the bend she came and hit the turbo. Nicole Cooke, of Wick and Wales. Nicole Cooke, of Great Britain. Nicole Cooke, Olympic champion. As she crossed the line she was not the only one shouting for joy.

---

12 AUGUST 2008

MY TEARS OF JOY AT SEEING RECORD FINALLY BROKEN

Anita Lonsbrough describes her 1960 triumph and long wait for a successor

Ever since 1972 and the first Olympic Games I covered for *The Daily Telegraph*, I have wanted to write about a female British winner at the

Games and yesterday that wish came true when Rebecca Adlington snatched gold on the final stroke of the 400 metres freestyle. As she raced down that final fifty metres I became emotional with a tear or two in the eyes and a lump in my throat. When she touched and her name appeared on the scoreboard the memories came flooding back. In Rome, in 1960, I was nineteen plus a few days, some six months younger than Rebecca. My mother, aunt and cousin Joyce all made the journey by rail to watch me swim. Apart from the fact that she raced over the 400 metres freestyle and I swam 200 metres breaststroke there are many similarities. We both qualified for the final in second spot behind the world record holder. We were both behind until the final length, though I did not leave it as late as Rebecca did.

But there the similarities end. Rebecca went quickly from television interview to radio, to agencies and rushed through the written media before being whisked away for the presentation. Then it was a short press conference before a long swim down. Not so for me. Swim downs were unheard of, though there was an interview with Alun Williams for BBC radio immediately after the race. After the presentation I was rushed to the BBC TV studios to be interviewed with no time to dry and change. So there I sat in a soggy swimsuit – there were no quick-drying ones in those days – under my tracksuit. I sat there for about half an hour with the media waiting outside. As the programme opened Peter Dimmock, the then presenter, held my gold medal for all to see before they played the tape of my race. My poor father, still at home in Huddersfield, had the embarrassment of having a film crew with him while he watched the programme.

Media duties done, I returned to the Village where the team had laid the red towels we had been given as part of our kit, to make a red carpet for me to walk up. At the headquarters, the *chef de mission*, Sandy Duncan, opened a bottle of Champagne for us all to celebrate. Modern technology meant that Rebecca could immediately receive texts and emails of congratulation. For me it was a pile of telegrams the next day; many from people I did not know. The morning after my race there was another round of interviews. Lottery money, in fact sponsorship of any kind, was not allowed so I worked as a clerk in the borough treasurer's office at Huddersfield Council. To prepare for Rome I had taken holiday and extra unpaid leave and somehow the media got hold of this and next day the headlines were all about how much it cost to win gold. I am so glad that swimmers and parents do not have to make sacrifices like this any more.

When the swimming is over Rebecca will be allowed to enjoy the rest of the Games and see something of Beijing. In 1960 we had one free day, and then it was off home. No doubt companies will be queuing up to sponsor Rebecca, and her Lottery funding will be increased. Good for her. But back in the old days we were true amateurs, with no gift larger than £5 allowed without permission. Ah, the good old days.

_____

16 AUGUST 2008
AINSLIE SECURES PLACE IN HISTORY
Andrew Baker in Qingdao

Ben Ainslie became Britain's most successful Olympic sailor when he guaranteed himself either a gold or silver medal in the Finn after another day of elusive and light winds. Following his golds in Sydney and Athens, and his silver in Atlanta, Ainslie now overtakes Rodney Pattisson in the pantheon. In today's final medal race, which will score double points, Ainslie will need to keep what he called a 'loose cover' on American rival Zach Railey to win gold. The Briton leads by twelve points, so can follow Railey home and still prevail, so long as he finishes no more than five places behind.

Ainslie, though, was quick to deny that the pressure was now off him. 'I wish it was,' he said. 'The job is only half done. I just hope that we have a good breeze for the final race so that I can go out and get the job done. It will be a difficult race if the wind doesn't blow.' Ainslie's task will be to stick to the American like glue, no matter how far down the fleet the two might fall in the process. The Englishman has previous form in this kind of situation, after he famously and successfully sailed the reigning Olympic champion, Robert Scheidt, down the fleet in the final race of the Laser class in Sydney to take his title. 'It certainly helps to have had that experience,' Ainslie, thirty-one, said. 'I just hope I can keep a cool head and not make any mistakes.'

Ainslie also played down the significance of overtaking Pattisson, who won gold medals in the Flying Dutchman in 1968 and 1972, and a silver in the same class in 1976. 'Rodney's achievements were amazing in his era,' Ainslie said. 'He was the best sailor of his generation by a long way.'

_____

'THREE BLONDES IN A BOAT' DAZZLE ON A GREY DAY

Andrew Baker in Qingdao

In conditions typical of a seaside Bank Holiday back home, Britain's favourite boating blondes yesterday triumphed in the first sailing final of the Beijing Olympics. Sarah Ayton, Sarah Webb and Pippa Wilson outflanked their Dutch rivals to win gold in the Yngling class on the turbulent Yellow Sea off the coast of Qingdao, five hundred miles south of Beijing. Ben Ainslie later followed up in similar style, taking the gold medal in the Finn class with a win in the event's final race to round off a wonderful day for Britons on the water.

Ayton and Webb won their second gold medals, having partnered Shirley Robertson to the Olympic title in Athens. 'It's awesome,' Webb said afterwards. 'Totally fantastic.' She and her crew-mates had vanquished fifteen rivals and weather conditions that might have prevented any sailing yesterday had the organisers, who had been traumatised by previous calms throughout the regatta, not wished to get at least one medal event away. The three British women were joined on the dockside by Robertson, who is working here for British television. There have been tales of ill-feeling among them, after Ayton and Webb recruited Wilson while Robertson took a break from the sport to have twins, but it is amazing what a gold medal can do for the spirit of amicability.

The whole 'Blondes in a Boat' media confection is ridiculous: how many other double Olympic gold medallists are defined by their hair colour? But Ayton and Webb shrug it off, as they shrugged off yesterday's torrential rain, and Wilson long ago admitted with a rueful grin that yes – of course – she only made it aboard the boat in the first place because of the colour of her hair. The trio, who were British Olympic Association Athletes of the Year last year, needed only to beat the Dutch yesterday to secure the gold medal. But rather than engage in a tactical battle, which might have been hazardous in such rough and blustery conditions, they elected to race for themselves and came home at the head of the fleet to earn their place on top of the podium in style. 'Being British, you know, we are used to rain and wind,' Ayton said. 'We're well trained in these sort of conditions. Winning a gold medal means that you are the best in the world at what you do. That feeling is particularly special.'

17 AUGUST 2008

'DAME' BECKY SWIMS INTO POOL OF FAME
Simon Hart in Beijing

She left Britain an ordinary teenager little known outside swimming circles and her native Mansfield. She will return a double Olympic champion, a world record-holder and with the tag of being the greatest British swimmer of all time. It's not been a bad week's work for Becky Adlington. Or make that Dame Rebecca, as she will now surely be known. On a remarkable day in the Water Cube, Adlington went to her starting block for the final of the 800 metres freestyle just minutes after Michael Phelps had equalled Mark Spitz's record of seven gold medals. By the time the 19-year-old had finished, eight minutes 14.10 seconds later, she had carved out her own piece of Olympic history. Not only did she win her second gold medal of the Games, following her 400-metres victory on Monday, she did so by annihilating the longest-standing world record in swimming – the eight minutes 16.22 seconds set by American Janet Evans in Tokyo nineteen years ago.

It was not so much a race as an exhibition of strength and technique by the young Briton. Adlington was never threatened, and by the halfway mark she was so far ahead that she knew it was all but over. What she was not aware of was the incredible pace she was setting and that the record she had dreamt of breaking one day was within her grasp. 'I can't believe it has happened,' she said. 'I obviously knew when I touched that I had won, and that was a great thing because I was just going for gold. But I didn't expect that record at all, and especially not by that much. It's just unbelievable.'

No British swimmer has won two gold medals at an Olympic Games in the modern era, and only middle-distance runner Dame Kelly Holmes has won two individual golds in the same Games in any sport. While David Wilkie's world record-breaking victory in the 200 metres breaststroke in Montreal in 1976 bears comparison as the greatest British swim of all time, Adlington's coach, Bill Furniss, was in no doubt about the enormity of her achievement. 'This has been an awesome Olympic Games,' he said. 'It's been frighteningly fast. But up there with all of it, that has got to be one of the all-time great swims. It's such a magnificent record and to take it down by so much is incredible. She just destroyed it.'

17 AUGUST 2008
LIGHTNING BOLT SETS THE TRACK ALIGHT
Mark Reason in Beijing

Usain Bolt became the first man in history to run under 9.7 seconds for the 100 metres, and he did it easing down. 'Lightning' Bolt slaughtered his own world record and crushed a world-class field beneath his golden spikes. Ten yards from the line Bolt looked at the clock and began to prance in front of ninety-one thousand open-mouthed spectators. The clock stopped at 9.69 seconds, but Bolt just kept on going, high-stepping towards the crazy faithful in the crowd. Bolt's mate Marc Burns, one of six men from the Caribbean to run in the final, said that the 21-year-old from Jamaica could have gone as low as 9.55 if he had run through to the line. He was talking gospel.

Right from the start Bolt was clearly on another planet from the rest of the field. As the two Americans and five men from the Caribbean ramped up the testosterone stare, Bolt was jigging around like a clubber on a Saturday night. He weaved a few shapes, smiled the shy smile of a teenager meeting a first date and then took up the statuesque pose of the archer. He may be the lightning Bolt, but the *Golden Shot* never saw anything like this. Second slowest out of the blocks – a fast start by his standards – Bolt then just smoked the field. 'I was havin' fun,' he said. 'That's just me. Just stayin' relaxed. I like dancin'.' Bolt stayed relaxed all day. Flanked by silver medallist Richard Thompson of Trinidad and bronze medallist Walter Dix of America, Bolt took a packed press conference through his day. He got up at eleven, watched some TV, had some nuggets, slept for a few hours and then had some more nuggets. At this point Thompson and Dix began to giggle. What was it with those nuggets, they wanted to know. They must have been golden nuggets.

One thing is for certain: Bolt has an immense talent. At school he was 'thunder' Bolt, a fearsome fast bowler who eventually turned to athletics. On the track he seemed even quicker. No teenager, not even Michael Johnson, has ever run a faster time for the 200 metres. Right up to the last moment there was doubt that he would even participate in the 100 at this year's Olympics. The 200 was his bag. But Bolt knew better. Already he had the golden shoes with the inscription, '2008 100m Beijing' on the heels.

PHELPS THE MACHINE HAS MORE MILEAGE
Jim White

The presentation party assembled to award Michael Phelps his eighth gold medal of these Olympic Games was so sizeable that the announcement of their names over the public address system went on longer than his final race. There was the executive vice-president of this and the newly elected chairman of that, all anxious to be there. And who can blame them? Whatever the claim and counter-claim of Phelps's standing as the greatest of all Olympians, even to be in attendance when his gold rush came to a triumphal end was to feel part of history. Imagine, then, how he must have felt, as he stood there on the podium for the eighth time after winning gold in the 4 × 100 metres medley relay. How he must have felt as he surveyed Beijing's Water Cube, the place that, over this past week, has become his kingdom, his domain. How he must have felt to achieve every one of the elevated ambitions he had written down on a sheet of paper and handed to his coach before the start of these Games a fortnight ago. Eight gold medals: it is no small achievement. 'Well, I guess I'm supposed to tell more about how it felt,' he said later. 'But what is there to say? It was fun.'

If that sounds trite, nobody sent Phelps to Beijing to talk. He is a man who reserves his articulacy for the water. That is where he comes alive. On the podium he cuts an awkward figure. His extravagant torso makes his legs look foreshortened, giving him an unbalanced, unathletic appearance. He looks adenoidal, too, as if his nose is permanently blocked, meaning his mouth hangs open like Gordon Brown with a heavy head cold. Put him in the water, though, and he is another being altogether. As he was in the last race of his octet of glory.

His was the butterfly leg in the medley relay. When his compatriot, the breaststroker Brendan Hansen, handed over to him, the United States team were lying third behind Japan and Australia. For a moment, just as it had in the freestyle relay and the 100 metres butterfly races, it looked as if the goal of eight was too greedy. By the time Phelps had completed his leg and passed responsibility to the freestyler Jason Lezak, however, the U.S. were so far ahead Lezak could have done an Usain Bolt, stopped swimming, punched the air and still won in world record time. Phelps put his team-mates in the ascendancy by doing what he has done all week, by the ruthless application of sustained power. Nobody has swum like him before. When he goes through the routine drugs test after each event, the suspicion must be that instead of providing a urine sample he will produce engine oil. In the water, the man is a machine.

———

20 AUGUST 2008

OHURUOGU TURNS ON THE POWER TO STRIKE GOLD

Tom Knight in Beijing

Christine Ohuruogu overcame a couple of sleepless nights and a bout of nerves to win Britain's first women's Olympic 400 metres gold medal in the Bird's Nest Stadium. It was a gold medal that was a long time coming for a team overshadowed at these Games by cyclists, swimmers, rowers and sailors, but it was the sweeter for all that. There will be those who doubt Ohuruogu's credentials because of her 12-month ban for missing three out-of-competition drug tests, but she proved that last year's world title in Osaka was no fluke and established herself as the ultimate championship performer with victory in a superb 49.62 seconds.

The media-shy and undemonstrative Ohuruogu prevailed in the most fascinating of races. It came as no surprise when the 24-year-old from London, whose career went into free-fall when she was banned in 2006, showed her emotion at the medal ceremony. She said: 'I'm just so grateful that I have been given an amazing talent and I'm just so happy that I'm able to come and perform.'

This gold medal was the result of a year of hard work designed to counter Sanya Richards's speed over the first two hundred metres. She had missed the 400 metres in Osaka after failing to qualify for the American team in the individual event, and in three subsequent races on the European circuit had handed Ohuruogu the most emphatic of wallopings. For Richards, the races were about restoring her reputation. Ohuruogu accepted the invitations in order to pay off the legal bills that had mounted while she fought her ban. Throughout it all, Ohuruogu and her coach, Lloyd Cowan, were convinced that the American was beatable. Her training was adapted to incorporate more speed work, as well as more 60-metre, 100-metre and 200-metre races.

Ohuruogu, the first Briton to win Olympic gold over this distance since Eric Liddell in 1924, trained in South Africa and California, raced sparingly and tried hard to keep a low profile. Everything she did was geared towards the three rounds of the Olympics. She said: 'My coach always says that you train for three days, and three days only. You don't train for grand prix races, you don't train for the trials. You train for these three days. If you're at your best for those three days, that's what it's about.'

Ohuruogu might not have followed the race plan devised by Cowan to the letter, but her timing proved immaculate. While Richards overdid her customary fast start, Ohuruogu concentrated on closing down Yulia Gushchina, the Russian in the lane outside her. As the eight finalists hit the final hundred metres, it was Richards who faltered as Ohuruogu powered down the home straight. At the line, the American was pushed into third place as Shericka Williams added to Jamaica's medal tally with silver. Ohuruogu said: 'I had a bad start but I just ran my own race. I could just see the Russian chasing Sanya down, so I kept running after her. If you're going to beat me then you have to fight very hard. Lloyd always said that the race would be won in the last fifty metres. It doesn't so much matter what you do before. You need to keep your cool and keep your composure for the last fifty metres and stay relaxed. That's when people start dying and everyone knows that I don't die in the last fifty metres. That's how I run and it obviously works.' It worked to perfection last night.

––––––––––

20 AUGUST 2008

HAT-TRICK HERO HOY SHOWS WHY HE'S THE LEADER OF THE PACK

Brendan Gallagher in Laoshan

Three Olympic gold medals in five days, eighteen straight victories en route – even Michael Phelps didn't win all his heats – and a thousand memories. Chris Hoy will never forget his Beijing Olympics and nor shall we. Not for one hundred years has a British competitor won three gold medals at a single Olympics – Henry Taylor in the swimming in 1908 – and in a century of British sporting endeavour Hoy's achievement here stands comparison with anything we have witnessed.

It was the perfect end to a nigh on perfect meeting for Britain's track cyclists who, led by Hoy, blazed their way to seven gold medals, three silvers and two bronzes. The biggest contribution to Britain's total medal haul by a single sport in modern Olympic history. Hoy was the linchpin. Never has a bike been ridden so fast so often with such certainty. The world's best sprinters could race Hoy from now until the Chinese New Year and end up empty-handed. The Scot is in his pomp and totally dominant. As he came into the pits after his final triumph one of the GB mechanics handed him his recovery drink and he automatically gulped thirstily from it only to nearly choke on the potion. They had filled it with potent Belgian beer, the first alcohol to pass his lips since the last night of the World Championships in March. It will be Champagne all the way for the rest of this week, and probably next week as well.

On Friday Hoy, Jason Kenny and Jamie Staff had won gold in the team sprint, breaking the world record as they did so, and on Saturday the rest of the cycling world appeared to be moving in slow motion as Hoy blasted his way to the Keirin title. Yesterday he finished the job in style, demolishing the field in the men's sprint, a campaign which culminated in victory over his young compatriot Kenny. Kenny dug deeper than anybody else but still had no answer as the 'Flying Scotsman' built up a head of steam on the back straight. Pistons pumping mightily, Hoy is a well-oiled speed machine who devours the ground like no other.

He never 'cracks' on the track but as he rolled around after victory last night the tears came. He has given this triple gold shot everything, mainly because that is his nature and partly as an emotional riposte to the International Cycling Union's decision to scrap his beloved kilo, which he won in Athens.

What he achieved here was amazing and the degree of difficulty was emphasised when that other great British rider of this generation, Bradley Wiggins, had hit the wall yesterday and failed to fire in the Madison as he would have wished. Wiggins had ridden six world-class four-kilometre time-trials in the previous four days, either individually or in team pursuit, including two world records, but this time he went to the well just once too often. These things happen, but Hoy on the other hand didn't miss a beat. He made the extraordinary look routine and he made Scotland and Great Britain proud. Hoy is Britain's new Redgrave figure, a tireless sporting superman who grows better with age and a knighthood surely beckons. If not, why not? An Olympian on and off the track, who never lets standards of sportsmanship and decency slip, Hoy could well be the totem pole around which all of British sport will gather heading towards 2012 when, aged thirty-six, he fully intends to contribute again. Steve Redgrave's British record of five gold medals could be in danger.

———

21 AUGUST 2008
RIVALS LEFT AWESTRUCK AS BOLT SCORCHES TO SPRINT DOUBLE
Tom Knight in Beijing

The world wondered what Usain Bolt could do if he ran flat out instead of showboating. Now it knows that 'Lightning' really does strike twice. Four days after smashing the world record for 100 metres, the Jamaican chose the eve of his twenty-second birthday to win the 200 metres in the Bird's Nest Stadium in 19.30 seconds to shatter the mark set by Michael Johnson at the Atlanta Games in 1996. Bolt became the first man to win Olympic gold medals and set world records in both sprints, and this performance could well live longer in the memory than Saturday's 100 metres.

Running in lane five, Bolt exploded from his blocks and in less than a dozen strides, the six foot five inch sprinter from Kingston was leading the field into the turn. As he entered the straight, Bolt's lead was five metres and growing and it was obvious that he was going to deliver on his promise to 'leave everything on the track'. This, after all, was his favourite event and the one at which he had won the world junior title when he was only fifteen. There were no glances at the stadium screen, no smiles and no gestures. The world's greatest sprinter was intent on seeing what was possible. With legs and arms pumping, he powered on, dipped probably a tad too early and only then did he look to his left at the digital reading on the finish-line clock.

He screamed in delight, spread his arms wide and kept on running, tugging at the word 'Jamaica' spelt out on his yellow and green vest as he lapped up the applause from another delirious crowd of ninety-one thousand packed into this magnificent stadium. 'I knew I could go that fast,' Bolt said. 'I've been running fast all season and shutting down. I knew that if I was going to get the world record, it was going to be here. The track is real fast and I wanted to give it everything I had. From the day I won the world junior title, I set my heart on winning this gold medal.'

Bolt shimmied around his lap of honour, draped in the national flag on another night of Jamaican gold. He danced barefoot and preened at images of himself on the stadium screen. He said: 'I was looking at myself and thinking, "That guy's fast".' Wallace Spearmon celebrated finishing third by dancing alongside Bolt. But his mood changed abruptly when he was told he had been disqualified for running on the line and stomped away from the celebrations. Officials then upheld the United States team's protest that second-placed Churandy Martina, of the Dutch Antilles, had also stepped out of his lane. So Shawn Crawford, the 2004 champion, was handed the silver medal and fellow American Walter Dix bronze as the U.S. rescued something from what has been a Jamaican blitz of the sprints. By this time, Bolt was taking a call from Bruce Golding, the Prime Minister of Jamaica, and probably relaying what he was to tell everyone else. 'I just blew my mind and blew the world's mind,' he said, and no one was arguing.

---

22 AUGUST 2008
PERCY AND SIMPSON IN GOLDEN FINALE
Andrew Baker in Qingdao

Victory for Iain Percy and Andrew Simpson in the Star class off the coast of Qingdao wrapped up the Olympic sailing regatta in an entirely appropriate manner. The Yngling trio of Sarah Ayton, Sarah Webb and Pippa Wilson started Britain's rolling wave of success here, winning the first gold of the sailing competition, and the two big men in the Star won the last. British sailors not only topped and tailed the regatta: they dominated the rest of it as well. Four golds, a silver and a bronze gave them twice as many medals, and twice as many golds, as their nearest rivals in the sailing competition, all the more satisfactory because those rivals happened to be Australia.

Percy and Simpson were in silver medal position at the start of their double-points medal race. The daily weather lottery of Qingdao had thrown up gale-force gusts and torrential rain: had it not been for the heat and the humidity, it could have been a grey day off Portland Bill. The two British Star sailors certainly seemed quite at home, surfing their heavy keelboat through the swell into second place at the second mark. They fell down the fleet to an eventual fifth place, but their decline coincided with an error by their main rivals, which saw the Swedes finish tenth and last. The gold was safe. 'We looked at the weather and thought, "Great",' Percy said afterwards. 'There has been no room for fun and games for us this week, no Olympic paraphernalia, no mucking around when other people have won medals. We have been full-on all week.' The same goes for the rest of the British sailing team. The medal winners have celebrated with a discreet beer or two, mindful of the need not to disturb those who were still competing. But now they are all done, and the party in the British house in Qingdao on Thursday night will be an epic. 'We're going to get in the house and shut the door behind us,' said Team GB sailing manager Stephen Park. 'And then we are going to do a little bit of partying.'

---

23 AUGUST 2008

THANK YOU BEIJING, BUT NOW IT'S OUR TURN

Sebastian Coe in Beijing

Around this time tomorrow, the world will know London is the next city to host the summer Olympic and Paralympic Games. This magical moment will happen during the closing ceremony of the Beijing Games when the mayor of Beijing hands the Olympic flag to Boris Johnson. We will then present our eight-minute show – a youthful, diverse and athletic performance that will act as our invitation to the world to join us in four years' time. From then on, the countdown to London hosting the Olympic and Paralympic Games in 2012 will be under way. And I know the excitement, expectation and value we will bring to the Games will build every day. The atmosphere and anticipation will become infectious. The talk will turn to Wembley and Wimbledon and the impressive new Olympic Park, while the Bird's Nest and Water Cube, inevitably, will become part of sporting history.

Beijing has been an extraordinary experience, particularly for Team GB, who have surpassed all expectations and excelled, day after day, on the biggest sporting stage in the world. We could not have asked for a better run-up to our time in the spotlight than Team GB's performances. In four years' time they will have the chance to do it all again, against iconic backdrops and spurred on by passionate, enthusiastic home fans. Our team's great performances at these Games is the amalgam of good administration within governing bodies, world-class coaching, elevated levels of funding and hungry and motivated competitors. If you bring those four things together you tend to get people up on to the rostrums. I take my hat off to the work that is being done in the governing bodies, because they have supported some extraordinarily talented competitors.

Beijing has given the entire 2012 team an enormous opportunity to see first hand the mechanics of running the biggest event on the planet. It has also been a magnificent celebration of sport for competitors and spectators. That's what the Olympic Games are all about. So thank you, Beijing, for being great hosts – now it's our turn.

---

24 AUGUST 2008

DEGALE RIDES STORM TO GOLDEN PEAK
Mike Lewis

James DeGale, the Artful Dodger from the streets of north-west London, countered, grappled, danced and shimmied his way to a famous victory at the Beijing Workers' Gymnasium to become only the third British boxer to win an Olympic title since 1956. Following a roughhouse contest, which at times resembled a scrap you might see outside a club in DeGale's native Harlesden, the Briton took a hard-earned 16–14 verdict over Cuba's Emilio Correa. Not since Chris Finnegan won at the Mexico Games of 1968 has Britain had an Olympic middleweight champion.

Afterwards it emerged that a two-point penalty Correa received for biting DeGale on the chest in round one proved crucial. Though the Cuban denied the offence, DeGale offered up his chest for inspection at the post-fight press conference to reveal a faint set of teeth marks. 'It was flowing and everything, I was getting into my southpaw style when he got me in a hold and bit my chest,' protested DeGale. Through an interpreter, Correa answered amid laughter: 'He came into me and I had my mouth open – to him it must have seemed like a bite.'

What began entertainingly swiftly degenerated into something more akin to wrestling, as Correa, desperate to claw back a five-point deficit at the end of the first, threw himself at DeGale, who met fire with fire. Both boxers repeatedly threw each other to the deck and after both earned warnings from Korean referee Kim Jae-Bong, DeGale received a two-point penalty for holding to bring the scores to 11–7. Correa, eager to emulate his father – also called Emilio – who won a welterweight gold at Munich in 1972, cut the gap to two points. But then DeGale, who again produced a series of his trademark lefts, crashed home a mighty right hook that had the Cuban hanging on for dear life.

Of the eight boxers who left Britain a month ago, DeGale was one of the least fancied. Favourite for the 2006 Commonwealth Games crown in Melbourne, he only came back with the bronze and had a reputation for freezing on the big occasion. Now his name will stand forever alongside past British Olympians, Terry Spinks, Dick McTaggart, Chris Finnegan and Audley Harrison.

---

25 AUGUST 2008

NOT EVEN BORIS COULD UPSTAGE SPARKLING BEIJING

Jim White in Beijing

The Games of the twenty-ninth Olympiad ended as they had begun, with a vivid demonstration of this irrefutable fact: there are an awful lot of people in China. As there had been for the opening ceremony, there were thousands of acrobats, dancers and unicyclists mobilised to the Bird's Nest Stadium for this closing occasion. The warm-up acts alone were more populous than Croydon. Astonishing acrobatics and visuals abounded. The fireworks were prodigious. And then there was Boris Johnson's role in the hand-over of the Olympic flag. Not attempting to upstage Beijing's valedictions, London played its part with a humorously low-key presentation which focused on the one thing Britain has that China doesn't: pop cultural celebrity. Though you wonder how the theme of youthful exuberance that is meant to be at the heart of 2012 was advanced by the appearance of Jimmy Page, plucking out the chords from a 40-year-old pop song that clearly no one in the crowd had heard before. Presumably everyone watching in China thought the elderly gentleman with the ponytail addressing his Gibson through *Whole Lotta Love* was the mayor of London and the scruffy chap with the shock of white hair who got his hands on the flag was merely some overgrown prep-school lad lobbying for conkers to be included in the 2012 Games. Still, judging by the cheers that greeted his emergence from the top deck of a red London bus, for many it was David Beckham's appearance that was the highlight of their Games. Standing there and smiling as the world went loopy around him: it wasn't a bad sales job for London from a man who earns his crust in Los Angeles.

As was traditional on these occasions, before he invited the youth of the world to convene in four years' time, the president of the International Olympic Committee gave his summation of the Beijing Games. 'Sixteen glorious days we will cherish for ever,' Jacques Rogge called them. He has a point. In many ways Beijing has hosted the most successful event in Olympic history. Thirty-nine world records were broken in the pool, at the velodrome and on the track. Commanding performances were delivered by Usain Bolt, Michael Phelps and the Chinese divers. And that is without mentioning Team GB, whose gold haul gave a lift to the national chin in the midst of a wash-out August. Names such as Rebecca Adlington, Tim Brabants and James DeGale, before these Games largely unknown beyond the confines of their own front room, have been elevated to the sporting pantheon. Their job in promoting London 2012 has been every bit as effective as Beckham's: we can hardly wait to see them in action once more.

And the million-plus volunteers smiled continuously, behaving with a deference that gave daily insight into what it must have been like to be a feudal lord. Nothing was too much for them. It was a battle at times to open a door for yourself. One evening, at about midnight, I picked up my washing from the 24-hour laundry in our village. The young student in charge was slumped in his chair, exhausted by the demands of his 12-hour shift. I tapped him on the arm and he snapped to attention. 'Sorry to wake you,' I said. 'No, Sir, it is no problem,' he replied as he dashed round the room searching out my load. 'It is an honour for me to work at these Olympic Games.' Others might have been disappointed by attending to the ablutions of sweaty newsmen rather than, say, operating the remote control cars in the stadium that bring back the discus after it has been thrown by some neckless Estonian, but he wasn't complaining. But then no one in China does much of that. One of the consequences of totalitarianism is that people do what they are told. And at times the endless smiles had the air of remorselessly taught behaviour. The striking thing was, when you got into conversation with those volunteers whose grasp of English went beyond 'have a nice day', few had the chance to witness any sport. Tickets were reserved for those with influence. The ordinary guy never got a look in. That is London's big chance. Nothing can top these Games, but, by paying attention to the people who really matter, the fans, London could do something equally memorable.